Tunxis
Community
College

Education That Works For a Lifetime

Dreamers of the Colorado:
The Mojave Indians

Part 1 – Their Land and Religion

Edited by Frances L. O'Neil and Paul W. Wittmer

Dreamers of the Colorado: The Mojave Indians
Part 1: Their Land and Religion

Tunxis Community College Publication
© 2013 by Tunxis Community College
All rights reserved. First Edition 2013

Copyedited by Frances L. O'Neil and Paul W. Wittmer
Cover and book design by Bryan R. Bonina
Project management by Deborah Young
Printed in the United States of America

Please direct comments and inquiries to:

Tunxis Community College Foundation
271 Scott Swamp Road
Farmington, CT 06032
(860) 255-3604
www.tunxisfoundation.org

Sunbelt Publications Inc.
P.O. Box 191126
San Diego, CA 92159-1126
(619) 258-4911; fax: (619) 258-4916
www.sunbeltbooks.com

17 16 15 14 13   5 4 3 2 1

Library of Congress Cataloging-in-Publication Data

Dreamers of the Colorado : the Mojave indians : part 1 their land and
religion / edited by Frances L. O'Neil and Paul W. Wittmer. :
      pages cm.
  Includes bibliographical references and index.
   ISBN 978-0-916251-27-7 (softcover : alk. paper) 1. Mohave
Indians--History. 2. Mohave Indians--Social life and customs. I. O'Neil,
Frances L.
   E99.M77D74 2013
   979.1004'975722--dc23
                              2013021537

Cover Photos:
Front cover background photo and top three photos by Jeffrey J. Garton;
Front cover lower photo by Peter Furst.
Back cover photo by Paul W. Wittmer.

Copyright Acknowledgments

Table of Contents: Part 1 – Their Land and Religion

Preface

These literary pieces were selected by the editors because they were particularly descriptive of the Mojave Desert in both its captivating beauty and its ever-present danger. This awe-inspiring environment has shaped the religion and lifeways of the Mojave people, who have live there since time immemorial.

Acknowledgments

We should like to express our deep gratitude to the Mojave people.
They have paid us the great compliment of treating each of us as one of their own.

Mojave elders, Betty and Lew Barrackman

Many thanks also to the following people for their contributions to this volume:

Cathryn Addy	Colleen Keyes
Paula Baird	Patricia Kuzianik
Patricia Bode	Diana Lewandowski
Bryan Bonina	Rosemary Nevers
Susan Christy	Behnaz Perri
Susan Dantino	Michael Rooke

Chapter One

Introduction and Overview

Photo by Jeffrey L. Garton

NA U KNOV EM (*I Am Going To Tell You Something*)

by Kelly Hills

Volume 1, Issue 1 • September 28, 2007

Fort Mojave Indian Tribe Changed Forever In The Year of 1957 With The Enactment Of The Mojave Constitution

The Fort Mojave Indian Tribe is located in the Tri-State area along the California, Arizona and Nevada Borders. The Fort Mojave Indian Tribe is also referred to and known as "Pipa Aha Macav"- people who live along the river.

The lands of the Mojave Indian Reservation extend across the three states with two-thirds of land located in the lower part of Mohave Valley, Arizona. The Fort Mojave Indian Reservation encompasses approximately 38,000 acres.

In the late 1890's, many of the Mojave Indians attended the industrial boarding school known as Fort Mojave Indian School. With the passing of the education law, the United States Government forced many of the tribal children back into school with the ultimate intention of eliminating native language and culture. Many of the Mojave Indians were whipped and locked in the attic for days, and given only water and a slice of bread for meals. This was the consequence for speaking the Mojave language. The Fort Mojave Indian School was closed in 1931, leaving many of the Mojave children to begin attending public schools

Fort Mojave Indian School Dormitory for Girls

The Mojave Indians lived for many years within a clan system. It consisted of 22 clans which are reduced today to less than 18. The clan system names were provided to each individual and represented the earth, sun, clouds and birds. The children within the clan system were given the name of their father's clan and only the women used the clan name in accordance with Mojave tradition.

Over many years, the tribe was governed through traditional tribal leadership. This was changed forever in the year of 1957 with the approval of the Fort Mojave Constitution creating a seven member tribal council.

Today, the Fort Mojave Indian Tribe continues to uphold the traditional ways of the Mojave people through language, song and dance.

Mojave People Are People of Dreams

The Mojave People are a tribe willing to protect their lands and willing to venture far from it. In accordance with history, the Mojave Indians traveled to the Pacific Coast becoming skillful traders of surplus crops for goods they desired and valued such as shells.

The Mojave people were people of dreams and visions. In the stories told by the elders of the tribe, the dreams would return to the time of creation. The great dreams and visions were related to the tribe's great spiritual visions. It was stated by elders that the dreams long ago were visions leading the Fort Mojave Indian Tribe in the path of new economic development.

Tribal Council Leadership: The Fort Mojave Indian Tribe has progressed with new economic development providing employment to tribal members within the tribe, as well as providing employment opportunities to individuals residing within the surrounding tri-state area.

Mohave

by Kenneth M. Stewart

Northernmost and largest of the Yuman-speaking tribes of the lower Colorado River in aboriginal times, the Mohave (mo'häve) comprise two divisions—former residents of the Fort Mojave Reservation in Arizona who have lived since the 1930s across the river in the town of Needles, California, and the Mohaves of the Colorado River Reservation, 60 miles downstream (fig. 1). These are approximately the same localities that the Mohave were occupying when the Spaniards first encountered them in the seventeenth and eighteenth centuries. The Mohave then constituted a true tribe, with a loose division into bands that did not weaken the tribal unity for purposes of attack or defense, possessing a national consciousness despite a minimal political organization.

The core and most heavily populated part of the Mohave territory in precontact times was the Mohave Valley, where no other tribe has ever been reported. The Mohave, if Schroeder is correct in identifying them with the prehistoric group he calls the Amacava, may have come out of the Mohave Desert to the west to settle along the river in the Mohave Valley as early as A.D. 1150 (Schroeder 1952b:29). Mohave settlements in the valley extended from about 15 miles north of the present Davis Dam down to the peaks known as The Needles, just south of Topock, Arizona. The Mohave apparently considered, too, that they owned the country along the Colorado south to the Bill Williams River, although in the nineteenth century they allowed the Chemehuevi, migratory desert Indians, to infiltrate and farm along the river in what is now known as the Chemehuevi Valley.

Mohaves were also living in the Colorado River Val-ley, near the present Colorado River Reservation, when they were first seen by Spaniards of the Juan de Oñate expedition in 1604 (K.M. Stewart 1969a). That valley was later in part occupied by a hostile tribe, the Halchidhoma, who after protracted warfare were finally expelled from the valley between 1827 and 1829. Some Mohaves then moved into the northern part of

the valley to establish possession once again. In 1859 a larger group of Mohaves was induced to move south from the Mohave Valley by Chief Irrateba (*irateve*), and others joined them when the Colorado River Reservation was established in 1865. A conservative faction, under a rival chief, *hamosé-kaahot* ('good star'), refused to leave their ancestral homeland in the Mohave Valley, and ever since that time the Mohaves have remained split into two groups, one in the Mohave Valley and the other on the Colorado River Reservation (K.M. Stewart 1969). Despite the differences between the two Mohave communities, there is considerable visiting between them and some intermarriage.

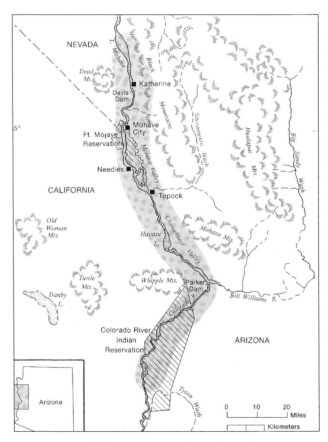

Fig. 1. Tribal territory in the mid-19th century (reservations and hydrography are modern).

External Relations

The Mohave were culturally very much like their Quechan friends and allies and were also similar in culture to the antagonistic Halchidhoma, Maricopa, and Cocopa. The Pima (and to a lesser degree, the Papago) were allies of the Maricopa and thus were considered to be enemies by the Mohave. The Yavapai, on the other hand, were friendly to both the Quechan and Mohave, whom they sometimes joined in expeditions against the Maricopa. Relations between the Mohave and the Walapai were mixed; at times they were friendly enough to permit trade, while fighting between them occurred at other periods.

The Cahuilla, Tipai-Ipai, and other Mission Indians of southern California were regarded by the Mohave as good people. In the deserts to the north and west of Mohave territory were the Southern Paiute, close relatives of the Chemehuevi. Poor and nomadic, the Chemehuevi were allowed to come on the river to farm in the early nineteenth century. But war broke out between Mohave and Chemehuevi between 1865 and 1867, and the Chemehuevi were temporarily driven back into the desert. They were allowed to return when peace was made, and they were later incorporated into the Colorado River Reservation community (K.M. Stewart 1968a).

Environment

The Mohave country is a region of mild winters, oppressively hot summers, and extremely low annual precipitation. Back from the bottomlands along the river, vegetation is prevailingly xerophytic. Were it not for the beneficence of the great Colorado River, the land would doubtless have been only thinly populated by hunters and gatherers. But annual flooding made possible relatively dense populations in the lush oases of the river valleys.

The Colorado River, originating high in the Rocky Mountains, is fed by numerous tributaries in a drainage area of a quarter of a million square miles. Emerging from the chasm of the Grand Canyon, it rounds a bend at the present boundary of Arizona and Nevada and turns southward, flowing alternately through constricted canyons and floodplains en route to the Gulf of California.

Once an untamed torrent, the silt-laden Colorado was prone to overflow its banks in the spring of the year, swollen with the melting snows of the Rockies. Ordinarily the floods were not destructive, spreading gently over the bottomlands for distances of as much as a mile or two from the river. In late June the waters began to recede, leaving behind a deposit of rich silt on the floodplains. In these alluvial sediments the Mojaves have planted their crops, which ripened rapidly in the intense summer heat.

In the bottoms are dense thickets of cane and arrowweed, and groves of cottonwood and willows. The terrain away from the river rises gradually to a sandy mesa, where there are stands of mesquite trees, which do not tolerate marshy conditions. Where the root systems can no longer reach the subsurface moisture, abrupt changes in flora occur. Beyond the arid mesa, where the vegetation consists mainly of cacti and creosote bushes, rise jagged and utterly barren mountains. Few larger game animals were found at the lower elevations, although deer occasionally strayed into the thickets near the river. More common were rabbits and various rodents. In the river were fish such as hump-backs and mullets, which have been supplanted by introduced species.

History

The Spaniards of the sixteenth and seventeenth centuries, far to the south in Mexico, knew of the Mohaves mainly by hearsay. Too remote from the Spanish centers of ecclesiastical and temporal influence to be very directly affected by the activities of the Spaniards, the Mohave were visited only at protracted intervals.

The first Spaniard known to have contacted Mohaves was Onate, who in 1604 met them near the junction of the Colorado and Bill Williams rivers and farther south. Father Francisco Garces was in 1776 the first Spaniard to reach the Mohave Valley. He estimated the Mohave population to be 3,000 (table 1).

No missions or Spanish settlements were ever established in Mohave territory; the Mohave maintained their independence throughout Hispanic times. The rather sparse accounts of the Mohave left by the Spanish explorers reveal a picture of Mohave life similar in its essentials to that later reported by ethnographers. There were few changes in Mohave culture during the Hispanic period. The Mohave obtained wheat at second hand from the Quechan, and they acquired a few horses, some of them obtained in raids upon the Spanish mission communities in California.

After Mexican independence from Spain in 1821, the Mohave for a while continued their traditional way of life without hindrance. But during the 1820s a new breed of aliens, the Anglo-American trappers and fur traders, began to travel through Mohave country. Among them were the parties of Jedediah Smith and James O. Pattie in 1826 and 1827. At this period the Mohave were unpredictable in their reception of strangers, and blood was spilled on several occasions (K.M. Stewart 1966). Some of the parties of Anglo-Americans passing through their territory in subsequent years also had trouble with the Mohave; for example, the Lorenzo Sitgreaves expedition, seeking a route for a transcontinental railroad, was attacked in 1851.

Table 1. Population

Date	Estimate	Source
1770	3,000	Kroeber 1925:883
1776	3,000	Garces (Coues 1900, 2:450)
1872	4,000 (828 on the Colorado River Reservation, 700 at Fort Mojave)	ARCIA 1872:58, 323
1910	1,050	Kroeber 1925:883
1965	1,500	Wallace (Spencer and Jennings 1965:273)

Other railroad explorers, including Amiel W. Whipple in 1854, and steamboat captains seeking to determine the navigability of the Colorado, among them Joseph C. Ives in 1858, penetrated Mohave territory at a time when the long period of intertribal warfare among the River Yumans was coming to an end. In 1857 the Quechan-Mohave allies suffered a disastrous defeat at the hands of a combination of Pima and Maricopa warriors. Still smarting from their defeat, and apprehensive about the increasingly frequent intrusions of Whites into Mohave country, the Mohave warriors in 1858 attacked a wagon train bound for California. As a consequence, a United States

military post, later to be named Fort Mohave, was established in the Mohave Valley. However, the Mohave were still defiant, and in 1859 a battle was fought in which the Mohave warriors were mowed down by the rifle fire of the soldiers. This defeat ended the resistance of the Mohaves and paved the way for their subsequent acculturation (K.M. Stewart 1969).

During the period between about 1870 and 1890 the Mohaves, plagued with disease and living in abject poverty, went through a demoralizing interlude. Around the turn of the century things began to improve for them somewhat, although many problems persisted. Recent years have brought increasing prosperity to the Mohave of the Colorado River Reservation in particular, with the development of irrigated farmlands and income from leases of reservation land to Whites.

Culture, 1860-1890

Settlement Pattern

The Mohave had no true villages but lived in sprawling settlements or rural neighborhoods that were scattered throughout the valleys near

Mus. für Völkerkunde, Berlin: IV B12910.

Fig. 2. Mohave appearance in the 1850s. The woman holds an infant on one hip and a basket on her head and wears a double skirt of bark fiber. The designs on her arms and cheeks were painted, while her chin may have been tattooed. The men wear long breechclouts and hair rolls, are painted on legs, chests, and arms, and wear feather head ornaments. Watercolor by Heinrich Balduin Mollhausen on Joseph C. Ives Expedition, 1857-1858.

arable land. The houses were usually situated on low rises above the floodplain. The houses of a particular settlement might be spread out over a distance of a mile or two, with perhaps four or five miles separating them from the next settlement. The settlement constituted a local group, the nucleus of which was an extended family, either patrilocal or bilocal, although because of much shifting around of population, and also because of marital instability, unrelated families might be resident in a settlement (K.M. Stewart 1970-1971).

Structures

During much of the year the Mohaves slept under flat-topped, open-sided ramadas (shades), resorting to their more substantial sand-covered houses only in cold weather. The winter houses (fig. 5) were low and rectangular in floor plan. Four large cottonwood posts supported a sloping roof of poles, which was covered with a thatch of arrowweed. The sides and ends of the house, consisting of vertical poles, were also sloping. A layer of sand and earth or river mud several inches in thickness was piled over the exterior of the house (Kroeber 1925:731-735). Native-style houses have not been built since the beginning of the twentieth century.

Subsistence

The Mohave were basically dependent upon farming in the bottomlands along the river, supplementing their diet by gathering wild plants, by fishing in the river, and by doing some

left. Bancroft Lib., U. of Calif., Berkeley: right. Boston Public Lib., Print Dept.

Fig. 3. Clothing of the 1860s. left, Woman at Ft. Mojave. Her torso and probably her arms and legs bear vertical painted stripes, and she wears a bark skirt overlaid by a decorative cloth. Photograph by R. D'Heureuse, 1863. right, Group at Ft. Mojave. The man standing beside Maj. William Redwood Price (8th Cavalry) wears a rabbitskin robe over one shoulder, while the Indian man at right wears a military coat and hat. The women wear bead necklaces and skirts made of twisted cloth and yarn strips tied with waist bands. Photograph by Alexander Gardner, while on the Kansas Pacific Railroad, early 1868.

hunting. The principal crop was maize, mainly flour corn of the white variety. Tepary beans of several varieties were second in importance, and pumpkins and melons were also raised.

Mohave agricultural methods were relatively simple. The men did most of the work in clearing the land, and in planting and cultivating the crop, often assisted by the women, who did much of the harvesting. The Mohave farmer used a planting stick with a wedge-shaped point, punching holes in the moist soil, four to six inches deep and a pace apart, making no attempt to align the holes in regular rows. A woman usually followed a planter, dropping a half-dozen seeds in each hole, then replacing the soil and pressing it down by hand.

No crop rotation was practiced, and artificial fertilization was superfluous, since the fertility of the fields was maintained by the deposition of silt in the annual overflows. The growing plants received little attention other than that required to clear away weeds with sword-shaped wooden hoes.

Harvesting of the main crop started in late September and continued into October. The corn was husked in the fields by the women, and that portion of the crop that was not roasted and eaten while still green was thoroughly dried in the sun on the roofs of ramadas. After that it was stored away in huge basketry granaries, woven of arrowweed branches with the leaves still on them, and so coarse in their weave that they have been compared to giant birds' nests.

A man might appropriate any piece of land not already in use, clearing the land by breaking down the shrubby growth and burning it. Once under cultivation, the land was regarded as private property. The shape of the fields varied in accordance with the topography, but the fields were rarely more than an acre or two in size. Boundaries were marked with ridges of dirt, or with arrowweed markers set up along the edges of the field. Disputes over boundaries sometimes occurred, when flooding changed the configuration of the land or obliterated the dividing ridges. A rough pushing match or stick fight between the disputants, each backed by supporters, might then be the way to settle the matter. Each party would attempt to drive the other back across the contested territory, thus definitely establishing claim to the land.

Famines were rare, and in normal years the Mohaves had enough to eat. But in years of drought the river might fail to rise sufficiently to flood the fields, and then the harvest was lean. At such times the Mohaves were obliged to rely more heavily for their food supply on hunting, gathering, and fishing. These activities were also

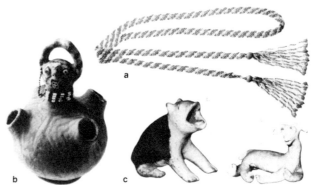

top, Southwest Mus., Los Angeles: 1376; Smithsonian, Dept. of Anthr.: a, 348,977; b, 278,080; c. U. of Colo. Mus., Boulder: 963.
Fig. 4. Tourist trade. top, Women selling bead necklaces to tourists. Photograph by Warren Dickerson at Needles, Calif., about 1890s. Crafts sold at the Needles, Calif., train station-a scheduled meal stop-included: a, necklace of braided strands of light blue and white seed beads accented with larger light blue beads; b, painted pottery vessel with 4 spouts and handle in shape of a human head with blue and white seed bead earring and necklace added (figurines similar to those of the Quechan were also made); c, whimsical animal figures that may also have been made as toys (Kroeber and Harner 1955:2). Length of a, 94 cm, collected before 1930. Height of b, 15 cm, rest to same scale, b and c collected by J.P. Harrington in 1911.

carried on at other times but became of crucial importance in times of poor harvest (K.M. Stewart 1966b; Kroeber 1925:735-737; Castetter and Bell 1951).

The women collected a variety of wild seeds in the bottomlands after the recession of the floods. They also went out in small parties to collect cactus fruits and other desert plants on the adjacent mesas. The most important wild food plants were the beanlike pods of

top left, Mus. fur Volkerkunde. Berlin, top right and bottom, Mus. of N. Mex., Santa Fe.

Fig. 5. Habitations. top left, Low-roofed winter house made of wattle-and-daub with earth-covered roof and open ramada. At left foreground is a basketry granary with 2 pottery vessels. A hoop-and-pole game is in progress. Watercolor by Heinrich Balduin Mollhausen, on Whipple Expedition, 1854. top right, A low-roofed house inundated by the annual spring flooding of the Colorado River. A basketry granary stands on the platform on left. bottom, Semisubterranean house under construction. The large posts are made from cottonwood trees and the covering is of arrowweed under a layer of sand. Thatch and sand remain to be added on the side walls (cf. Kroeber 1925:731-734). Corn is drying on the house roof as well as on the storage platform to right. The men wear long breechclouts and the traditional hair rolls. In front are pottery vessels of at least 5 shape types including a large shallow parcher for corn and wheat (cf. Kroeber and Harner 1955). top right and bottom, Photographs by Ben Wittick, 1890s.

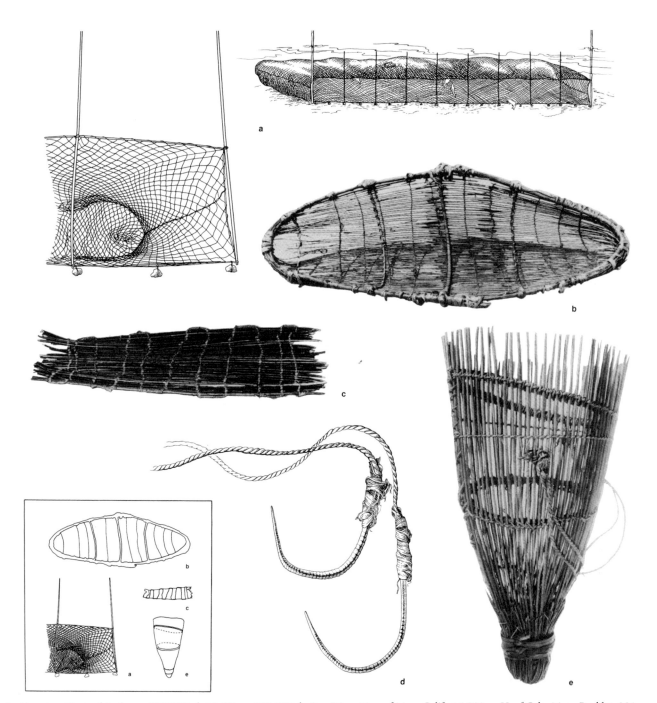

Smithsonian, Dept. of Anthr.: a, 277.907, d, 24,181; e. 278,007; b. San Diego Mus. of Man. Calif.: 16.838: c. U. of Colo. Mus.. Boulder: 981.

Fig. 6. Fishing equipment. Fish were caught in the Colorado River and in the lagoons and sloughs left by its spring flooding. One of the most common techniques used a seine or drag net (a) with poles attached to each end and sticks spaced vertically across the net with stones serving as weights. The net was worked by 2 men at opposite ends who dragged it through the water. A large basketry scoop (b) of willow lashed with bast would have a long handle attached across the center and was used by one man, although not on the river. Fish were also caught in sieves (c), dip nets, and weirs, and were shot with bow and arrow (Wallace 1955; K.M. Stewart 1957). Angling was not so common, but fishhooks (d) were made from cactus spines that had been moistened, heated, and bent. They were attached with fiber line to willow poles. A conical basket of willow twigs (e), carried on the back, was used to hold fish. d, collected by Edward Palmer in 1871; c, collected by J.P. Harrington and Junius Henderson in 1911; a,b,e collected by J.P. Harrington, b in 1914, rest in 1911. a, length of stick 120 cm; b, length about 183 cm; c, length 66 cm; d, length 5 cm; e, length 68 cm. Key at lower left indicates relative sizes (except for fishhooks)

the mesquite and screwbean (tornillo) (K.M. Stewart 1965; Castetter and Bell 1951).

Fish were the principal source of flesh food in the Mohave diet, although the fish native to the Colorado were rather soft and unpalatable. They were taken in dip nets, with seines or drag nets, in traps, or weirs, or with large, canoe-shaped basketry scoops with long handles, both in the river and in muddy sloughs and ponds (fig. 6). The fish were eaten fresh, after broiling on hot coals or boiling with corn in a kind of stew that the Mohaves particularly relished (K.M. Stewart 1957; Wallace 1955).

Hunting was of relatively little significance to Mohave subsistence, since game was scarce along the river, and the Mohave only occasionally went farther afield to hunt. The Mohave had only a feeble development of hunting techniques and devices, making no use of pit-falls or deerhead disguises. The deer hunter either waited in ambush or stalked the animal with a bow and arrow. Deer hunters sometimes made special excursions to the mountains east of the river. The hunter traded the game to other Mohaves for fish and farm products, since it was believed to be bad luck for a hunter to eat his own kill. Rabbits were caught in snares or nets, or shot with bows and arrows, or bowled over with curved throwing sticks, sometimes in communal rabbit drives (K.M. Stewart 1947b).

Technology

Artifacts, for the most part unadorned, were fashioned to meet only minimum requirements of utility. Little value was placed upon anything technological, but the Mohave indifference to craftsmanship may be in part attributable to the fact that all the property of an individual was destroyed at his death, and there was thus no inheritance of personal possessions. Mohave basketry was carelessly woven, and pottery (fig. 7) was no better than mediocre. Few artifacts were made of stone or bone, and the craft of woodworking remained rudimentary (Kroeber 1925:737-740).

Clothing and Adornment

Since the weather was hot or warm for the greater part of the year, a minimum of clothing was necessary. Children went naked, and the garments of both men and women were scanty. Men wore breechclouts, woven of strands from the inner bark of willow. Women were clad in knee-length skirts of willow bark.

Both sexes took pride in the glossy appearance of their long hair, which for cleansing

Calif. Histl. Soc., Los Angeles: Title Insurance Coll., 1908.

Fig. 8. *Nopie wearing strands of rolled hair wound around his head. He also has a bone nose ornament through his nasal septum. A ramada is behind him. Photograph possibly by Charles C. Pierce or George Wharton James, 1890s.*

Smithsonian, Dept. of Anthr.: 278,042. 10.320.

Fig. 7. *Painted pottery. left, Bowl, k aoki val'tay 'big bowl', painted with red geometric pattern on interior, with fiber wound around the rim for strengthening. Water was added to pounded mesquite beans in the bowl and, after stirring, the slightly sweet beverage was drunk. right, Water bottle with red on buff design. left, Diameter 30 cm (other to same scale), collected by J.P. Harrington in 1911; right collected by Edward Palmer in 1871.*

purposes was frequently plastered with a mixture of mud and boiled mesquite bark. The hair of the women hung in a loose mass over their shoulders, while men's hair was rolled into some 20 to 30 ropelike strands that hung down the back (Kroeber 1925:729).

Transport

Despite the importance of the river to the subsistence of the Mohave, they had no true boats. They were good swimmers, and often swam across the river, a swimmer sometimes ferrying goods or small children by pushing them ahead of him in a large pottery vessel. A man might straddle a single log to float downstream, and occasionally log rafts were made when an entire family wanted to travel downriver. On foot, the men could cover great distances across the desert in a single day, sometimes as much as 100 miles, in a steady, jogging trot. Women carried burdens in a rough, netted structure that was supported by a framework of sticks and was attached to a tumpline passed over the woman's forehead (Kroeber 1925:738-739).

Political Organization

The Mohave, regardless of place of residence, thought of themselves as one people, living in a true nation with a well-defined territory. Despite a loose division into bands and local groups, the tribal cohesion was such that the Mohave were able to present a united front in warfare against all enemies. At least three bands within the Mohave tribe have been identified: *matháladom*, the northern division; *hatópa*, the central division; and *kavéladom*, the southern division. Each band was subdivided into settlements or local groups. To the Mohave, the locality of residence was unimportant in contrast to membership in the tribe, and people moved freely from one locality to another within the tribal territory.

The Mohave had a head chief for the tribe, although it is uncertain how long the status had existed prior to extensive contact with Whites. The chieftainship may have developed out of the status of local group leader. Although the head chief was supposed to have dreamed his power, which is in full accord with Mohave

ideology, the office also became hereditary in the male line, which is un-Mohave-like. It is clear, in any case, that despite the tribal cohesiveness, the governmental machinery of the Mohave was minimal, with relatively slight institutionalization. No one individual or group of persons was in a position of significant authority over other Mohaves. There was no organized tribal council, although the chief might at times ask the prominent men from each settlement to meet with him for informal discussion of matters of importance. The chief had little authority but was expected to look after tribal welfare. He exerted a moral rather than a commanding influence over the people. The chief's importance increased for a brief period around 1859, when Mohave independence was coming to an end, but factionalism subsequently developed, with rival claimants to the chieftainship.

There were subchiefs in the several bands of the Mohave: one in the north, one in the south, and five in the more populous central division, according to informants. In the various settlements also were an indefinite number of local group leaders who, like the chiefs, were believed to have attained their positions by dreaming. They were expected to be skillful speakers, who addressed the people from the rooftops in the morning. People deferred to their wishes because they respected them, not because they had any real authority.

The main religious leaders were the *kohóte* ('the one who is good'), of whom there were several in different parts of Mohave territory. They performed religious functions that were believed to strengthen the integration of the tribe, and they were also festival chiefs, giving feasts and arranging victory celebrations. They, too, were speakers, addressing the people at funerals and on other occasions. They may at one time have been the principal tribal leaders, but their importance declined considerably during the early contact period, as that of the chief increased (Kroeber 1925:725, 745-747; K.M. Stewart 1970-1971; Fathauer 1954).

Mohave warfare was carried on primarily by the *kwenemí* ('brave, willing'), those men who had experienced "great dreams" conferring power in battle, although in a major expedition men who had not had the proper war dreams might also participate. In Mohave belief, warfare was instituted by the culture hero, *mastamhó*, who decreed that in each generation some men would have dreams giving power in war. Thus the *kwenemí* were eager to validate their dreams, so to speak, by demonstrating prowess in battle. A few *kwenemí*, those with stronger dreams, were recognized as war leaders.

A raid might be undertaken by 10 or 12 *kwenemí* whenever they wished to go out and fight, but more preparation preceded a major campaign. Scouts or spies, who had dreamed specific powers, first reconnoitered the route to be traversed, locating water holes and enemy habitations. Attack on an outlying enemy settlement was at dawn, by surprise, but if the Mohave continued farther into Maricopa territory they might encounter a battle array of Maricopa and Pima warriors. Challengers from the opposing sides would then meet in single combat before a general melee started. The Quechan usually joined the Mohave for campaigns, and sometimes they invited the Mohave to come down-river to join them in an attack on the Cocopa.

The Mohave had a divided armament in which some warriors bore long bows with untipped arrows of sharpened arrowweed, while others carried hardwood clubs, which did most of the damage in hand-to-hand fighting. Most effective was a mallet-headed club (fig. 10) shaped like an old-fashioned potato masher, which was wielded by the *kwenemí*.

On each major expedition a special scalper, who had dreamed his power to scalp, treated warriors who had fallen ill because of contact

top, U. of Ariz., Ariz. State Mus., Tucson: E-4971: bottom. Yale U.. Peabody Mus.: 19127.

Fig. 10. War equipment. top, *Warrior's traveling kit consisting of bow with twine string and arrows with sharpened tips, painted ends with 3 feathers. Attached to bow are items a man would need: cloth cap, hide sandals, wooden club painted black except for red ends, gourd water bottle with wood stopper hung in twine netting, hair ornament of flicker feathers. Missing is a small bag of mesquite beans for food. Made by Romeo Burton.* bottom, *War standard, made of pointed stick with feathers attached. Quills are bound with red yarn to either end of a short string, which is then tied to the staff by a continuous cord. This example was probably made for use at a mourning ceremony since those used in battle were usually heavier (Spier 1955:12). Each war party had a standard bearer who carried no other weapon and was obliged not to flee (K.M. Stewart 1947:265-266).* top, *Length of bow 120.0 cm, bottom to same scale, collected in 1962; bottom collected by Leslie Spier in 1932.*

(Facing Page) top right and bottom left, Mus. of N. Mex.. Santa Fe: School of Amer. Research Coll.. 15959. 15956; bottom right, Smithsonian. NAA: 2801-b-6: top left. Douglas Co. Mus.. Roseburg. Oreg.

Fig. 9. *(Facing Page) Adornment. Both men and women customarily had tattooed chins and frequently wore elaborate facial painting in a large variety of designs (see Taylor and Wallace 1947; Kroeber 1925:730, 732-733 for other patterns). top left, Olive Oatman, a White woman who was tattooed by the Mohave while she was a captive among them 1852-1856 (K.M. Stewart 1969:220); photograph by Powelson of Rochester, N.Y., about 1858. top right, Unidentified woman from Needles, Calif.; photograph by Ben Wittick, about 1883. bottom left, Hanje; photograph by Ben Wittick, about 1883. bottom right, Unidentified woman; photograph by Ben Wittick, 1880s. Two of the women wear jew's harps suspended from their multi-strand bead necklaces.*

with the evil power of the enemy. The return of the warriors was celebrated with a victory dance around enemy scalps mounted on poles. Prisoners were almost exclusively girls or young women, who were given to the old men as an insult to the enemy (K.M. Stewart 1947; Fathauer 1954; Kroeber 1925: 751-753).

Social Organization

Marriage among the Mohave was casual, arranged without formality by the couple themselves, subject to the observance of clan exogamy and the avoidance of marriage between close relatives. Wedding ceremonies were lacking; the couple simply began living together. Most marriages were monogamous, although polygynous unions occurred occasionally. There was no mandatory rule about place of residence after marriage. Where the newlyweds lived seems in practice to have been a matter of preference or convenience. The Mohave had neither in-law avoidances nor prescribed behaviors toward affinal relatives. Marital instability was common, divorce entailing merely a separation at the will of either party (Kroeber 1925:745; K.M. Stewart 1970-1971).

Status differences between families were insignificant. The nuclear family was the essential unit in daily social and economic life, although the members of an extended family sometimes cooperated in tasks such as farming (K.M. Stewart 1970-1971).

While lacking both phratries and moieties, the Mohave had a rather unusual system of patrilineal, exogamous clans. Whatever functions the clans may have had in the precontact period have been lost, other than the sometimes-ignored exogamic prescriptions. There were no clan leaders, and the clans played no significant part in either religious or secular life.

The Mohave word for a clan is *símul* (also 'clan name'; cf. *imul* 'personal name'). The names of the clans, 22 in number, were believed to have been given by the deity *matavíle* in the mythical period. All the women of a particular clan were called by the clan name rather than by a personal name, while the men were silent carriers of the name, being known by nicknames. The clan names were of totemic import, pertaining to plants, animals, or natural phenomena, although the words were archaic rather than those in current usage. There were no taboos on killing or eating the totems, nor were the totems venerated. Not all members of a clan lived in the same locality (Kroeber 1925:741-744; Spier 1953; K.M. Stewart 1970-1971).

Religion

Mohave religion featured an unusual conception of dreaming, which was in fact a pivotal concept in their culture as a whole, permeating almost every phase of Mohave thought and endeavor. All special talents and skills, and all noteworthy success in life, whether in warfare, lovemaking, gambling, or as a shaman, were believed to be dependent upon proper dreaming.

Dreams were constantly discussed and meditated upon by the Mohave. This intense preoccupation with dreams was accompanied by an indifference to learning. The Mohave were aware, of course, that skills could be improved by practice and that songs and myths could be assimilated by listening to them. But the acquisition of knowledge in such ways seemed of little value to the Mohave, since information and skills were regarded as ineffectual unless a person had the requisite power-bestowing dreams.

Although the Mohave were interested in dreams of all kinds, they made a clear distinction between ordinary dreams and the "great dreams" that brought power. All dreams were believed to have a meaning, so the ordinary dreams were regarded as "omen dreams," which when properly interpreted might foretell coming events.

The "great dreams," called *sumác ahot* 'good dream', came to relatively few people, but the chosen ones who had them were the leaders in Mohave society-chiefs, braves, shamans, singers, and funeral orators. The dream was thought to occur first while the unborn child was still in the mother's womb.

In Mohave belief the prenatal dream was forgotten by the dreamer but was dreamed over again later in life, usually during adolescence. The youth, conditioned throughout his life by the cultural emphasis upon dream power, longed for and anticipated having a "great dream." Having heard others tell their dreams, again and again, in the stereotyped mythological pattern, the boy might have, or believe that he had, similar dreams. The test of the authenticity of his dreams depended upon whether he was able to validate them in successful undertakings.

Public ceremonies were almost totally lacking among the Mohave, and even dancing occurred only incidentally as an adjunct to the singing of certain song cycles. The Mohave had no masks, almost no ceremonial regalia and paraphernalia, and practically no symbolism or fetishism. There were no rituals intended to bring rain or promote the growth of crops.

Instead, the Mohave emphasized the recitation of dream experiences and the singing of song cycles. The song cycles, numbering about 30 in all, were supposed to have been dreamed by the singer. Each cycle consisted of from 50 to 200 songs, and the singing of a complete cycle required an entire night or more. The singer alternately sang and recited mythological episodes, for some cycles accompanying his singing by shaking a gourd rattle or beating rhythmically with a stick on an overturned basket (Kroeber 1925:754-755; Wallace 1947; K.M. Stewart 1970-1971; Devereux 1956, 1957).

Mythology

Mohave myths were extremely long and detailed, and the narrations were replete with details of name and place and trivial events. In general, they described the journeys of mythical personages and told of their eventual transformation into animals or landmarks.

In the Mohave cosmogony, Sky and Earth were male and female respectively. From them was born the deity *matavíle* who built a sacred house, the Great Dark House, where Mohave dreamers would later receive power. He offended his daughter, Frog Woman, who bewitched him, causing his death. *Matavíle* was cremated, and the Great Dark House was burned, setting the precedent for future Mohave funerals.

A younger deity and culture hero, *mastamhó*, then assumed leadership and proceeded to put the land into shape, making the Colorado River and heaping up the sacred mountain, *avìkamé*, where he conferred upon the unborn souls the powers of which they would later dream. *Mastamhó* taught the people to speak, to get food, to cook in pottery; he also instituted the clan system and separated the various tribes. His work completed, *mastamhó* transformed himself into a fish eagle and flew away. Since *matavíle* and *mastamhó* no longer existed as divinities, the Mohave neither worshiped them nor invoked them in prayer. Other supernaturals were not numerous and did not figure prominently in Mohave myths (Kroeber 1925:770-775, 1948, 1972).

Shamanism and Sorcery

Shamans, who were believed to have received their power from *mastamhó* at the time of creation, had perhaps the most elaborate "great dreams" of any Mohaves. The Mohave shaman (*káoidé*) was typically a specialist, who had dreamed the power to cure only one or several kinds of illness, such as sickness attributed to contact with aliens, to "bad dreaming," to loss of one's soul, to witchcraft, to sickness caused by ghosts, to arrow wounds, or to the bites of rattlesnakes and other poisonous animals. The shaman's power to cure depended upon which portion of the creation myth he had dreamed, and upon which powers *mastamhó* had conferred upon him. When curing, the shaman would brush the patient with his hands, blow a spray of saliva over him, and sing the songs learned in his "great dream."

A shaman could cause disease as well as cure it. Mohaves were apprehensive that a doctor might become a witch as he grew older, being most apt to bewitch his own relatives, or those of whom he was fond, or to whom he was attracted, in order to segregate them in a special place as his "followers." There, he was believed to be able to visit them in dreams. A shaman was thought to be powerless to bewitch anyone who was "mean," or whom he hated or disliked. The Mohave distinguished between "fast witching," in which the witch shot power into a person, killing him almost instantly, generally at a public gathering such as a funeral, and "slow witching," in which the witch came to the victim in dreams and caused him to gradually waste away and die. Successful treatment of a bewitched person was possible if not too long delayed.

The shaman lived a precarious life, since if he were suspected of witchcraft, or if he lost too many patients, he might be killed. Usually, the braves were the witch-killers. Shamans are said to have met their fate with an accepting stoicism, sometimes even deliberately provoking people and inviting them to kill them. The reason for the shaman's indifference to death was that a special fate was believed to await him in the afterworld, but only if he died in a violent manner. If the death were too long delayed, his retinue of "followers" might be kidnapped by another witch, or if he died a natural death the souls of the bewitched were automatically released to pass on to *salaáyte*, the land of the dead (K.M. Stewart 1970, 1973, 1974a; Kroeber 1925:775-779).

Life Cycle

Mohave observances in connection with pregnancy and birth were of a simple and nonritualistic nature. But the period of pregnancy was significant to future life, since it was believed to be then that the "great dreams" first occurred, with the soul of the dreamer being impelled backward in time to the "first times." Also, the fetus was believed to have a conscious existence of its own, and it could cause difficulty for the mother if it were unhappy or angry.

The enculturation of the young Mohave was informal and gradual, and the parents were indulgent and permissive throughout the childhood of their offspring. Disciplinary methods were mild, and were mostly of an admonitory nature.

Children spent much of their time in play activities, many of which were in imitation of adult occupations. Education of the child was casual, and little pressure was put upon the children to acquire skills rapidly. Specific instruction was minimal, since in Mohave belief myths and songs were dreamed, and special abilities could be acquired only in dreams.

Puberty rites had only a feeble development among the Mohave. The very minor observances at the time of a girl's first menstruation were considered a private, family affair, and they were not occasions for singing, dancing, or public performances. For four days the girl was secluded in a corner of the house, remaining quiescent and eating only sparingly, while avoiding meat and salt. Each night she lay in a warmed pit. Her dreams at this time were considered significant as omens of the future (Wallace 1947a, 1948; Devereux 1950).

Sociocultural Situation in 1970

By 1970 little of the traditional Mohave culture remained, and the Mohave had been largely acculturated to the Euro-American way of life. Although pride in identity as Mohaves persisted among the people, many were apprehensive that the identity would be lost in the near future, as intermarriage with other ethnic groups became more common, and as Whites moved into Mohave territory in increasing numbers.

Even the Mohave language was lapsing among the younger people, although their elders still conversed in it frequently. Most of the Mohaves have attended school and were able to read and write in English.

The old mode of subsistence was gone: fishing, hunting, and gathering were no longer of importance. Some farming was still done, but with canal irrigation and the use of modern implements and techniques. Most of the food was purchased in grocery stores.

The old material culture had disappeared almost entirely. Craftwork was of negligible importance. The Mohaves were living in wooden cottages or modern houses of cement-block construction. The White styles of clothing alone were worn.

There had been no successor to the last chief, who died in 1947. Both reservation communities were governed by elected tribal councils with chairmen, under the provisions of the Indian Reorganization Act of 1934.

The clan system was being rapidly forgotten, and many people disregarded exogamy or did not even know their clan affiliations.

Belief in the Mohave religion persisted among some of the older people, although many Mohaves had been converted to Christianity, affiliating mainly with the Presbyterian, Nazarene, or Assembly of God churches. Some had resisted conversion, and some older Mohaves maintained that they believed in both the Mohave religion and the Christian religion and tried to equate them.

One elderly shaman still occasionally treated people on the Colorado River Reservation, although most people went for treatment to the government hospital. Some of the older people speculated about whether certain youngsters might have had the proper dreams for curing power, but had not yet "shown themselves." Older people, at least, continued to believe in witchcraft, and certain individuals were commonly suspected of being witches.

Marriage and divorce were conducted by legal methods, often through the tribal council, but marital instability was still rather common. Many Mohaves had been married more than once.

Native games were seldom played any longer. Few singers of the ancient song cycles were still living, and only a few older people remembered fragments of myths and folktales. It was doubtful that anyone any longer experienced a "great dream," although the Mohaves were still very much interested in dreams as omens. But the manifest content of the dreams had come to reflect contemporary conditions rather than the traditional Mohave culture.

Most Mohaves were still cremated on funeral pyres, to the accompaniment of wailing. Some of the property of the deceased was still being burned, but houses were no longer put to the torch. The commemorative mourning ceremony was no longer held.

Approximately 1,000 Mohaves were living on the Colorado River Reservation, and some 500 former residents of the Fort Mojave Reservation were living on the outskirts of Needles, California. A higher standard of living had been attained by many Mohaves during the 1960s, when it became possible to lease reservation lands to development corporations and large-scale farming operations. By 1970 most of the Mohave income was in wages and land-lease money, with a lesser income from farming (K.M. Stewart 1970-1971).

Synonymy

(This synonymy was written by Ives Goddard, incorporating some references supplied by Kenneth M. Stewart.)

The Mohave have generally been referred to by variants of their name for themselves, *hàmakháv*. Many Mohave speakers identify the syllable *ha-* with the word *ahá* (or *há*) 'water', but linguists have not recorded the apparent form *ahàmakháv* given as the "true Indian name" by Sherer (1967:2, 28-29, phonemicized), though explained as pronounced "so that it sounds as though it begins with an H." Some speakers give no literal meaning to this name, others translate it as 'people who live along the water' or relate it to an old word for the traditional grass skirt. The shortened form *makháv* is also in use (Pamela Munro, communication to editors 1974).

The translation of the name Mohave as 'three mountains' (Gatschet 1877-1892, 1:378; Hodge 1907-1910, 1:919) is a guess based on knowledge of the Mohave words *hamók* 'three' and *aví* 'mountain', but these words do not appear in *hàmakháv* and would in any case have to be used in the order *avíhamók* to give the meaning 'three mountains' (Sherer 1967:4; Pamela Munro, communication to editors 1974).

The earliest known recording of *hàmakháv* is as Amacava, 1605 (Escobar in Bolton 1919:28), later Spanish spellings being Amacaua, Amacaba, Amacabos (Sherer 1967:5-6, 29), and the Jamajab of Garcés, 1776 (Coues 1900, 2:443), and Jamajá of Font, 1776 (Bolton 1930, 4:484). The first recordings by English speakers refer to incidents in the late 1820s: Ammuchabas and Amuchabas, 1826 (Jedediah Smith), Mohawa (J.O. Pattie), Mahauvies, Mohauvies, and Mohavies (G.C. Yount as recorded by O. Clark), and Mohave (Christopher Carson as recorded by D.C. Peters; all in Sherer 1967:8-13, 30-32). Later forms are Mohahve (obtained by J.C. Frémont in 1843, probably from Carson), and in the 1850s Mojave, a Spanish or pseudo-Spanish spelling first used by Whipple (1941), 1853-1854, and found interchangeably with Mohave since (Sherer 1967:11-18). Other forms are given by Hodge (1907-1910, 1:921) and Sherer (1967). The spelling Mojave has been officially adopted by the Fort Mojave and Colorado River tribal councils; Mohave is used by the Bureau of

Indian Affairs.

Related or borrowed forms of the name Mohave in other Indian languages include the following: Havasupai *wamkáv* (Leanne Hinton, communication to editors 1981); Walapai wa-mo-ka-ba (Corbusier 1923-1925) or wamakav or wamukava (Kroeber 1935:39); Yavapai makhava (Gifford 1932:182, 1936:253); Quechan *xamakxáv* (Abraham M. Halpern, communication to editors 1981); Maricopa *xamakxava* (Kroeber 1943:38) and *makxav* (Lynn Gordon, communication to editors 1981); Cocopa *xamkxap* (Kroeber 1943:38); Hopi *amakava* (Harrington 1925-1926). Other names are Pima-Papago *naksad* or the English loanword *maháwi* (Saxton and Saxton 1969:156), and the historical Spanish Soyopas, 1774 (Bolton 1930, 2:365).

top, Colo. River Tribal Lib.-Mus., Parker, Ariz.: BBB-14-823; center, Smithsonian, Dept. of Anthr.: 210,954.

Fig. 12. Beaded collars and belts. *top, Cha-cha Cox (d. 1941), Irrateba's granddaughter, wearing an elaborate netted bead collar of the type that became popular in the late 19th century. center, Beaded collar. Netted openwork body of blue and white seed beads in fret pattern with drawstring neckline and fringe of strands of seed beads ending with large white glass beads. Depth 23.0 cm, collected before 1901. bottom, Flora Sands beading a belt at the home for the elderly on the Colorado River Indian Reservation. Photographed by Jerry Jacka, Nov. 1977.*

Sources

The early Spanish chronicles contain rather meager descriptions of the Mohave. The best account of the Mohave in Hispanic times is that of Garcés (Coues 1900). The writings of the Anglo-American fur trappers in the early nineteenth century contain scant ethnographic information, since the trappers were little given to the observation of cultural details, and their encounters with the Mohave were often hostile (K.M. Stewart 1966).

For the mid-nineteenth century there are accounts of railroad explorers and steamboat captains, as well as Stratton's (1857) sensationalistic and in part inaccurate book on the captivity of the Oatman girls among the Mohave. And, from the Annual Reports to the Commissioner of Indian Affairs between 1865 and 1892 it is possible to glean a fragmented conception of the culture and conditions of the Mohave during the early reservation period. The nearest approach to an anthropological account of the Mohave during the nineteenth century was Bourke's (1889) article, based on a brief visit in 1886.

The basic and definitive ethnographic work among the Mohave was done by A.L. Kroeber between 1900 and 1911. His chapters on the Mohave (Kroeber 1925) remain the standard and most complete source on this tribe.

No phase of Mohave culture has been neglected by anthropologists, who have generally written articles on particular aspects of Mohave culture rather than comprehensive books or monographs. The few books on the Mohave include Devereux's (1961) work on ethnopsychiatry. Mohave subsistence is explained by Castetter and Bell (1951). The information in print on Mohave culture is actually rather copious, but it is widely scattered in many journals, some of which are relatively obscure and available only in large libraries with extensive holdings. The most important articles on the Mohave have been written by Kroeber (1925, 1948, 1972), Devereux (1937, 1950, 1951, 1951a, 1956, 1957), Sherer (1965, 1966, 1967), Fathauer (1951, 1951a, 1954), Wallace (1947, 1947a, 1948, 1953, 1955), K.M. Stewart (1946, 1947, 1947a, 1947b, 1957, 1965, 1966, 1966a, 1966b, 1968, 1969, 1969a, 1969b, 1970, 1970-1971, 1974, 1974a, 1977), and Spier (1953, 1955).

The best museum collections of Mohave artifacts are at the University of California Lowie Museum, Berkeley, and the National Museum of Natural History, Smithsonian Institution, Washington.

Chapter Two

❖

The Land

Photo by Jeffrey L. Garton

The Teatime Moon and the Setting Sun

From *Outposts of Eden* by Page Stegner

Reprinted with permission of Don Congdon Associates, Inc. Copyright ©1989 by Page Stegner

"Everyone knows Desert Solitaire *as the title of Edward Abbey's first and best book, published in 1968 and still being savored by new geneartions of readers. But it also heads the first chapter in Page Stegner's* Outposts of Eden, *a collection of essays published in 1989—coincidentally the very year that Abbey died.*

Like Abbey, Stegner's love for the wildernesses of the West is tempered by pessimism about their survival, and his attitude ranges from curmudgeonly to combative. But his sense of humor is always lying in wait, ready to pounce." –L. W. C.

For the third week in a row the mid-morning temperature in Parker is over 110 degrees. While I wait for gas I stand in the shade of a Mobil station canopy, squinting across the sagebrush to the line of tamarisk and willow along the Colorado River that marks the border between Arizona and southern California. Beyond the river lies the great desert, twenty-five million acres of barren, bleak terrain that makes up one-quarter of the land surface of America's most populated and geophysically diverse state. Three deserts, actually: the Colorado, Mojave, and Great Basin, each blending into the other and distinguished by major increases in elevation as one moves north. The Colorado desert (generally below three thousand feet) extends from the Mexican border to an imaginary line drawn between Los Angeles and Phoenix. The Mojave continues for some two hundred miles north before giving way, in turn, to the higher, colder Basin and Range province associated primarily with Nevada and western Utah. Colder, it should be said, is a relative term.

A growing sensation at the top of my cherubic cheeks begins to announce itself as the searing metal frames of my glasses undergo rapid thermogenesis outside the air-conditioned cab of my truck. I remove them when the temple wires become molten and my sideburns begin to fry. A damp, pink man with a bumper sticker on his pickup that reads "Sierra Club, Kiss My Axe" fills his tank in the aisle next to me and comes back to polish the windshield of the boat he's towing—a candy-apple red projectile with a white tuck-and-roll interior and a half dozen chrome pipes sticking out of the engine casing like rocket launchers. He observes my California plates and asks if I, too, am in Parker

for the jet boat races. I tell him no, I'm just down checking out my desert—seeing if it needs watering or anything like that.

"Your desert," he says. "Ha ha ha."

I don't know what's so funny. It is my desert. It's *his* desert, too. Over three-quarters of the region is federally owned lands, some of it (two and a half million acres) in national monuments and state parks, a bit more (three million acres) in military reservations, the rest of it (twelve and a half million acres) Bureau of Land Management (BLM) territory administered for the American people by the Department of the Interior. Except where the Pentagon plays furtively with explosives and supersonic toys it is "public domain," though the general public's interest in *this* domain seldom extends beyond calculations of speed and distance—how fast it can be crossed.

Not surprising. The California desert is replete with uninviting place names like Death Valley, Devil's Playground, Furnace Creek (where the hottest temperature officially recorded in the United States occurred on July 10, 1913—134 degrees Fahrenheit, in the shade), Badwater (where it is historically four degrees hotter than Furnace Creek, and where there is no shade), Funeral Mountains, Dead Mountains, Styx, Poison Wells. While it is actually more inhabited than one might expect-particularly where San Bernardino and San Diego have sprawled eastward into the Coachella and Imperial valleys around Palm Springs, Indio, and El Centro—settlement is sparse by any standards. And the majority are contained in a relatively small area southeast of Los Angeles. The interior is not for everybody. Practically anybody.

Certainly it is not for my friend at the Mobil

station in Parker. He tells me he crossed "all that greasewood" in four hours flat and advises me to do the same, then tows his boat off toward the local marina to spend a restful weekend tearing up and down the Colorado, spewing gasoline fumes and oil slicks, splitting the quietude of canyon and river with the screaming fury of high tech engines wound to their breaking point. Some fun. Unfortunately he is an increasingly common type. He has his counterparts in the operators of off-road vehicles (motorcycles, dune buggies, four-wheel drive jeeps, trail bikes) who are as destructive to the desert ecology as he is to the river. Together they represent a phylum of Americans whose love of the outdoors is expressed solely by the various ways they tear it up with an internal combustion engine. They constitute as great a threat to wilderness as all the mining, energy, and livestock interests who destroy it for profit.

Ah well, another grumping environmentalist. I cross the bridge into California and head west toward Joshua Tree National Monument, one of three major desert parks in the region and about midway between the Arizona border and the Pacific coast. A hot wind buffets the truck, whipping the creosote brush along the road, whirling off across the sand like some mad dust devil executing entrechats and pliés through the cactus. Nasty stuff, creosote brush, and not to be confused with that sweet-smelling inhabitant of high altitude deserts-sage. The creosote bush, also known as greasewood, exudes a toxin into the ground to kill off all potential competitors for the infrequent rains that sustain life. It will poison its own offspring, given half a chance, and tastes so foul even cattle don't like to eat it. Which no doubt explains why it is the most conspicuous plant

throughout these arid lands.

All around me the dun-colored plain is periodically broken by low ranges of mountains that seem as barren and inhospitable as the parched

ground from which they rise–or from which I presume they rise. A hundred feet in front of my bumper the highway vanishes in a mercuric line of shimmering heat and I am surrounded by an opalescent sea of thermal waves that ebb and flow with each change in the road. At times it seems more like crossing an estuary than a desert. Cholla, yucca, beaver-tail cactus, and the ubiquitous greasewood poke up above the puddles. Somewhere to my right the Colorado River aqueduct snakes through jagged ridges that appear to float on the basin floor like islands. Big Maria Mountains, Turtle Mountains, Old Woman Mountains, Coxcomb Mountains.

Mountains? Yes, indeed. Some of them four and five thousand feet high. The present configuration of the Mojave is thought to have been formed during the Cenozoic era from uplifting associated with movement of the many thrust faults that strike across it in a predominantly north-south direction. The Garlock and San Andreas faults are the most infamous, but there are at least thirty others of less impressive dimension. Sometime during the Oligocene epoch the earth's crust, tortured by the stress of plate movement, broke into great blocks that were forced upward to form the high ranges and deep troughs that were then subjected to forty million years of erosional processes. The troughs between the ranges gradually filled with material that crumbled down from the slopes, and a once-mountainous topography was all but erased, buried in its own debris. And the process is hardly complete, as any desert traveler can plainly see. Wherever these old molars have been wrinkled and cut by the forces of wind and rain, alluvial fans flow out of the canyon mouths like gravel aprons, sloping gently toward the center of the basins they have been slowly filling since the last days of the dinosaur.

It is late when I arrive at Joshua Tree and I am forced to lay out my gear by the lights of my truck. The Park Service provides a table and a fire pit with a grate, but I converted my operation to a propane camp stove long ago, and have no need of these amenities. Not very aesthetic, propane, but it saves scrambling over five hundred acres of rattlesnakes and scorpions in search of the twelve remaining twigs in the area not discovered by previous campers. It also saves me from contributing to one of the less appealing features of the modern American campsite—a pigsty of charcoal and ashes ringed by a splatter of half-burned garbage. People who otherwise understand that it is wicked to leave a sack of trash in their wake will nevertheless try to burn wet newspaper, soggy lettuce, steak bones, beer cans, gin bottles, and other assorted nonflammable components of their wilderness experience. Wood fires should be banned from the national parks, never mind how cheerfully they dispel creatures who go bump in the night.

Joshua Tree encompasses an area of nearly a half million acres and provides within its boundaries an excellent contrast between Mojave and Colorado desert ecosystems. The eastern half of the monument lies below three thousand feet and is dominated by creosote brush, small stands of spidery ocotillo (that looks like some kind of multilimbed sea worm) and jumping cholla, a deceptively benign-looking cactus with a single trunk and a number of short lateral branches on top that are so closely set with straw-colored spines they appear soft and cuddly. They aren't. In the higher, slightly cooler areas, twisted rock and granite monoliths create a broken terrain where the *yucca brevifolia* thrives. Early Mormon travelers crossing the California desert thought it looked like Joshua leading the Israelites out of the wilderness and so named it in his honor. It looks like a bad drug trip to me. Especially those samples bordering my campsite, their twisted, contorted branches silhouetted against the night sky. The Joshua tree is a member of the lily family (which it in no respect resembles), grows to thirty feet, and when looked at in the daylight reminds me strangely of thorn trees dotting the Serengeti Plain of northwestern Tanzania-widely spaced, solitary, yet totally dominating the low horizon.

Because I am not clouding the atmosphere with wood smoke I am treated after dinner to a bowl full of stars to light my way into bed. Leave my tennis shoes in the back of the truck to discourage wandering scorpions. Pull a tarp over my sleeping bag and lie on top because it is still too hot for covers. A coyote barks somewhere up on Sheep Pass, answered by a relative off in the low hills to my left. Good hunting, guys. Keep the racket down. A meteor drops like a hot spark, punctuating consciousness. Later, around the first light of dawn, I wake for a moment and catch in the corner of my eye a shadow trotting through the pinon scrub separating my camp from the park road. Friend coyote heading home with what appears to be the remains of an unlucky jackrabbit.

Unless one has the night vision of an owl, and a disposition for wandering around dark places where every scrap of plant life is a pincushion of spines, needles, thorns, one is not likely to see much in the way of desert fauna. But it's out there, and in a profusion that would startle most travelers who regard the Mojave as a wasteland. Coyotes, of course, and bobcat, desert bighorn sheep, desert tortoise, antelope, ground squirrel (often mistaken for a chipmunk), round-tailed squirrel, grasshopper mouse, white-footed mouse, harvest mouse, little spiny pocket mouse (who comes about the size of a walnut and can jump three feet in the air), cactus mouse, brown-footed wood rat, dusky-footed brush rat, and everybody's favorite-the kangaroo rat. This fuzzy little rodent with feet the size of a spatula looks as if he was invented by a Walt Disney cartoonist.

When I am finally forced from my bed by the bright morning sun I find his tracks in the sand all around my sleeping bag. Checking me out to see if I'm edible, the nocturnal snoop. It's comforting to recall that he is strictly vegetarian. Not so comforting however, the discovery that my tennis shoes have been kidnapped from the tailgate of the truck. Probably lie murdered under some prickly pear. Unlucky jackrabbit, indeed.

Leaving the park after breakfast I head north over the Sheephole Mountains and across Bristol Dry Lake to Amboy, a tiny railroad junction for the Atchison, Topeka, and Santa Fe line, and a place of residence for a number of workers who mine the lake bottom for calcium chloride. This is truly a less accommodating landscape than the surface of the moon. Bristol is like almost all the lakes scattered throughout the Mojave and Great Basin, internal drainage bottoms, dry on the surface and bottomless muck underneath. Trenches are dug as deep as twenty feet into the sludge, allowed to fill with subsurface water from which salts are then precipitated. Pools of alkaline scum. Chemical slag heaps that look like dirty snow. At the northern end of the basin the dark cinder cone of the Amboy crater projects its perfect volcanic snout above the flats—a relative newcomer, geologists believe, having exploded and spewed its molten lava over a five-mile area within the last thousand years.

Small wonder, I suppose, that a lot of people regard proposals for the protection of this kind of country as a dementia of the environmental lunatic fringe. The California Desert Conservation Area Plan, mandated by Congress in 1976, written by the Bureau of Land Management after five years of "intensive" study, approved in 1981, has been under constant attack from mining interests, livestock interests, and off-road vehicle (ORV) clubs who would like to (and probably will) amend it out of existence. Particularly operators of motorized gadgets who seem to feel that it is their God-given right to run their machinery whenever and wherever they please, regardless of their effect on wildlife habitat and fragile soils and plants. "I don't tell you where to drive your car, do I?" one truculent dune buggy owner tells me during an inadvertent lunch counter interview I conduct over an Amboy burger in the town of the same name.

"Give me your address," I tell him. "Next time I'm in your town I'll come over and drive it on your lawn."

The Amboy burger is a discouraging affair. Preparation seems to have coincided with the birth of the crater for which it is named. One more salvo at the dune buggy driver and I belch on over Granite Pass toward Kelso, Cima, and the Ivanpah Mountains along the Nevada border. Somewhere between the Devil's Playground and the lava beds north of Kelso I stop to stretch the legs and climb a low gravel hump for a better view of the great sand dunes that lie in a basin between the Bristol and Soda Mountains. I am, frankly, in the process of contributing to the moisture content of this arid land when the ground under me seems to list to starboard and then suddenly subside about a foot and a half. I find myself on my knees looking at a network of small holes my blundering presence has evidently destroyed. Kangaroo rats again. They have honeycombed the area with the burrows, and I can hear the local inhabitants chiding me for my intrusion from deep in their tunnels, a sound that reminds me of the flutter of quail wings.

Two-thirds of the mammals that inhabit the California desert are rodents or gnawing animals, survivors because they have adapted to heat and drought in ways that other creatures could not. They come out of their holes only after dark. Unlike their bungling visitor they pass very little urine. They have no sweat glands and consequently lose no body liquid through perspiration. Many never drink at all, metabolizing what water they need out of the seeds and grasses on which they live. In a region that receives less than ten inches of rainfall a year (much of it less than five, and some of it as little as an inch and a half) this is a biological endowment that is critical. Sorry about the damage here, folks. I hope you have insurance....

The teatime moon has won its argument with the setting sun. Time to move on. The teal-wing mountains have gone black, their bright backdrop turned copper, lavender, indigo, before losing the cosmetic blush and melting into the etched lines of the ridge tops. Back on the highway, I am reduced to white knuckles and bulging eyeballs, hurtling along the center lane, terrified I am about to become a scrap of Toyota ham in a big rig sandwich. I can hear them downshift behind me as we fly over the summit at Mexican Well and rocket down into the Shadow Valley toward

Baker, Barstow, San Bernardino.

Humanoids are as abundant as kangaroo rats in Baker, a mid-Mojave pit stop along Interstate 15 that cuts northeast from Los Angeles and ends at the Canadian border near Glacier National Park. Cadillacs, Lincolns, Buicks, motor homes, trailers,

stream through town, most headed for the gambling pens in Las Vegas—HOWDY PARDNER—windows closed, air conditioners blowing frost into the perms of brittle-eyed gents in seizure suits, while Ms. Spandex sucks down another Virginia Slim and rides, bored, in the passenger seat, waiting for the desert to pass, waiting for glitter gulch to appear on the horizon. No biological adaptation here....

I stop only long enough for gas, then hightail it north through bone-dry hills toward Death Valley. The Great Basin Indians who first came here around a thousand years ago called it *Tomesha*, a word that supposedly means "ground afire." By rights it isn't a valley at all, but a graben—a depression that occurs between two parallel faults when the earth's convulsions force great blocks of tortured, twisted rock into mountains. Death Valley is bounded by the Amargosa and Panamint ranges, the peaks of which rise on the east to five and six thousand feet, and on the west as high as 11,000 feet. Between the two lies the collapsed sinkhole of salt, mud, gravel, sand, and blast furnace temperatures that most people think is the major attraction of the California desert, and some would argue is the major attraction of any desert in the world. But then most people see it largely from behind the tinted glass of a climate-controlled vehicle-a visual rather than a thermal experience.

Spectacle is perhaps a more accurate word than *attraction*. Whether Death Valley inspires one's poetic imagination or makes one shudder and step on the gas is pretty much a matter of disposition. I'm of both persuasions. Coming into it from the south, after a night unwittingly spent camped on an anthill, the mountains seem to fall in on each other, tumbling down from 3,315 feet at Salsbury Pass to a point on the valley floor that is below sea level—254 feet below sea level, to be exact, the lowest point in the United States. Parallel escarpments over a mile high are separated by a dry chemical lake nearly a hundred miles long and ten miles wide, all of it shaking and wobbling in the saffron heat of mid-afternoon. The overwhelming impression is that nothing is alive here in this chaos of warped and folded rock except a few stalks of creosote brush, pickleweed, and salt grass.

This is not true, exactly. The famous botanist

Frederick Vernon Colville, whose 1891 expedition into Death Valley is still the foundation of all ecological study in the eastern California desert, listed 1,200 species and varieties of plants in the area, and when one remembers that the park traverses vegetation zones from the lower Sonoran to the subalpine, these numbers are not difficult to believe. But then I'm told that the rocks lying at the base of the Black Mountains right over there to my right are early Precambrian—which is to say anywhere from a billion to 600 million years old-—and I believe that too. With about the same degree of understanding and capacity to conceptualize. I'll believe anything, but I still say it looks mighty dead down here.

From a point at the foot of the pass where the valley floor narrows between the Black Mountains and Owlshead Mountain I look north across a vast, smoky, pale distance: hemmed in by steeply sloping alluvial fans, sulfur-colored walls shading into mauve, rose, charcoal, and creased by a thousand welts and folds. Beautiful and ugly. Inviting and terrifying. They look sore in this light, like a nasty bruise. They look cracked and parched like the rotting hides of indecipherable, hairless animals. They look like some kind of malignancy that could draw me in and snuff me out.

Evidently the Park Service thinks so too. It has erected a wooden box by the side of the road with a sign attached, *Death Valley Survival Hints*. Why so coy? Why not just come right out with it? For survival stay in the shade and drink lots of water. Better yet, stop in at your friendly Fred Harvey bourgeois burrow at Furnace Creek Inn and Stovepipe Wells. Belly up to the bar for a cool one. Take a cue from the snakes and lizards and stay in a hole until dark.

Furnace Creek, one of the two places in the national monument that offers accommodations (Fred Harvey, concessionaire), is an oasis of date palm, cottonwood, and tamarisk. The springs that irrigate this small area in the center of the valley bubble up from an underground aquifer that lies along the base of the nearby Funeral Mountains. They are the only significant potable water resource available, but they are sufficient (or so I am told by a park ranger) to provide for the ten thousand visitors who arrive at peak usage times over the Christmas and Easter holidays, as well as for normal consumption on a year-round basis. How

long this can continue is anyone's guess. How big is that subterranean lake? With average rainfall in Death Valley at 1.7 inches a year, how fast can an aquifer recharge? How many showers and flushes and trips to the ice machine are there left before Furnace Creek Springs burps up one last quart of sulfuric brine and goes dry?

Well, for the moment, anyway, we have palm groves and lawns, an Olympic-size swimming pool, an eighteen-hole golf course, stables, bikes, lighted tennis courts—all of which the Fred Harvey brochure proudly tells us, "is just the beginning of Furnace Creek Resort life." One is tempted to ask what a "resort" has to do with a national park or monument, and to wonder whether we really need golf, tennis, and poolside dining in the world's hottest, driest place. Why is an inability to distinguish between a natural preserve and a playground endemic to the American mind? Some American minds; Departments of the Interior minds. No wonder a night at the inn costs $150 for a single.

I take my curmudgeonly carcass out near the foot of the Cottonwood Mountains, squat over my propane stove and cook a surly can of beans. Tomorrow I'll head west, over the Panamints and down into the trough of the Panamint Valley, over the southern extension of the White Mountains and down into the Owens Valley where the great wall of the Sierra Nevada rises abruptly out of the shadscale and sagebrush to block in its rainshadow everything that lies to the east for nearly five hundred miles. The ultimate range, and personally responsible for this gravel pit where I cook my supper. Tonight, however, I'm willing to forgive. I take my afterdinner cigar and stroll a bit out into Mesquite Flat toward the dunes above Stovepipe Wells. Scraggly plant life gives way to sand, gracefully embroidered here and there with the tiny tracks of circus beetles, and as evening settles down the last of the sunlight sets fire to a few high wisps of cloud, turning the mangled old ridge of the Amargosa Range into one radiant moment etched against the darkening backdrop of space. Not a bad piece of real estate. Glad I own it.

❋ ◆ ❋ ◆ ❋ ◆ ❋ ◆ ❋ ◆ ❋ ◆ ❋ ◆ ❋ ◆ ❋ ◆ ❋ ◆ ❋ ◆ ❋ ❋ ◆ ❋

Raging Arroyo

Flash Flood from *Sonoran Desert Summer* by John Alcock

Ineffably beautiful though it is, the desert is not a benign land, graciously welcoming the intrusion of human beings-the one resident species not biologically adapted to live in it. The desert has a remarkably long list of ways to discourage the presence of Homo sapiens, *from the heart-stopping buzz of a rattlesnake to a slow, agonizing death of anyone stranded without water and directions.*

Van Dyke appeared to describe one of these perils, the flash flood, in the voice of a remote observer. In this chapter from Sonoran Desert Summer, *John Alcock, a professor of zoology at Arizona State University, relates a closer encounter he had on a hike in southern Utah. –L. W. C.*

In May it is almost impossible to imagine water flowing down the washes near Usery Mountain and around the hackberries growing there. The monsoon season seems light years away and the sand of the washes as ancient and dry as a Saharan dune. But in August enough rain may fall in a short enough period to send a few inches of water surging along channels that drain the Usery Mountain watershed. Driving out to the desert the day after such a rain, I will see sheets of damp sand deposited on the blacktop and ditches that have been gouged a little deeper by rushing water. But the streams run for only a short time, and the only sign of water will be a brown pool or two along the roadside. The pools quickly evaporate, leaving a residue of smooth mud in their place.

The brevity and modest flow of most flash floods in central Arizona is such that I rarely have seen a dry wash flowing and I never have seen a true wall of water coming down a dry wash at the start of a flood. But once in southern Utah, on a grey monsoon day in early August, I almost became a part of a flash flood.

Clouds had coalesced over the Bear's Ears Mesa miles to the east of White Canyon; while sheets of rain soon blocked neighboring hills from view. At the trailhead, however, skies were only overcast; there was an occasional sprinkle, but the day was calm. In the flat, sombre light the shadowless canyon seemed more monumental than ever, even intimidating in the grand scale of its construction. The trail left the juniper-dotted plateau and dropped down through white, cross-cut canyon walls to reach the dry creek more than

five hundred feet below.

Once at the bottom of the narrow canyon, the trail skirted the empty streambed, cutting from one side to the other. Slickrock walls towered above the little strip of willows, oaks and cottonwoods growing along the watercourse. About fifteen minutes down the trail I heard an unfamiliar sound that I decided must be a wind sweeping high overhead off the plateau. The noise was not loud, but it was persistent, steady, odd. I walked on unconcerned. For a minute or two the whispering noise held steady, but as the flood flashed round a bend upstream the sound became horribly louder all at once.

When I realized that an indeterminate but clearly considerable amount of water was headed my way like an express train, I was on a little meander in the canyon on a stretch of sand and scrub bordered on one side by the wash and on the other by canyon walls. In the few moments before the flood reached me I ran in panic downstream along the wash looking for a way up the canyon on my right, but the sheer rock walls leaned out toward the wash, forming an unclimbable obstacle. I then had the choice of trying to cross the wash to reach the other side before the water thundered through or of heading for the highest point on my side of the stream. The thought of being caught midstream was so unappealing that I stayed on my side and scrambled frantically through a patch of scrub oak about thirty feet from the edge of the wash next to the imprisoning grey canyon wall. After climbing the biggest oak, which was disappointingly small, I was about six feet off the ground just as the wall of water came around the last bend upstream. Because of the screen of vegetation, I could not see the flood from my vantage, but as I contemplated the vagaries of existence I could hear with terrible clarity the crunch of boulders smashing along the streambed and the crack of limbs ripped from trees.

Seconds later the roar of the flood's leading wall traveled past and around the downstream bend, leaving me alive but shaken by the experience. I waited a bit before descending to inspect the flood. A light rain misted my glasses. Where streambed had been, there was now a torrential rush of water from ten to forty feet across and about four feet deep. The rampaging stream consisted of one part of Navajo red sandstone, finely ground, to one part of water, topped with foam, the whole thing whipped into a frenzy. It would have been suicidal to try to cross the stream at once, and I knew that the waters would recede eventually.

For the time being I was trapped, and if another storm hit the Bear's Ears there could be another flood. I most definitely did not want to be up the little oak tree if the main event was preparing for a grand entry somewhere up the canyon even then. Hustling about my little Devil's Island, I discovered one barely possible route to a spot high on the canyon wall that I might head for if I heard the big one coming down White Canyon. I did not look forward to becoming a rock climber under these conditions. As I waited on a little ledge above the floodplain I admired a nicely sheltered spot an easy climb one hundred feet up a sloping hillside across the impassable stream, and I reproached myself for not immediately seeking safety as soon as I had heard that strange whispering sound.

The floodwaters carried with them an unusual and unpleasant odor, slightly acrid, a bit like witch hazel, a smell of fear and anxiety. The red-brown waters thudded into the rock walls that checked their course and pulled at the willows in their way.

The drizzle stopped and the roaring stream receded with painful slowness. As the afternoon passed torturously and grim shadows filled the canyon, a rock squirrel came out from somewhere to forage on the sandy meander and tiny red-dotted toads sat in moist crevices in the canyon wall. Ten feet above the current flood, masses of flotsam from a much more impressive flood in the past gripped cottonwoods in a fierce embrace. Had a wall of water of similar dimensions come down the canyon while I was there I knew I would have been on my way to feed the fishes in Lake Powell dozens of miles downstream.

In the late afternoon I gingerly waded across the relatively subdued stream. Silt clung to my legs up to my thighs when I left the water.

By the next morning the torrent had disappeared, leaving behind stranded logs, a trickling stream, and great rippled flats of fine sandstone mud. Dancing sunlight reflected from the remnant watercourse to overhanging canyon walls. A desert primrose poked out of the mud with leaves mangled and muddied, its stem draped with flash-flood debris. The plant had bloomed overnight and its cheerful yellow flower faced upstream, looking toward the Sun and the source of future floods.

Travels with Charley
by John Steinbeck

Reprinted with permission of Viking Penguin, a division of Penguin Group.

John Steinbeck fought the first impulses we all feel in the desert: that it is hostile, that it is our obligation to pacify it. Unlike the other writers in this collection, he never lived in the Southwest, but in Travels with Charley (1962) he wrote perceptively as he passed through. His error was in repeatedly characterizing the desert as an "unwanted" land. The exploding populations of Tucson, Phoenix, Las Vegas, ElPaso, and Albuquerque today testify to the contrary. —L. W. C.

I bucketed Rocinante out of California by the shortest possible route—one I knew well from the old days of the 1930s. From Salinas to Los Banos, through Fresno and Bakersfield, then over the pass and into the Mojave Desert, a burned and burning desert even this late in the year, its hills like piles of black cinders in the distance, and the rutted floor sucked dry by the hungry sun. It's easy enough now, on the high-speed road in a dependable and comfortable car, with stopping places for shade and every service station vaunting its refrigeration. But I can remember when we came to it with prayer, listening for trouble in our laboring old motors, drawing a plume of steam from our boiling radiators. Then the broken-down wreck by the side of the road was in real trouble unless someone stopped to offer help. And I have never crossed it without sharing something with those early families foot-dragging through this terrestrial hell, leaving the white skeletons of horses and cattle which still mark the way.

The Mojave is a big desert and a frightening one. It's as though nature tested a man for endurance and constancy to prove whether he was good enough to get to California. The shimmering dry heat made visions of water on the flat plain. And even when you drive at high speed, the hills that mark the boundaries recede before you. Charley, always a dog for water, panted asthmatically, jarring his whole body with the effort, and a good eight inches of his tongue hung out flat as a leaf and dripping. I pulled off the road into a small gulley to give him water from my thirty-gallon tank. But before I let him drink I poured water all over him and on my hair and shoulders and shirt. The air is so dry that evaporation makes you feel suddenly cold.

I opened a can of beer from my refrigerator and sat well inside the shade of Rocinante, looking out at the sun-pounded plain, dotted here and there with clumps of sagebrush.

About fifty yards away two coyotes stood watching me, their tawny coats blending with sand and sun. I knew that with any quick or suspicious movement of mine they could drift into invisibility. With the most casual slowness I readied down my new rifle from its sling over my bed—the .222 with its bitter little high-speed, long-range stings. Very slowly I brought the rifle up. Perhaps in the shade of my house I was half hidden by the blinding light outside. The little rifle has a beautiful telescope sight with a wide field. The coyotes had not moved.

I got both of them in the field of my telescope, and the glass brought them very close. Their tongues lolled out so that they seemed to smile mockingly. They were favored animals, not starved, but well furred, the golden hair tempered with black guard hairs. Their little lemon-yellow eyes were plainly visible in the glass. I moved the cross hairs to the breast of the right-hand animal, and pushed the safety. My elbows on the table steadied the gun. The cross hairs lay unmoving on the brisket. And then the coyote sat down like a dog and its right rear paw came up to scratch the right shoulder.

My finger was reluctant to touch the trigger. I must be getting very old and my ancient conditioning worn thin. Coyotes are vermin. They steal chickens. They thin the ranks of quail and all other game birds. They must be killed. They are the enemy. My first shot would drop the sitting beast, and the other would whirl to fade away. I might very well put him down with a running shot because I am a good rifleman.

And I did not fire. My training said, "Shoot!" and my age replied, "There isn't a chicken within thirty miles, and if there are any they aren't my chickens. And this waterless place is not quail country. No, these boys are keeping their figures with kangaroo rats and jackrabbits, and that's vermin eat vermin. Why should I interfere?"

"Kill them," my training said. "Everyone kills them. It's a public service." My finger moved to the trigger. The cross was steady on the breast just below the panting tongue. I could imagine the splash and jar of angry steel, the leap and struggle until the torn heart failed, and then, not too long later, the shadow of a buzzard, and another. By that time I would be long gone—out of the desert and across the Colorado River. And beside the sagebrush there would be a naked, eyeless skull, a few picked bones, a spot of black dried blood and a few rags of golden fur.

I guess I'm too old and too lazy to be a good citizen. The second coyote stood sidewise to my rifle. I moved the cross hairs to his shoulder and held steady. There was no question of missing with that rifle at that range. I owned both animals. Their lives were mine. I put the safety on and laid the rifle on the table. Without the telescope they were not so intimately close. The hot blast of light tousled the air to shimmering.

Then I remembered something I heard long ago that I hope is true. It was unwritten law in China, so my informant told me, that when one man saved another's life he became responsible for that life to the end of its existence. For, having interfered with a course of events, the savior could not escape his responsibility. And that has always made good sense to me.

Now I had a token responsibility for two live and healthy coyotes. In the delicate world of relationships, we are tied together for all time. I opened two cans of dog food and left them as a votive.

I have driven through the Southwest many times, and even more often have flown over it—a great and mysterious wasteland, a sun-punished place. It is a mystery, something concealed and waiting. It seems deserted, free of parasitic man, but this is not entirely so. Follow the double line of wheel tracks through sand and rock and you will find a habitation somewhere huddled in a protected place, with a few trees pointing their roots at under-earth water, a patch of starveling corn and squash, and strips of jerky hanging on a string. There is a breed of desert men, not hiding exactly but gone to sanctuary from the sins of confusion.

At night in this waterless air the stars come down just out of reach of your fingers. In such a place lived the hermits of the early church piercing to infinity with unlittered minds. The great concepts of oneness and of majestic order seem always to be born in the desert. The quiet counting of the stars, and observation of their movements, came first from desert places. I have known desert men who chose their places with quiet and slow passion, rejecting the nervousness of a watered world. These men have not changed with the exploding times except to die and be replaced by others like them.

And always there are mysteries in the desert, stories told and retold of secret places in the desert mountains where surviving clans from an older era wait to re-emerge. Usually these groups guard treasures hidden from the waves of conquest, the golden artifacts of an archaic Montezuma, or a mine so rich that its discovery would change the world. If a stranger discovers their existence, he is killed or so absorbed that he is never seen again. These stories have an inevitable pattern untroubled by the question, If none return, how is it known what is there? Oh, it's there all right, but if you find it you will never be found.

And there is another monolithic tale which never changes. Two prospectors in partnership discover a mine of preternatural richness—of gold or diamonds or rubies. They load themselves with samples, as much as they can carry, and they mark the place in their minds by landmarks all around. Then, on the way out to the other world, one dies of thirst and exhaustion, but the other crawls on, discarding most of the treasure he has grown too weak to carry. He comes at last to a settlement, or perhaps is found by other prospecting men. They examine his samples with great excitement. Sometimes in the story the survivor dies after leaving directions with his rescuers, or again he is nursed back to strength. Then a well-equipped party sets out to find the treasure, and it can never be found again. That is the invariable end of the story—it is never found again. I have heard this story many times, and it never changes. There is nourishment in the desert for myth, but myth must somewhere have its roots in reality.

And there are true secrets in the desert. In the war of sun and dryness against living things, life has its secrets of survival. Life, no matter on what level, must be moist or it will disappear. I find most interesting the conspiracy of life in the desert to circumvent the death rays of the all-conquering sun. The beaten earth appears defeated and dead, but it only appears so. A vast and inventive organization of living matter survives by seeming to have lost. The gray and dusty sage wears oily armor to protect its inward small moistness. Some plants engorge themselves with water in the rare rainfall and store it for future use; animal life wears a hard, dry skin or an outer skeleton to defy the desiccation. And every living thing has developed techniques for finding or creating shade. Small reptiles and rodents burrow or slide below the surface or cling to the shaded side of an outcropping. Movement is slow to preserve energy, and it is a rare animal which can or will defy the sun for long. A rattlesnake will die in an hour of full sun. Some insects of bolder inventiveness have devised personal refrigeration systems. Those animals which must drink moisture get it at second hand—a rabbit from a leaf, a coyote from the blood of a rabbit.

One may look in vain for living creatures in the daytime, but when the sun goes and the night gives consent, a world of creatures awakens and takes up its intricate pattern. Then the hunted come out and the hunters, and hunters of the hunters. The night awakes to buzzing and to cries and barks.

When, very late in the history of our planet, the incredible accident of life occurred, a balance of chemical factors, combined with temperature, in quantities and in kinds so delicate as to be unlikely, all came together in the retort of time and a new thing emerged, soft and helpless and unprotected in the savage world of unlife. Then processes of change and variation took place in the organisms, so that one kind became different from all others. But one ingredient, perhaps the most important of all, is planted in every life form—the factor of survival. No living thing is without it, nor could life exist without this magic formula. Of course, each form developed its own machinery for survival, and some failed and disappeared while others people the earth. The first life might easily have been snuffed out and the accident may never have happened again—but, once it existed, its first quality, its duty, preoccupation, direction, and end, shared by every living thing, is to go on living. And so it does and so it will until some other accident cancels it. And the desert, the dry and sunlashed desert, is a good school in which to observe the cleverness and the infinite variety of techniques of survival under pitiless opposition. Life could not change the sun or water the desert, so it changed itself.

The desert, being an unwanted place, might well be the last stand of life against unlife. For in the rich and moist and wanted areas of the world, life pyramids against itself and in its confusion has finally allied itself with the enemy non-life. And what the scorching, searing, freezing, poisoning weapons of non-life have failed to do may be accomplished to the end of its destruction and extinction by the tactics of survival gone sour. If the most versatile of living forms, the human, now fights for survival as it always has, it can eliminate not only itself but all other life. And if that should transpire, unwanted places like the desert might be the harsh mother of repopulation. For the inhabitants of the desert are well trained and well armed against desolation. Even our own misguided species might re-emerge from the desert. The lone man and his sun-toughened wife who cling to the shade in an unfruitful and uncoveted place might, with their brothers in arms—the coyote, the jackrabbit, the horned toad, the rattlesnake, together with a host of armored insects—these trained and tested fragments of life might well be the last hope of life against non-life. The desert has mothered magic things before this.

Lost & Found

The Mystery of Louise Teagarden is Not What Became of Her But Why She Disappeared

by Ann Japenga

It's a fantasy many desert hikers share that one day they'll look under a ledge and find an intact olla brimming with wild apricots. Peering into dark corners for clay pots or arrowhead just become automatic. Vicki pear had acquired this habit from years of wandering in the Santa Rosa Mountains above Palm Springs, California. One day in 1991, she and a companion were boulder-hopping up a little-used draw when she glanced up and saw stones stacked by hand, reinforcing a rock shelter.

Naturally, Spear had to look. Most caves yield nothing, so she certainly wasn't expecting what she found. Years later she says of that moment: "You don't want it. It can't be happening."

Want it or not, it was hers: a skull, an arm bone, and the rest of a skeleton tucked in a shredded sleeping bag. Rodents had scattered the cave's content, but lying near the body was a hand-drawn map and a calendar from a Whittier bookstore, with dates marked off from December 17, 1959, to February 20, 1960. Judging from a box of Kotex also found in the cave, the bones were a woman's.

Spear made a decision that may seem peculiar to the rest of us but is in keeping with the unwritten laws of the Santa Rosa Mountains. Odd thing turn up in those hills, and the finders keep their mouths shut. Spear had found headless skeletons from a long-ago Indian massacre and didn't tell authorities. Another local found a skull with a bullet hole in it far in the backcountry and let it be. "The thing up here is to leave things alone," Spear says. The cave dweller had died a long time ago, so the discovery seemed to appear more like an archaeological find than a crime scene. Probably no one was looking for the woman. Spear and her friend walked back to the trailhead, agreeing to keep silent.

We know the story: A young man walks off into the wilderness, never to return except into the ranks of folk heroes. Most famous are Christopher McCandless (the subject of Into the Wild) and Everett Ruess, an artist and writer who disappeared in the Utah canyonlands in the 1930s. Both helped shape their own mythology, leaving behind reams of Unabomber-like ideology and colorful alter egos: Alexander Supertramp and Lan Rameau, respectively.

This time, however, the wilderness wanderer is not an adolescent joyrider but a mature woman who turned 40 in her rock tomb. Her name is Louise Teagarden. She invented no aliases and if she wrote a manifesto, it hasn't survived. Two brothers out deer hunting, John and Bill Sloan, came across her discarded diary in the 1960s near where her car was found. It was full of girl things, they said, worries about family and relationships. (The brothers have since died, and no one knows what became of the diary.) While the McCandle and Rues stories grew louder and more public over time, Teagarden's has retreated into privacy and silence. Almost no one—even in Palm Springs—knows her name.

"When Auntie Louise disappeared, it was just hush-hush," say her niece Barbara Barnes. "Nobody in the family wanted to talk about it."

Some of what we know about Teagarden comes from a family history written by her father, Albert. She was born in 1920 and grew up in a close middle-class family living here and there in Southern California: Hollywood, Highland Park, and Whittier. Of three sisters, Teagarden was the only one who never married and thus was expected to be her family's helper-coming home as an adult to nurse one sister through an infected cat bite and her father through prostate cancer.

Teagarden had discovered the freedom of the wilderness as a child on family camping trip to Bryce Canyon, Yosemite, and Sequoia National

✳ ✦ ✳ ✦ ✧ ✳ ✧ ✦ ✳ ✦ ✧ ✦ ✳ ✧ ✦ ✳ ✧ ✳ ✦ ✧ ✦ ✳ ✧

A happy moment in Louise Teagarden's beloved Santa Rosa Mountains. She is the woman at center; the man is Wilson Howell, her roomate in the tiny Southern California town of Ribbonwood. The woman at left may be Betty Moore.

Parks. Sometime around 1949 she moved to Ribbonwood, a tiny settlement on Highway 74—also called the Palms to Pines Highway, the serpentine drive depicted in chase scenes in the 1963 comedy It's a Mad, Mad, Mad, Mad World. She moved into the storeroom of the Ribbonwood general store, a little ramada where travelers, would stop to purchase curios (Teagarden made buttons from manzanita wood) or a Nehi soda.

The proprietor, and Teagarden's roommate, was Wilson Howell, a vegetarian proto-hippie who kept a huge garden, befriended skunks, and lived mostly on sunflower seeds. He was also friends with local Indians, who taught him how to make soup from native yucca blossoms. Up here Teagarden was accepted, even though she was in a relationship with a woman, not a common arrangement in the 1940s. Mountain resident Harry Quinn knew Teagarden and remembers her girlfriend, Betty More, an amateur archaeologist who'd show up at digs in Barstow and Tehachapi driving a military jeep equipped with a trailer, cots, backup fuel, and water tanks.

To this day Quinn is impressed with Teagarden's survival skills. His opinion is backed by his own outdoors cred: He taught wilderness survival in the Army, worked in remote Alaskan camps as a geologist, and survived crashes of three helicopters and two fixed-wing planes. Teagarden knew where to find wild strawberries on the back side of the Santa Rosa Mountains, he says, and could locate tiny seeps where she'd insert a straw and an hour later have a quart of water. She'd disappear on solo backpack trip for weeks at a time and stop by the Quinn family cabin on her way home. While skirting questions about where she'd been, he did let Quinn—then just a boy—study her hand-drawn topographic maps, with their penciled notations of elevations ranches, locked gates, and the all-important springs and streams. A series of circle she'd drawn along a trail corresponded to a mesquite grove—a native food source she may have learned about from Howell.

Teagarden' family may not have shared Quinn's respect for her backwoods knowledge. Her choices baffled them; some would later tell authorities that she was "moody." Her father, at least, loved and struggled to understand her. In his memoir, Albert often mentions dropping by Ribbonwood to visit "our Louise." Anxiety creeps in as she becomes more insistent on her solo walkabouts. "Now I must tell of Louise's year of wandering away from home," he writes.

In 1954, two years before his death from cancer, Albert wrote that his daughter "holds to the thought that she is happier there [the Santa Rosas] than she would be anywhere else and that she would not fit into the social life of any city or town. So we must be content to wait, hope, and pray that she may lead the life that will make her the happiest."

In December 1959, Teagarden told Howell she was driving to Hemet to go Christmas shopping. When she failed to return, a search turned up her car parked at an abandoned gold mine in Garner Valley. Teagarden had drained the radiator and placed the radiator cap on the driver's seat, just as Howell had taught her to do in the days before the common use of antifreeze. To Howell, that meant she was coming back.

From the Gold Shot Mine, Teagarden hiked through head-high thicket of red hank along the Pacific Crest Trail and picked up one of several paths leading toward Palm Canyon, an area pocked with grinding holes and other reminders of Cahuilla Indian occupation. The cave where she settled was low ceilinged and just big enough to stretch out in. Above her, the sweeping agave-dotted plateau of the desert merged into the snowy flanks of the Santa Rosa peaks. The brushy crowns of palm trees peeked from a nearby oasis that was like the set of a jungle movie, with deep pools (good for bathing), fat lizard, and vines. At night the light of Palm Springs sparkled some seven miles below her shelter.

Moving-in day must have been a relief. While she had never fit in with her peers from the city, out here she was more able than any of them.

Temperatures dropped to the teens, setting records for cold. Days before she disappeared, it had snowed in nearby Idyllwild. But Teagarden knew how to keep warm; the newspaper accounts her disappearance called her a "competent woodsman." Anyway, it was probably better being chilly in a cave than at home with her family for the holidays. Her father had died three years before, followed soon after by her sister Virginia. Her girlfriend Moore had moved away. Now her mother's health was declining, and Teagarden was again under pressure to come home and care for

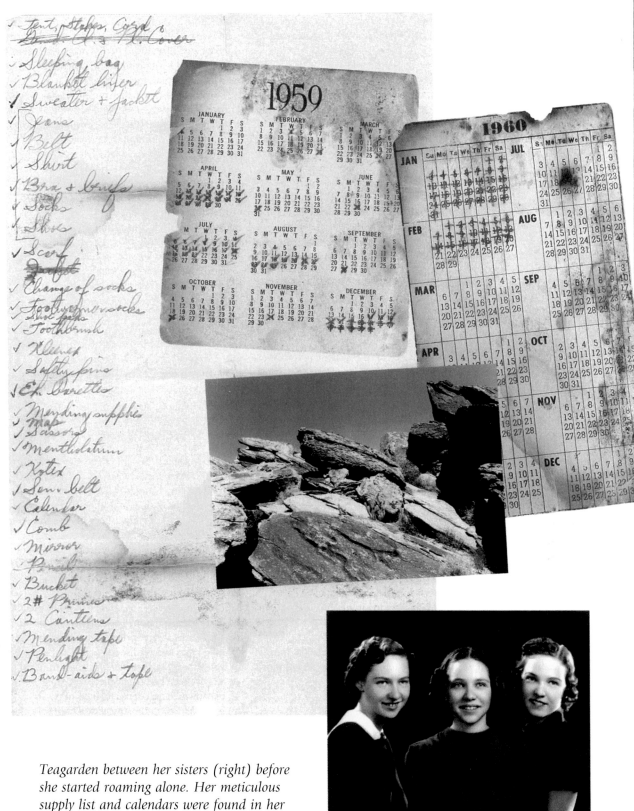

Teagarden between her sisters (right) before she started roaming alone. Her meticulous supply list and calendars were found in her cave (above) in 1991. She had marked the days of her final walkabout, from her disappearance on December 17, 1959, until February 20, 1960.

her. After all, as her surviving sister surely pointed out, Teagarden had no responsibilities. At an age when others were raising families, she was running around the mountain like a make-believe Indian, black braids flying.

Her staples—Zwieback and Hershey's bars—must have soon run out. New Year's 1960 brought more snow, but Teagarden survived and survival was perhaps a goal to her, a challenge to stay on. The last date crossed out on her calendar was four days after her 40th birthday on February 16. Teagarden was likely thinking in her final days about her mother and sister and how she'd let them down. Howell had respiratory problems and relied on her for trips to the doctor. He and others were undoubtedly upset with her for disappearing. The longer she stayed, the harder it was going to be to explain her absence—plus, spring in the desert comes early. Easier to stay for now.

Teagarden's remains might have stayed hidden for another 30 years if it hadn't been for Spear's low-life hiking companion. Unbeknownst to her, after their discovery he had doubled back to the cave and taken Teagarden skull. Days later a sheriff's deputy found it in the cabin of a local who had likely purchased it from the grave robber. The skull triggered a coroner's investigation that led officials to Teagarden's shelter.

Authorities had no idea, however, to whom the remains belonged. The riddle was solved when Barbara Barnes—who was only 15 when her aunt vanished—produced a wedding album with Teagarden's signature. The handwriting sample matched the writing on a list of supplies found in the cave.

For more than two months, Teagarden survived in the cold beauty of the Santa Rosas

The coroner listed the cause of death as unknown. There were no broken bones, no sign of trauma or foul play. But there was this tantalizing find: The teeth found in the cave showed an unusual staining pattern on the front central incisors. "Staining of this type is not commonly found in modern populations," wrote forensic anthropologist Judy Suchey.

In another surprise, an enlarged deltoid tuberosity—a muscle attachment in the arm—suggested a musculature more like that of an Aleutian kayaker than a 40-year-old suburban woman. The discoveries suggest that Teagarden might have lived like a primitive, growing strong from foraging and staining her teeth on chia, agave, and mesquite.

In mid-winter, though, cactus would have been the only wild food available to her. She may have died of starvation. Or, as her niece and mountain residents speculate, she could have succumbed to a snakebite, appendicitis, hypothermia, or suicide.

Whatever the cause, we know how Teagarden's final solitary walkabout ended. Death looms so large in these tales that we forget it's not the main point. The point is the urge to go into the mountains or desert alone, a necessary and creative response to being human. That's why Ruess and McCandless have spawned so many imitators—young seekers who follow Ruess's steps across the redrock or trek to the Alaskan school bus where McCandless lived. They would understand something about Teagarden, something her father and girlfriend also knew. She wasn't running away; she was going toward something.

Teagarden had wanted to live like a native on the land and she'd done it. She owned it all—the seeps at Madwoman Springs, the basketball-size grinding hole near Bullseye Rock. The beauty of the backcountry too was hers. The last things she would have seen before she died were stone pools full of snowmelt and dense thickets of cholla cactus wearing halos in the low winter light. No one knows what her last days were like. Maybe she was freezing, fevered, or depressed. She may have regretted many things about her life, but going to the mountain was probably not one of them. It was the thing she did right.

Chapter Three

Religion and Myth

Dreamers of the Mojave

by Kenneth M. Stewart

The Mohave Indians near Needles, California, once a proud warrior race, are falling behind in the struggle to better their lives in the white man's world. A basic reason for this failure may be an ancient belief still prevalent in the conscious and subconscious manifestations of their ancient culture – that to succeed one need not work or train or learn – one merely need have the proper dreams.

I sat on a rock, watching the flickering campfire of mesquite wood. To my right loomed the dark bulk of the truck. The Coleman lamp illuminated a small circle of sandy mesa beyond which lay utter blackness. The moon was a thin sliver, and the stars added little illumination. Save for the crackling of the fire, and the heavy breathing of my fellow anthropologists in the tent, the desert was still. Far away in town, a dog howled.

The desert was new to me, a city dweller, but I had vicariously anticipated this atmosphere for a long time, and now I was reveling in it.

It was a great relief to be camped on the clean desert after a miserable night in a flea-infested auto court on our arrival in Needles, California, for anthropological field work with the Mohave Indians. The court was near the switchyard, with its clangor and hissing, while traffic whizzed by on the nearby highway.

I despaired of further sleep, and dressed for a sunrise walk along the Colorado River, watching the reddening skies above the gray mountains to the east. Making my way through thickets of rushes, I watched the turbid, silt-laden stream flow relentlessly in its channel, eddying around sandbars, dallying in lagoons, and I thought of the days when broad-shouldered Mohave Indians, naked to a G-string, ferried their children and household goods across the river, pushing large pottery vessels before them as they swam.

The day before at the railroad station I spoke to stocky Mohave

women in bright calico dresses, selling beaded curios. I learned from them that my best source of information would be the old chief, a man of more than 80 years, yet in full possession of his faculties and well-informed about the Mohave way of life in the old days.

An hour later I found this man.

"I dreamed that my spirit was floating in the sky, far above the clouds," he said in a gentle tone, as his bright eyes gazed beyond the river toward the jagged peaks, seeing things to which my own eyes were blind.

I was silent, not wishing to interrupt his flow of memory.

"Truly, it was a great thing. I saw two big hawks, flying swiftly through the air. That made me very happy. It meant that I would become a kwanami, a great warrior."

The days passed as I interrogated the old chief, attempting to draw out information about the former life of the Mohaves. This was never a difficult task for he spoke freely, and my pencil moved rapidly in taking notes.

I learned that before the wagon trains of the whites rumbled through Arizona, upsetting the ancient Indian way of life, the Mohave were known by other tribes as a nation of dreamers. The Mohave believed that to achieve attainment in life one must dream properly.

A Mohave must have the proper dreams to be successful as a medicine man, a warrior, a gambler, to acquire any desirable ability. And there was nothing a man could do to induce the right dreams. He either had them or he didn't.

Mohave dreams would baffle a psychoanalyst, since they supposedly begin in infancy, or even before birth, while the unconscious embryo is yet in his mother's womb, or even earlier, while the soul of the future Mohave was with the gods at the sacred mountain north of Needles known as Avikwame, or Ghost Mountain.

This prenatal dreaming was in a sense predestination, since knowledge and skills were acquired through dreams and not by reflection, practice and hard work.

As I listened to the old chief, I concluded that the Mohave were so preoccupied with dreaming that they had little interest in material things, and this was reflected in a great indifference to the arts and crafts. Their basketry was sloppily executed and their pottery did not rise above the level of mediocrity. The simple rectangular house was constructed of logs, brush and mud, with a floor of dirt and an earth-covered roof, while during the steaming summer months the Indians moved out under ramadas, fiat-topped shades without walls which permitted the free circulation of breezes.

Today, too, the Mohave show little evidence of a materialistic orientation. Many of them live in shacks on the outskirts of Needles, in an area often partially flooded by the river, and their yards are littered with tin cans, rusty jalopies, and other rubbish of western civilization. Meticulous housekeeping is rare among the Mohave.

Little time was lost from dreaming in making clothing. For men, the wardrobe consisted of breechclouts and fiber sandals; for women, a short skirt of fibers. Hairdress, too, necessitated a minimum of effort. Both sexes wore their hair long in back, with that of the women cut in bangs, while that of the men was sometimes rolled into "pencils" which hung down the back. On occasion the long hair was plastered with mud as protection against insects, suggesting the turbans of the Near East.

Even dreamers require nourishment, but the food quest along the lower Colorado was not an arduous one. In spring the mighty river, swollen by the melting snows of the Rocky Mountains far to the northeast, burst its banks and flooded the bottomlands. Then as the waters receded, the Mohave planted corn, beans and squash in the rich mud, and harvested the crops after their rapid growth under the fierce summer sun. Jackrabbits were hunted in the thickets along the river, fish were taken in huge basket scoops shaped like canoes and a few hunting specialists (who had, of course dreamed their power over the game) went to the mountains in the vicinity of present day Oatman and Kingman to hunt deer and antelope.

Government was a casual matter, and held little interest for the Mohave. The tribal chief was respected, but the great warriors, the kwanamis, were at the pinnacle of prestige in the tribe.

The only activity which ranked with dreaming in the Mohave conception of things was warfare. But dream-life and warfare were closely related—a man could not be successful in battle unless he had experienced the proper dreams for war. These kwanamis were the great men of the tribe. The Mohave enjoyed fighting, and terrorized neighbor tribes for hundreds of miles around, smashing their enemies with vicious wooden clubs shaped like old-fashioned potato-mashers. Periodically, bands of Mohave raiders departed on a grueling six day journey across the desert to descend on the Maricopa southwest of Phoenix, killing, scalping, plundering and capturing women and children for slaves.

Sometimes even marriages resulted from dreaming. If a girl and a young man dreamed of each other, it was regarded as an indication of the will of the god Mastamho that they marry. Marriage and divorce were extremely casual affairs, with a couple simply deciding to live together. The marital bonds were severed by the simple departure of either partner.

When the death of a Mohave approached, friends and relatives assembled and began an eerie wailing, which might continue for days, if death were slow in coming. The corpse was cremated on a funeral pyre, while mourners cast the possessions of the deceased into the flames. In former times, they were sometimes too precipitate in their actions, and there are reports of "corpses" suddenly sitting up in the midst of the leaping flames.

The death of the old chief had been anticipated after he had suffered a stroke shortly before my arrival at Needles. Relatives had been summoned from the Colorado River Reservation, 50 miles downstream at Parker, Arizona; the funeral pyre was ready beside the house, and ceremonial replicas of the ancient weapons, the war club, the long bow and the feathered pike, had been prepared. But the patriarch's vitality was great, and he fooled the mourners. By the time of my arrival, he was able to sit up and talk for hours at a time.

Mohaves, like so many other Southwestern Indians, fear the dead and anything connected with death. After a person has rejoined the gods at Ghost Mountain, his name should never again be spoken and it is a great insult to a Mohave to mention the names of his dead relatives. The Mohave resent having their pictures taken, fearing that someone may see the photo after their death.

On one occasion, my fellow anthropologists and I accompanied some Mohaves to the site of old Fort Mohave, on the Arizona side of the river. Walking through the thicket in single file, we were spread out over a distance of 30 or 40 yards. I began to whistle, and a Mohave woman in the rear of the column became frightened.

"I hear a ghost," she cried. It seems that, in Mohave belief, ghosts whistle, and to hear whistling at night is particularly terrifying.

Mohave life today goes on at a leisurely pace, with much free time for dreaming. Employment for many of the men is not steady, and they lounge on the grass in back of the railroad station at Needles, perhaps dreaming of the old days and the god Mastamho. Many of them are rather bitter about the white man's encroachment upon their land, and his discrimination against the descendants of a tribe once generally feared and respected. And discriminated against they are. For example,

they are required to sit in a Jim Crow section at the local theater. In a certain department store in Needles, the Mohaves trust only one clerk, and will wait silently until he is free to wait on them.

Approximately 400 Mohaves live in and near Needles, while 600 reside on the Colorado River Reservation. The ones on the reservation farm irrigated lands and are more progressive than the die-hards at Needles, who insist on staying where they have always lived, even though it may mean poverty and hardship for them. The old chief once said to me, "That's like a prison down there at Parker." But it seemed to me that those at Parker were happier and more prosperous by having adjusted to altered conditions instead of clinging tenaciously and futilely to a vanished past.

Change is inevitable and is accelerating. In 1956 Mohave children attend school, play football, watch movies and young men are drafted into the armed forces. Mohaves drive automobiles, use modern methods of farming and work in the railroad shops or on the tracks at Needles. Warriors no longer campaign against the Maricopas.

But dreams persist, in spite of a nominal acceptance of Christianity by many of the Mohave. The old people are nostalgic for a time when the river was wild and unhampered by dams, when the white men were not yet numerous in the region, and when the desert was not scarred by the material things of civilization.

Source: *Desert Magazine*: November 1956

Mojave Dreams of Omen and Power

by George Devereux

The Mohave Indians live on both banks of the Colorado River, in Arizona and California. They are an agricultural and war-like nation imbued with a sense and pride of nationality and wholly unlike the layman's conception of the stolid "cigar store Indian." Their culture is singularly barren in rituals; instead, dream occupies the focal position in their culture. Mohave attitudes toward dreams, as toward everything else, are always a mixture of great practicality and of a headlong plunge into the inner world of fantasy.

Thus, the wife of a medicine man who was present while I was discussing dreams with her husband, remarked: "We don't dream when it is hot because we do not rest well. But if we do dream and rest in the heat, we may have nightmares—because we ate too much. Or else maybe we have good luck dreams. We jump up and walk around in the middle of the night if we ate too much."

Then her husband continued the discussion as follows: "When I was fourteen or ten years old, I obtained mysterious life and power. I married nine times and never had *hikupk* (venereal disease.) Some of the old seem to crawl on all fours now, but I got my strength. I might come to the end (of man's maximum life span?)—I dream I had long whiskers [the Mohave very seldom have whiskers], and a cane when I dream and lots of young people tell [call] me in dream, 'Grandfather.' I hear it in my ear. It is spirit power. It came to me in dream and happens in daily life. Good dreams—sumatc ahot—about one in a hundred have it."

Then referring to a dream of mine, which I had told him, and which, in Mohave terms, was a bad dream, he said : "If you have an evil dream, sumatc ala: yk, you die. Sumatc itcem—a bad dream—means illness. Since you did not die someone took your place and he died in your place."

This conversation reflects the mixture of great practicality and extreme fantasy characteristic of Mohave attitudes toward dreams. It is quite typical, save perhaps for the very last sentence, which may reflect one of this particular shaman's private theories.

Dreams Promise "Capacity"

Broadly speaking, the Mohave differentiate between ordinary dreams and great dreams. However, they hold that all dreams have a meaning, although it is not always understood. In that sense then, every dream is an omen dream though it does not necessarily reflect what will actually happen, but what could happen. For example, my interpreter told me of a dream which meant that if she were to gamble, she would be lucky. However, she did not go to gamble, but came to interpret for me, as usual. Perhaps a belief in the meaningfulness of all dreams results from ascribing prophetic qualities to a dream after an event occurs that seems to have been predicted or foreshadowed by the earlier dream.

In other instances the omen-element is quite obvious. Thus in the dream about having long whiskers and carrying a cane, we are confronted with obvious attributes of old age, further underscored by the fact that young persons call the dreamer "Grandfather." Among the Plains Indians, a young man may have a vision of a buffalo, which opens its mouth and shows that it has no teeth—as old persons have no teeth—thus indicating that the visionary will have a long life. However, we must note that even omen dreams may indicate only a potentiality, which, in some instances, the dreamer must actualize.

In this tentative sense, then, omen dreams are related to power dreams, which bestow upon those who have them certain qualities or powers, or else insure that some events of *major* importance will take place. By contrast, omen dreams seem to refer to specific and more restricted types of occurrences. Thus, a woman may have a power—dream in adolescence which indicates that she is to have children—surely a major event in the life of a woman. By contrast, during pregnancy she may have an omen-dream—dreaming of male or female regalia—which forecasts the sex of the child about to be born.

A young man may have a dream giving him the power to become a great warrior—and may also, on various occasions, have omen dreams foreshadowing the outcome of some military venture. On the whole, no major feat is possible in life without having had an appropriate power-dream, which bestows upon the dreamer the capacity to become a shaman, a warrior, a fertile woman, etc. By contrast, many concrete events of a more restricted scope may occur without their being predicted by an omen dream.

The Role of Myths

According to Mohave belief, there appear to be structural and psychodynamic differences between ordinary (omen) and great (power) dreams. Ordinary dreams appear to be genuine dreams, experienced in a single night. They come from the Day or from the Night, defined as personified entities-depending on whether one has the dream during the night or during a nap in the course of the day. As stated before, these dreams may, or may not, be understandable on awakening; their intelligibility depends on the presence of conventionalized omen symbols or—perhaps—upon the subjective impression which they make on dreamers or listeners.

Unlike the dreams of ordinary people, those of twins come from, and pertain to, Heaven, which is their real home. Objectively speaking, this origin of the dreams of twins is an imputation since Heaven is just like earth—only better—so that nothing in the "setting" of twin's dream indicates that it pertains to Heaven, save only the fact that this dream is that of a twin. The same dream dreamed by an ordinary mortal would come from the Day or from the Night.

The nature and divine origin of power dreams is more complex, especially in the case of medicine men (shamans) and, to a lesser extent, in the case of singers, of funeral orators—who are often also shamans—of warriors and of other personages prominent in Mohave culture. The most elaborate form of the power dream is experienced by the shamans, and offers us a comprehensive example of the type. What is true of these dreams also applies to other power dreams, although in a simplified form.

The most crucial factor in shamanistic power dreams is the role of myths, especially the Creation Myth, which establishes a set of precedents for everything that happens in human life. In Mohave belief, the future shaman dreams of that portion of the Creation Myth, which pertains to his future "specialty," while still in the maternal womb. However, even shamans who specialize in the same kind of cure do not necessarily have identical dreams. Their dreams will, however, fit the general pattern of the pertinent portion of the Creation Myth.

As a singularly perceptive non-shamanistic informant said: "Their accounts of the relevant portion of the Creation Myth will differ as your account of a car accident which you witnessed may differ from my account, who have also witnessed it." In other words, they recognize that the personal factor modifies or slants what is, supposedly, an objective experience. This fits perfectly the fact that singers—who specialize in narrating all myths—tend to recite somewhat different versions of the same basic myth—a flexibility entirely in harmony with the non-obsessive, non-compulsive, and non-ritualistic Mohave character. (This characteristic is so pronounced that when I tried to collect data on Mohave psychopathology, each diagnostic picture I painted for them was immediately recognized and illustrated with cogent examples, except for my descriptions of obsessions and compulsions. The latter only elicited the comment: "I know just what you mean—the chief of the tribe is always thinking of the welfare of the nation!")

Oddly enough, shamans seem to be the only ones who attach much importance to the exclusive correctness of their "experience" of the Creation, which they supposedly actually witness in utero. Thus, while singers do not seem to be angered by the fact that another singer tells the same myth somewhat differently, shamans are angered by the accounts of other shamans which differ from their own. Hence, no shaman will tell of his "experiences" or perform his cure—which includes a narrative of the mythical precedent—in the presence of another shaman, lest the latter be angered by divergences and bewitch him.

The "Devilish Child"

After supposedly witnessing an enactment of the Creation in the maternal womb, the future shaman after his birth forgets ("represses") this intra-uterine dream for several years. During this period he is simply a "devilish child" and a troublesome pre-adolescent. Then, suddenly he begins to have dreams which he "recognizes" as those he had in the maternal womb.

He has these dreams repeated and narrates them to suitable authorities, who may point out that there is something amiss with some portion of the dream. In fact, a singer specifically reports that his deceased father and brother formally tutored him in dreams, setting him right regarding various details of the myths which he was to "know" and recite. Such adolescents also follow attentively the performances of shamans specializing in the cure of ailments in which they, themselves, will eventually specialize.

The preceding paragraphs indicate clearly how the myth intrudes into dreams of this type and organizes them. What probably happens is this: An adolescent, who has been a very turbulent child, has a dream which seems to resemble a standard portion of the Creation Myth, which he has heard before. At this point he may recall that he was frequently spoken of as a future shaman, simply because his behavior was so turbulent. He is therefore inclined to view this dream as the first intimation of budding shamanistic powers.

The second fact is that the dream itself, and the myth-linked associations which it evokes, strikes him as familiar. However, because of his culturally determined expectations, and probably also because of genuinely psychological repressions, he does not ascribe this sense of "familiarity"—of *déjà vu*—to repeated listening to singers and witnessing of actual shamanistic cures. Instead, he projects it back to the remote past, and comes to believe that, in accordance with cultural expectations, he has had this same dream already in the maternal womb.

Formation of a Power Dream

Constant preoccupation with the dream, and with daydreams related to it, and with memories of what he actually learned and witnessed—all these elements, plus, possibly, actual "tutoring" by experts, help him to add new elements to the real remembered dream. He structures this sum of dream elements and learned material into a whole which fits cultural expectations related to shamanistic power dreams. In the end, the shaman comes up

with a suitable and complete "dream," which he now believes to have dreamed in its entirety both in the womb and, again, during adolescence.

It is this dream, including both medical theories and cures, which he then proclaims as his power dream and that he narrates during the cures he performs. Officially at least, as far as he and the tribe are concerned, all that which *matters* about this dream was learned in the course of an "actual" dream. Actually of course, the Mohave —both as regards shamans and as regards the laity—understand very well that much of this final product was learned in a matter of fact way. That, however, seems quite irrelevant to them, since that which truly matters was, by definition, learned in dream. Indeed, the Mohave emphatically specify that anyone can, simply by listening, learn the medical portions of the Creation Myth and the songs used in curing rites. However, even though such a person may be "letter perfect," his knowledge is simply not effective. He has the objective knowledge, but not the power which makes this knowledge effective, and which must come in dream. In fact, the Mohave hold that if a layman, who did not have the proper dreams, was presumptuous enough to sing a shaman's songs, he would bring untold calamities upon himself.

Indeed, one reason why so many Mohave were convinced that the writer was a shaman, is that, while recording them in writing, he sang certain curing songs without catastrophic consequences. Interestingly enough, there is also a reverse side to this medal: If someone receives the appropriate powers, but does not choose to practice his curing craft, he will go insane. In this respect too, power dreams differ from omen dreams, since the woman who had a dream of being lucky at gambling had nothing to fear because she chose the safer way of earning money by serving as my interpreter.

Success Proves the Shaman

There is sound evidence that power dreams of a specific type come to those who seek them, be it only unconsciously. Thus, Young Quail specialized for years in the cure of supposedly "venereal" diseases, before becoming also an obstetrician. He received obstetrical powers after his wife died in childbirth. He could *not* deliver the infant, which could be seen moving in its dead mother's body, while everyone stood around helplessly, since the

Mohave do not know how to perform Caesarean operations. Shortly after this tragic occurrence, Ahma Huma: acquired in middle age—itself a rather noteworthy and a typical occurrence—the power to function as an obstetrician.

While all *bona fide* shamanistic power dreams are valid, not all are equally effective. This explains why, of a group of obstetrical specialists, one may be highly esteemed and deemed to be consistently successful, while another' may enjoy little prestige. Presumably the dream of the first was complete and highly "loaded" with power, while that of the second was relatively incomplete and therefore less power-laden. Likewise, a new self-proclaimed shaman must first "earn his spurs" by a series of successful cures.

It is necessary to return once more to the basic importance of power obtained in dream, as against the ritual behavior related to cures. What matters is exclusively the power, and not the knowledge of the songs and other elements of the curing rite. Indeed, there are today practicing shamans who do not know traditional curing songs, because the last shaman who knew the songs pertaining to a certain illness died before he could transmit this knowledge. Such modern shamans recite instead a condensed version of their "dream" (myth). This is held to be quite as effective as if they had actually sung the relevant songs.

It is important to stress that Mohave shamanism, and the whole matter of curing powers, is still very much alive; gradually, it has absorbed elements related to occidental culture. New diseases are believed to have come into being as a result of eating occidental, store-bought, foods and these illnesses baffled the established therapists. Eventually, however, someone may receive in dream knowledge of the relevant—but hitherto unrevealed—portion of the Creation Myth, and acquire the ability, to cure illnesses resulting from eating canned food.

Witchcraft: Murderous Impulse

These data are of more than casual interest. They reveal the extraordinary adaptability of the basic Mohave pattern, whose strength lies in its non-rigidity. New parts of the Creation Myth may be revealed in dream at any time, to fit new situations, including situations resulting from contact with occidental culture, and suitable new types of dream power may thus come into being. In fact, it may well be said that as long as there is a single Mohave who still believes in Mohave mythology, Mohave mythology cannot become stagnant, it remains a growing and changing thing.

We cannot speculate in so brief an article about the psychodynamics of Mohave power dreams. We can, however, confidently state that they are appreciably motivated by aggressive elements. Indeed, it is of the essence of shamanistic powers that he who can cure disease X can also cause it; in fact, it may be said that he can cure it, precisely because he can cause it. It is a major tenet of Mohave beliefs concerning witchcraft that some shamans become witches in their old age, as do the singers of certain so-called "shamanistic song cycles."

Such persons are said to bewitch people they like, in order to have an imposing retinue in the other world. However, in order to keep their hold on their ghostly followers, they themselves must die a violent death. Hence, when a witch feels that he has acquired an adequate following of victims, and is haunted by longing for them, he will deliberately provoke the surviving relatives of his victims into killing him, so as to join them and enjoy his leadership and their company. This explains why many of the shamans who are killed as witches either deliberately provoked their killers or else made no effort whatsoever to escape them, even if they knew that there were killers on their way to their house.

These findings could be documented by some twenty detailed case histories of shaman killings. We may therefore view the curing activities of shamans as "reaction formations" against destructive impulses that first showed themselves in a turbulent childhood. Eventually such infantile murderous impulses find their way into behavior in the form of witchcraft; this, in turn, creates guilt feelings and causes the witch to seek death—punishment by getting himself murdered.

Much valuable work has been done by deservedly respected scholars on Mohave dreaming, shamanism and witchcraft. However, until at least one medicine man has been analyzed, nothing more can be done than outline the most basic and most obvious psychological factors which underlie these cultural beliefs, and motivate individuals to become shamans.

Mojave Pottery, Mojave People

by Jill Leslie Furst

Reprinted with permission of the School for Advanced Research, Santa Fe, New Mexico. Copyright ©2001

Mojave history consisted of the Great Stories—narratives of events in the mythic First Times, before the world assumed its present form, before humans and animals were differentiated, and before the Sun and Moon shone in the sky. The Great Stories told the origins of the first beings, human and animal, and of all significant objects and implements later owned and used by the Mojave people. They also described how the physical landscape was formed and confirmed the validity of Mojave custom and ritual practice.

Black Canyon on the Colorado River, by F.W. Egloffstein, from a sketch by Joseph C. Ives. Matavilye, the first Creator and organizer of the Mojave world, built his home in this canyon, which the Mojaves considered the center of the earth. The Mojaves apparently identified some of the vertical rocks with the two wooden supports at the fronts of Mojave houses (Ives 1861, General Reports, plate V.)

The Mojaves recounted the Great Stories in songs that were performed at public events called Sings. The Great Stories also were the basis for dreams, which were crucial to Mojave life. A dream revealed a person's skills and abilities and summoned a shaman, a scalper, or a warrior to his calling. Without a dream, a person could accomplish virtually nothing.

The Mojaves told many variations of the Great Stories, and no single authoritative version of any part of the creation and origin cycle existed. Instead the people shared a series of similar variants that differed according to the version the Singer learned, the extent of his knowledge, and even the family and community from which he came. Complicating our picture of the Great Stories is the fact that no anthropologist has attempted to collect anywhere near the complete corpus of Mojave Sings. We have only bits and pieces of what was an extensive and rich body of oral literature.

At the end of the nineteenth century, U.S. Army Captain John J. Bourke collected fragments of origin stories. Alfred Kroeber set down some of the longer narratives in the early decades of the twentieth century. Psychological anthropologist George Devereux studied dreams and their significance in Mojave life from the 1930s to the 1950s. George H. Fathauer's work on religion also dates to the same time.

In the First Days, the Mojaves said, only Earth and Sky existed. Earth was female, Sky was male, and nothing grew until a single drop of rain fell from Sky to Earth. The Earth conceived her children, one of whom was a son named Matavilye. He immediately set about creating various geographical features and populating the Earth with people, who appeared in the form of birds and animals, but who thought, spoke, and acted as would later-created human beings Matavilye led his followers to "house-post water" (Aha'av'ulypo), a site on the Colorado in Black Canyon north of the Mojave lands that the people later said was the center of the earth. There he built a sacred structure called the Great Dark House.

Matavilye had a daughter, Kathena (Frog Woman), and a son, Mastamho. (Some stories identified Kathena and Mastamho as Matavilye's siblings rather than his offspring.) The siblings had no mother because Matavilye made them from his own body. One day Matavilye accidentally offended Kathena, who, in turn, bewitched him by swallowing his feces and causing his death. He died on the Colorado River near Cottonwood Island. Matavilye's passing was the first death in the world, and sorcery caused it.

The people cremated his body and burned the Great Dark House to the ground. Nevertheless, Matavilye's shade stayed in the ruins and continued to be accessible there. The Mojaves pointed out stone pillars in Black Canyon as the remnants of Matavilye's first dwelling to travelers along the Colorado River at the end of the nineteenth century. Today, this and some other Mojave sacred sites lie below the waters of Lake Meade.

Matavilye's demise and subsequent immolation established the pattern for human death and funerals. The Mojaves later cremated the adult dead and destroyed by fire virtually all the deceased's property, including the house. Frog Woman, who caused Matavilye's death, was sometimes called the Queen of the Sky and lived in the heavens. Perhaps she was identified as a constellation.

Before Matavilye perished, he handed over responsibility for finishing the world and caring for human beings to his son, Mastamho, whose

Cottonwood Valley; Matavilye died on the Colorado River near Cottonwood River near Cottonwood Island. Today the northern dams have changed the river's shape and depth, and many islands are no longer submerged for all or part of the year (Ives 1861, figure 21).

exploits were the subjects of various stories with differing details. Whatever variants the Mojaves told, they agreed that Mastamho instituted nearly all significant rituals, patterns, and things in the ancient First Times and gave them names in a special ritual vocabulary as well as names in everyday language.

In a story recorded by Bourke in the 1880s, when Matavilye died, all was dark because the Sun and Moon had not come into being, and day and night did not exist. Mastamho did not want the Sun to shine, because then his father's remains would lie exposed and visible to all. At this time, the First People all lived together at Date Creek, Arizona (probably the rivulet between Parker and Prescott that flows from east to west out of the Rawhide Mountains, rather than the small town east of Parker later founded and named for the creek). The Colorado River had not yet come into existence.

Decades later, Kroeber's informants told him that, before placing the Sun in the sky, Mastamho decided to create the Colorado River by plunging a cane staff into the ground four times. After each strike, a flood of water bearing a different kind of fish gushed from the hole. Then he created four ducks for the Mojaves and said that he would teach the people how to fish and trap aquatic creatures in the future. He directed the flow of water with his staff and made the Colorado River. In other stories, he blew into his cane, and the Colorado rose from his breath and spittle. Mastamho was of gigantic stature, and he had a correspondingly huge boat. After creating the river, he climbed into his craft, taking his people with him. They sailed south, and the boat's turnings and twistings determined the course and width of the Colorado. Mastamho decided that such vessels were not for the Mojave people but should be given to the men who would later come from Europe.

This story explained why, before European contact, the Mojaves did not use boats to cross the Colorado but instead rode logs or rafts, or put their goods in large pottery vessels and floated them across. Mastamho had willed it so. The people were also good swimmers and often swam and ferried their children in cradleboards across the Colorado. The story also explained why Euro-Americans possessed objects that the Mojaves did not have: Mastamho had willed that, too.

In a similar narrative told to Bourke, when

Mastamho and the ancestral people arrived at the mouth of the Colorado, the waters began to rise to cover the earth. He gathered up the First People, carried them in his gigantic arms, and waved his hands, commanding the water to return to the ocean. As Mastamho turned his back to the sea and started north carrying his human charges, the river reached all the way to his neck. When he came to the site where Fort Yuma would later be built, it was only chest high. Where Fort Mohave was later constructed, it was below his knees.

Kroeber's informants said that, after Mastamho brought his human beings to the northern end of Mojave lands, he heaped up dirt to make the sacred site of Spirit Mountain (Avikwa'ame), also called Dead Mountain. Spirit Mountain was, and continues to be, one of the most (if not *the* most) important landmarks in Mojave territory. It was the site of many events in the ancient times, and Mastamho retired to its summit after his demise. The Mohave's believed that the souls of men, and sometimes women, went there in their dreams to visit him and to obtain crucial information about their roles in life. Spirit Mountain also appears in the legends of other Yuman speakers, including the Diegueños, Walapais, Maricopas, and Quechans.

Other legends collected by Bourke about the First Times suggest that Mastamho's journey reflected not only Yuman migrations along the Colorado River but also the displacement of

The mouth of the Colorado River, by J. J. Young, from a sketch by H. B. Möllhausen. The river's mouth lay to the south, in Quechan territory, but it played an important role in Mojave ancient history. Mastamho, the son of Matavilye and the second creator and organizer of the world, traveled to this spot and ordered the river to fall to reveal the land as he walked back to the north. (Ives 1861, General Report, plate I)

older populations and the division of the Yumans into distinct groups. For example, one story said that the Mojaves and the other Yumans were undifferentiated in the beginning. They and the related Apaches, Walapais, Pimas, Quechans, Cocopahs, and Kamilyas (a small band in lower California) emerged together near a large stone that sat above Cottonwood Island on the Colorado River. When Mastamho returned from the mouth of the river with the ancestral people, he found other human beings already living along its banks. They were men and women of the same blood as the Yuman ancestors, and some spoke the same language. These people did not want the newcomers to settle there because the land could not support them all. The two groups fought, and the returning people killed those already living a sedentary life. The victors then scattered to different places in order to have sufficient land to live. The Apaches traveled north from the Needles Peaks to Date Creek, while the Walapais went down the Colorado and joined the Maricopas, one of the earlier sedentary people who survived. Afterwards the Walapais journeyed to the Apache-Mojave country to the south-east and moved north and down into the Grand Canyon. Some Mojaves went to the Four Peaks and the Tonto Basin of central Arizona. Bourke suggested that this variant of the origin story described the return of a band of Mojaves from the south and memories of floods along the Colorado River. The arms of Mastamho, he believed, were river-worthy rafts.

Still other details suggested to Bourke that the Mojaves originated in central California. In one story, his informant said that Mastamho brought the people from the west. He led them northward from a site close to San Bernardino, past the area around today's Barstow, and then northeastward through the Camp Cady vicinity. The people arrived at the Three Peaks near Needles and traveled up the Colorado River to Spirit House and Cottonwood Island. Then Mastamho walked north, south, east, and west, and back to the center of the island, apparently establishing the land as the Mojaves'. Bourke believed that this journey reflected Mojave migration from a spot near San Bernardino, in part, because his aged informants knew that remote territory in greater detail than he thought they should have. One man, for example, told him of a phallic shrine between San

Bernardino and Camp Cady. On the other hand, the old men's knowledge of California landmarks may indicate no more than familiarity with the Mojave River Road, an old trade route between the Colorado River and the Pacific coast.

Yet another legend, also recorded by Bourke, suggested that some Mojaves came to the Colorado River from the east. It told of a time long ago, when the Mojaves lived in stone houses built into the cliffs on the other side of Spirit Mountain. The big chiefs who dwelled there had earlier led the Mojaves westward from Date Creek (where the original people lived) to the Colorado River. There they miraculously turned to stones that, in the nineteenth century, the Mojaves identified as Witchy-witchy-yuba and Matnapocua. These natural features were the homes of the trans- formed chiefs. The tall, natural stone pillars along the river looked much like the two wooden posts that stood in front of Mojave houses and *ramadas*; perhaps this story reflects not an actual migration but an explanation for these striking stone features.

To return to Bourke's version of the Great Story of origins, once Mastamho had a home, it was time to create light and dark. Mastamho did not fashion the heavenly bodies from fire or other materials; instead, he asked the people to shout. Four times they made a mighty noise, and at the last, the Sun and Moon appeared in the sky.

Mastamho heaped up a small pile of stones, and Bourke, who visited the area in the 1880s, wrote that the heap could still be seen near an iron column the U.S. government erected to mark the California-Nevada border. At this spot, Mastamho called on the First People to decide how they would live ever after. He assigned them their names, but he did not know what function each would fulfill. He asked the assembled creatures which of them would survive without working by eating any food that man tossed its way. One agreed, and Mastamho decreed that the creature would be the dog, which would live with men and women, receive handouts, and not toil. The Mojaves did keep many canines and often shared their last food with them. But they also ate dogs when the need arose.

Mastamho then dove into the water and ordered that everything that would swim in the future should follow him. Thus fish and turtle chose their proper abodes. Finally, he ordered a

race with the newly risen Sun to determine which creatures would walk and which would fly. The slowest land animals halted the soonest. The birds covered more territory, although they could not catch the Sun. Where each stopped determined its place on land or in the sky.

At the pile of stones, nineteenth-century Mojaves celebrated with dances and games when the Colorado receded. They purified themselves in the sweat lodge first and then plunged into the water in imitation of Mastamho. Bourke identified the ritual as a Creation Dance that reenacted the origin legend. He added that small rock piles at intervals of five to twelve paces marked places where a medicine man halted to perform the story, dressed as one or another animal that had failed to complete the running competition with the Sun.

In the area around Fort Mohave, according to both Bourke and Kroeber, Mastamho created the first agricultural implements and gave them to the Mojaves, instructing the people to plant crops. He made corn, tobacco, and mesquite for his children and established proper human social relationships and organization. He granted special powers to some people, who would become shamans, warriors, and scalpers, that is, men who scalped enemies during raids and brought these trophies back to their villages. Such people earned greater respect and higher status than their fellows, although prior to

Spirit Mountain, or Dead Mountain, by J. J. Young, from a sketch by H. B. Mollhausen. Mastamho created Spirit Mountain in the ancient First Times. Some Mojaves believed it was his home after he completed his work and transformed into an eagle, and shamans traveled to the mountain summit in dreams to receive knowledge from him. (Ives 1861, General Report, plate IV)

the coming of Euro-American culture the Mojaves drew no firm, permanent class distinctions, and the influence acquired and cultivated by a capable father could easily be dissipated by a lazy son.

At Mastamho's orders, some of the First People were transformed into birds, and he taught them to speak to one another in their own chirping and squawking languages. The birds would later serve as signs in the physical world and in human dreams to warn men and women of disaster or to signal impending good fortune. In fact, Mastamho established the meaning and importance of interpreting signs at the same time.

In the early twentieth century, Kroeber's Mojave informants identified the other Yuman-speakers as their older brothers, who had a better claim to Mastamho's attentions and bounty. Yet the Mojaves believed they were favored by Mastamho. They were his youngest children, and he doted on them by giving them more and better land along the fertile Colorado River. When Mastamho assigned the proper languages to the Mojaves, Walapais, Yavapais, Chemehuevis, Kamias, and Quechans, he told each group what foodstuffs it could eat. To the Mojaves he gave the choice cultivated corn, beans, and melons, and he specified the colors of corn and beans they would enjoy. Mastamho also divided food plants into those that should be eaten cooked or raw.

Then Mastamho snipped fingers into the hands of his beloved youngest children to enable them to count and create tools. He showed them how to farm and how to cook using pottery. He named the types of cooking vessels. Since he did not decree that the Mojaves should perform rituals, say prayers, or practice taboos on food or sexual intercourse before or during planting, the Mojaves did not do these things. Mastamho did advise the Mojaves to stay within the boundaries of their own lands, and he granted them their territory as long as they heeded the messages that he and other supernaturals sent to them in their dreams.

The instructions in the Great Stories reflected where people actually lived along the Colorado and were the basis for deciding what territory any group of people could hope to conquer or defend. Land not given in the First Times did not belong to squatters or victors. Mastamho's commands had the practical effect of ensuring that various groups did not consume and exhaust the same resources. The fragile high-desert environment could not withstand large numbers of people cutting or digging the same plant or hunting the same animals. The restrictions were also cultural markers. People knew one another by where and what they hunted and what they did or did not grow or consume.

With these gifts, Mastamho also established women's work. For the Mojaves, this consisted largely of caring for home and children and harvesting, preserving, and preparing food. Mastamho gave them vessels of specific shapes and assigned special names to these forms, in addition to their designations in every day speech. Women were to make the pottery for their households.

Once Mastamho had completed the task of ordering the natural and human worlds, it was time for him to leave. He went to the banks of the Colorado River, stretched his arms into wings, and lifted into the sky, changing from human form into a bald eagle. With this transformation, the Mojaves said that he became ignorant and "infested with vermin. He lived, hunted, and behaved as this bird, and when a bald-headed eagle flew from the high hills down to the river and back, shamans identified it as Mastamho paying his people a visit. Mastamho continued to live in the world, but he did not remember who he truly was.

More Mohave Myths

By A.L. Kroeber

THE INFORMANT

This "creation tale" was secured in March 1902, from Nyavarup, near Needles. Jack Jones interpreted.

Nyavarup was an old man and a confessed doctor. This latter is in accord with his being willing to tell about first origins, which most Mohave are afraid to narrate—at least avowedly and systematically—and sometimes even fear to hear told, because this lore is associated with doctoring or being a doctor. I suppose the association and reluctance are because the central theme of the earlier part of the Origins myth is the illness and death of Matavilya, the great first god that died. Personally, however, Nyavarup, as an old man, had little to fear from practice as a curing doctor or from his avowal thereof. In fact, as will be seen, he spoke of his shamanistic power with a certain pride.

Nyavarup was also a historic character, though I did not know it at the time of our acquaintance. He is mentioned several times, as "Navarupe;" in Mollhausen's 1860 account in German of the Ives ascent of the Colorado River in 1858 in the steamer "Explorer," as being a friendly young fellow who voluntarily attached himself to the expedition. When the steamer had to turn back, a German cook volunteered to go on up with Nyavarupe on foot to see if they could reach the Virgin River upstream on the right bank. They left on March 14, 1858, and rejoined the steamer on March 18 with a successful report. Next day, Navarupe was sent downriver ahead of the steamer with a message to chiefs Kairook and Mesikehota.

In 1902, Nyavarup said this about himself:

I saw all that I am telling about Mastamho: I was there when it happened. Only some men were there, those who are doctors. I shall see it all again tonight, when I dream.

No, doctors do not learn from older doctors: they are born to be doctors; they learn only from Mastamho.

There are four sicknesses I can cure:

1. Pains in the back.

2. When a baby gets sick with a cough from its father or mother eating the black seeds called kovo.

3. From getting hit with a stick.

4. A small child sick from eating food cooked with the wood of kutsie"rse, a plant with hooked thorns [cholla cactus- catsclaw acacia]. There are other sicknesses I can treat.

5. A baby passing blood from its father having eaten the remnants of birds killed but only partly devoured by a "chicken hawk" [atsyore, falcon, probably] or large hawk [sokwilye-akatai].

6. Sickness from eating birds, rabbits, or deer killed by oneself, or fish one has caught. This sickness is painless; one lies around, sleeps, does not feel right. A man may eat his own fish if the net in which he has caught them is old; but if it is new, he will go out of his mind and will work his hands as if making a net. He becomes sick because the ghosts (nyavesi) of the fish he caught take away his shadow (matkwisa), and he becomes weak and sleepy. Then I bring back his shadow by singing what Mastamho told me to sing for this, and by blowing saliva on him.

These six illnesses I cure: I have a song for each. I learned the songs from Mastamho. He sang them to me as he stood by me, and told me for what to use it. I would not have known them if he had not taught them to me. He also said to me to blow my spittle white [frothy], not black [clear]. He told me to keep this in my heart. If Mastamho had told me to cure like the white people, with medicine, I would have known how to do that; but he did not tell me.

He also told me how to catch fish. He told me to take a pointed stick of arrowweed and pierce the lower jaw of the fish as I took them from the net. He called this stick tinyam-esirqa. So

I am good at fishing; I can always make a catch.

I can go at any time to ask Mastamho whatever I want to know: I could go tonight. It does not take me long to reach him.

When a baby is still in the belly, and also after he is born and lies there looking up, that is when he goes to Mastamho at Avikwame, every night. When he is larger, he begins to understand; when he is so big [gesture] he knows; when he is an old man, he knows it fully.

Besides this semipersonal information, Nyavarup imparted to me the Alyha myth, here included as No. 10; an account of Mountain Lion's and Jaguar's (or Wolf's) institutings, No. 16A; and a brief Coyote tale, No. 16B.

THE ORIGIN MYTH
Part A: Matavilya

1. Ammaya, Sky, was a man, the father of all; Amata, Earth, a woman; all beings were born from them in the same day-Matavilya, Mastamho, people, plants, and everything else. They were born far west across the ocean at Pi'in, in darkness: there was no day then. Matavilya was the first to be born; the others followed. Now he came from there, from the west, leading the rest. He did not walk in coming here; he moved without stepping, turning to the right and left, to right and left, four times [like sliding]: in four motions he arrived here, and all the people followed. At Pi'in Sky and Earth are still having intercourse; Sky constantly comes down to Earth and rises again.

2. When Matavilya reached this land, he had no wife, but he said, "This is my daughter, Blue-green Flat, Havasum-kukelape!' He was a young man, Mastamho, a little boy, Frog, a girl. Hiqo came with them from the west. To the east the world is high; toward the west it is low. They had climbed up eastward until they came near the center of the earth. Now Matavilya was measuring with his hands outstretched: one of them did not reach to the end. Then he moved on a little, measured again, and each hand touched: so he knew that where he stood was the middle of the earth. He said: "This is the middle: here I will stay and build a house." There he built it; at Ha'avulypo.

3. When Matavilya built his house there, it was dark, but he had no wood for it: he made the timbers out of nothing. Now he was lying near the center of the house; his daughter lay with her head to the south, just west of the door. Matavilya went out to relieve himself, crawling on hands and knees, and in passing in the dark he put his hand on her privates. Outdoors, he turned west. Frog sank down into the ground and traveled along. After a time she came up and looked for Matavilya; sank again and traveled on until she came up under him. He did not see her: his feces dropped into her gaping mouth and she swallowed them. Then she returned to the house and lay down. Soon Matavilya came back also. He was sick, and crying from pain: "Eh! eh! eh!" Frog said: "My father, what is the matter?" He said, "I am sick." He lay down with his head to the east. Then he lay with his head to the north: he spat blood. Thereupon he lay with his head to the west: now he spat his white saliva. Hiqo knew that the red which he spat was gold and that the white was silver; but the people did not know it. Then Matavilya lay with his head to the south and sweated. His sweat is ore: it is mined in the mountains. He said: "I cannot endure this any longer. I am going where it is dark. I will be gone." Then he died.

4. As Matavilya had lain dying, he covered himself with a net, ihulye, and said: "I am content." He called the net uyatetonikwanyai. He called it also ihatskutsule. That is why people have nets now.

5. When Matavilya became sick, he said to one who was sitting on the west side of the house: "Come here: sit close by." He was Hiqo, but Matavilya called him Koro-koro-pa. Now Frog, his daughter, put her hands on Matavilya's breast. She said to Koro-koro-pa: "Come, Matavilya is nearly dead"; but Koro-koro-pa, sitting there at the west of the house, said nothing. He made a hole, sank down out of the house, and went off westward, making a loud noise. He went back to Pi'in where Matavilya and all of them had been born. He did not remain to see Matavilya and his house burned: that is why the whites do not burn the dead or their houses.

6. Matavilya did not speak loudly, and no one heard him. When he said: "Mastamho, come here," Mastamho paid no attention, for he was

playing about. When Matavilya spoke to him again, he still did not listen. But when Matavilya was sick, he said once more in a low voice: "Come here: Listen. I want to give you my instructions." Then Mastamho came and stood by him and leaned toward him to listen with his right ear.

7. The sun, the moon, and the stars were made by Mastamho. Matavilya had told him to make them. He said to him: "Do what I am telling you now. These people are unable, but you can do it."

8. If Matavilya had lived, everyone would have lived forever; but because he died and was burned, everybody dies. The small lizard said, "I wish people to die. If they all keep on growing, there will be no room. There will be no place to go to; if we defecate, the excrement will fall on someone's foot" So people began to die. If lizard had not said this, no one would die.

This same lizard was later sent eastward by Mastamho to see if the ma-selye'aye seeds were growing. Another lizard, Kwatulye, was sent westward by him to see how the kwaoepilye seeds were growing.

9. Frog was afraid that she would be killed for having been the cause of Matavilya's death. So she sank back into the ground and fled from Ha'avulypo. She came up to the south, at Na'aikunyilaqa, and opened her mouth wide to cool it. Then she sank down again and came up across the river at Hanyikoits-gwampa. When she emerged there, she still heard the people crying for Matavilya and continued afraid. So she went back into the ground and traveled on. She came up again at another Hanyiko-its-qwampa, to the south of the first. But she sank down once more, and finally emerged far southeast. She said: "I will not go farther. I will always stay here. This mountain will be called Ikwe-nye-va!"

*Toy cradle with pottery doll.
Mohave. 17 3/4 x 4 3/4".
Denver Art Museum (Cat. No. QMo–1)*

*Colorplate 30 from American Indian Art
by Norman Feder.*

Mojave Indian Shamanism

By Kenneth M. Stewart

The Shamans *(kwathidhe)* of the Mojave Indians of the lower Colorado River were believed to obtain in prenatal dreams their power to cure and to perform other shamanistic functions. Since in the Mojave conception all power and exceptional abilities depended upon proper dreaming, the shamans were not sharply distinguished from others who had experienced great dreams *(sumach ahot)*. But the power-bestowing dreams of the shamans were the most elaborate of those of any Mojave.

Dreaming, as was reported by the eminent

SCENES OF EARLY MOJAVE LIFE

In the photograph at top is shown a typical Mojave desert camp near Needles, California, taken about the turn of the century. Below is an unusual photograph of Mojave Indians holding a mourning ceremony for their dead chief Sutuma, a rite presided over by the shaman. (From the C. C. Pierce collection of historical photographs in the Southwest Museum).

anthropologist A. L. Kroeber, occupied a focal position in Mojave culture.[1] The dreams were believed to be first experienced while the unborn Mojave was yet in his mother's womb, only to be forgotten at birth. Later in life the dreams were remembered or dreamed over again. In a typical Mojave power dream the "shadow" *(matkwesa)* of the foetal dreamer was impelled back in time to the beginning of the world, when the "shadows" of the future Mojaves were with the deities at the sacred mountain, *Avikwame* ("Spirit Mountain").[2] At Avikwame the culture hero Mastamho built a sacred house and, according to Kroeber, "it is of this house that shamans dream, for here their shadows were as little boys in the face of Mastamho, and received from him their ordained powers."[3]

Mojave shamans were usually specialists[4], and each shaman was able to cure only certain illnesses, depending on the nature of his dreams.[5] In the words of a Mojave informant (PL), "There were different kinds of doctors. Each doctor had a certain power to cure certain sicknesses; they were specialists in curing wounds, snake bites, or insect bites"[6]. Among the specialists were the "ghost doctor" *(nyavedhi sumach)*, who cured sickness attributed to dreaming of the dead, the arrow wound doctor *(ipa sumach)*, and the rattlesnake bite doctor. The scalper *(ahwe sumach)* had the power to cure "enemy sickness," which was believed to be caused by contact with aliens. Also the *kohota* ("festival chief"), although not primarily a shaman, had some power to cure. The *kohota* was in addition entrusted with the custody of prisoners of war (young females and little boys), who were believed to cause "enemy sickness" unless they were decontaminated, so to speak, by his ministrations. Some shamans dreamed the power to cure more than one kind of illness, and it should be further noted that, depending on his dreams, a Mojave might occupy more than one status. Thus, if he had dreamed it, a man might be both a shaman and a brave *(kuanami)*.

Mojave conceptions of the causation of

disease included soul loss (the most common explanation), dream poisoning, contamination by contact with enemies, and object intrusion, although the concept of intrusion was of the aberrant type described by Forde for the Yuma.[7]

The soul of a Mojave might be kidnapped by a witch or ghost and taken to the land of the dead (Sila'id), which was believed to lie to the south.[8] "Ghost sickness" might be caused by dreaming of deceased relatives, who attempted to lure the dreamer to join them in Sila'id. Or the illness might be the result of bewitchment by a sorcerer (a malevolent shaman), or a consequence of a breach of the taboos attending funerals and mourning ceremonies. Some ailments and some deaths were attributed to natural causes, such as accident or old age.

The Mojave shaman did not ask the patient to describe his symptoms but made his diagnosis by feeling all over the body of the sufferer to ascertain what was making him ill. If the shaman diagnosed the ailment as of a type which he was not competent to treat he would refer the patient to another practitioner who had dreamed the power necessary to cure that particular illness.

In the most usual method of curing the shaman sang the songs that he had dreamed, describing how he had acquired his power. He blew tobacco smoke over the patient to drive away evil or bring back the patient's soul.[9] Sometimes a shaman sprayed saliva over a patient. Other curative procedures included massage or brushing with the hand, and the prescription of bathing and food taboos. Some doctors sucked on the bodies of their patients to draw out evil influences, but they did not suck out disease objects. Nor were Mojave shamans possessed by spirits while curing.[10]

There were no associations composed of doctors, but a shaman was regarded by other Mojaves as "different." Shamans sometimes showed vicarious suicidal tendencies, as Dr. George Devereux has described.[11] A shaman might say, "I do not wish to live very long," or he might try to provoke others into killing him by intimating that he had bewitched their relatives. As he grew older a shaman might become a witch. Such shamans were thought to be most apt to bewitch their own relatives and friends, in order to take them to the afterworld as "followers."

A shaman was paid a fee, but only if he performed a successful cure. If, on the other hand, a shaman was suspected of practicing witchcraft or withholding his power to heal, he might be slain. The killing was done by braves. In fact, shamans sometimes invited others to kill them. The explanation of this is that a special fate was believed to await the shaman in the hereafter, but only if he died a violent death. Furthermore, his retinue of "followers," the ghosts of those whom he had bewitched, was believed to be awaiting his arrival in a special place in the Shadow Land. There the ghosts would undergo several metamorphoses, finally becoming charcoal on the desert. If the death of a shaman was too long defered his "followers" might already have passed on to another stage.

The Ghost Doctor. The "ghost doctor" was called *nyavedhi sumach*, which according to LW means "dream of the old dead people in the family." LW also said that "These certain doctors use owl feathers.[12] When someone dreams of the old dead people it makes them kind of crazy; they cry. He doctors them at night and cures that kind of illness. The doctor wears feathers in his hair and a little red paint." Fathauer has described the symptoms of "ghost sickness": "People afflicted with ghost sickness were afraid of darkness, experienced nightmares, were unable to sleep at night, and cried for long periods of time."[13]

Arrow Wound Doctor. An arrow wound doctor (*ipa sumach or ipa kusumanya*) always accompanied a war party, which according to one informant also included a doctor who specialized in treating club wounds.

"There was a special doctor for arrow wounds. He would pull the arrow out and suck the blood so it wouldn't affect the body" (AL).

"Doctors go along on a war party like the Medical Corps in our Army. They worked on the wounded and took them out of the fight if they were really badly hurt. There was a special doctor for arrow wounds. He pulled the arrows out and sucked on the wounds. On the way to the enemy the doctor does all the talking. He made a few speeches on how to act, how to conduct themselves. He tells his dreams. He tried to work magic against the enemy and put them all to sleep. He tries to hypnotize them so they will fall down. Another medicine man at home works magic if they get lost. People go to him to find out things. He had a certain way of doing it in the night, to find someone who's lost. But he didn't go on a war party. He tells when the lost one will be home. The arrow doctor is a specialist, doctors nothing else. He goes on each war party. Maybe several in the tribe, but they just take one at a time. He takes care of the wounded, but he doesn't doctor during the fight. When they return and reach the first night's camp, he washes the wounds and sings" (PL).

Rattlesnake Bite Doctor. The rattlesnake bite doctor also sang while curing.

"While the doctor is on his way to the victim he sings so the man won't suffer. Meanwhile, the victim's family won't drink water. I heard that the doctor sang around until the victim didn't suffer. He didn't suck the bite and didn't blow on it, but just sang. I saw one man who got bit. His arm was swollen all the way up to his neck. The doctor came and put his hands over the arm and the swelling disappeared. I don't know how he did it" (AL).

Scalper. The scalper (*ahwe sumach* or "enemy dream[er]") was an important member of a war party.[14] He cured the "enemy sickness" that was believed to be a kind of contamination resulting from contact with aliens. One informant (LW) described the scalper as a "kind of half medicine man."

The scalps were considered to be magically contagious and extremely dangerous, and only one who had dreamed the appropriate power could take a scalp. If a warrior without proper dreams should scalp he would go insane from "enemy sickness," and "holler in the night."

"If a warrior is sick, the *awe sumach* doctors him. If an enemy slayer gets sick on the way home, the others can't carry him; it's too dangerous. If he's sick, the *ahwe sumach* doctors him, and he has to bathe for eight days" (AL).

"The scalp man understood and had a little power against the enemy. When warriors were coming home, they would be kind of a little insane from the enemy's power. There would be one or two scalp men in the tribe, but only one would go on a war party" (LW).

The scalper cleaned the scalp with mud to "tame" it, or purify it, and then turned it over to its permanent custodian, the *kohota*. Even the scalper had to undergo purification lest he fall ill with "enemy sickness."

"If they didn't wash, they would go crazy. He goes away to purify himself, even cleans his fingernails" (TB)

"After scalping he stayed out and went without food and water for eight days. On the eighth day, if he found water on a hill, he could bathe in it. On the fourth day of the scalp dance, he had to put

in another four days without eating salt. He also had to smut himself for another four days. He got a weed like tumbleweed on the mesa. It's kind of soapy when rubbed together. Rubbed his body all over with it like soap, and then bathed in the river. If he didn't purify himself, it would kill him" (PL).

The scalper also functioned as a funeral orator.[15]

"They made a date for the funeral, about four days later, if men had been killed. There was always a man who made a speech at the funeral. Just like a preacher. Never gives them bad feeling. Made a nice speech that they know he was brave, defending the home folk. The people wail. All the relations come in. All the people sit out and cry" (PL).

"Everyone is quiet and listens to him. He has that dream. Nobody laughs at him. He speaks at funerals and memorials" (LW).

After a funeral the mourners were under restrictions for four days and had to purify themselves by bathing. If a person did not observe the funeral taboos he would fall ill and would have to be treated by a "ghost doctor."

The scalper also conducted the mourning ceremony (*nyimichivauk*), which was held to honor dead chiefs and warriors and which featured a dramatization of warfare.

"The *ahwe sumach* is the medicine man in charge of Memorial Day" (PL).

"He's the medicine man with a feather headdress at the mourning ceremony. He's the one who sings about the *okwilya* (feathered pike) and war bonnet, and he tells about arrows, clubs, and canteens. He doesn't use a rattle, but he sings about rattles. He sings while the ten runners are standing resting."[16]

Kohota (or *kwaxot*). The *kohota* has been been variously described as a "dance director," "manager of entertainments," and "festival chief."[17] In some instances the *kohota* seems also to have been a shaman, or had at least dreamed certain powers of curing. The *kohota* cured "enemy sickness."[18] He was also the custodian of the scalps, and was responsible for taking charge of the prisoners and ridding them of the malevolent enemy power.[19]

The kohota's role as custodian of the scalps was also described by my informants.

"The keeper of the scalps was called *ahwe kusumanya*. There were two in the tribe. They take care of the scalps. He keeps the scalps in a corner of the house where he sleeps. The house is called *kwaxot niya*. The *kwaxot* kept them. He's the same man who gives parties. When any ceremony comes, the *ahwe kusumanya* cleans the scalps. *Ahwe kusumanya* and *kwaxot* are the same man. He knows how to avoid sickness, never gets sick from the scalps. He'd hold another scalp dance every summer" (AL).

"The *ahwe kusumanya*—he's the man who keeps the scalps. He puts them in a hut and keeps them. Maybe on certain days he prays over them and washes them" (TB).

"When the scalp keeper died, they burned the scalps. His son didn't inherit the position. He had to get the power" (LW).

"The *kohota* used greasewood or arrow-weed gum to seal up a gourd containing scalps. He arranges the victory dance for the returning warriors. He'd give another scalp dance at harvest time. He washed the prisoners when they were brought back. Gave them power to be related to the Mojaves. They were magically dangerous if not washed right away. The enemies had dangerous magic on them, so he washed and smutted them with soaproot and arrow-weeds. They had to bathe daily for four days" (PL).

"The keeper sometimes washed and brushed the scalps and dyed the hair and did it up in mud and painted the hair. When he was through, he always took a bath, and then he did without salt for four days" (LW).

On the basis of the present data, and without further field studies, it would be hazardous to attempt to estimate the degree to which shamanistic beliefs and practices currently survive among the Mojave. But Dr. George Devereux in 1956 stated that"... Mohave shamanism and the whole matter of curing powers, is still very much alive."[20] The old people, who experienced the traditional Mojave way of life in their youth, and who later served as informants for anthropologists, have now passed on to *Sila'id*. The Mojaves of the younger generations are now much more acculturated than were their elders, although many Mojaves have never been converted to Christianity. It is doubtful that people any longer get power from *sumach ahot*, although the Mojaves are still very much interested in dreams as omens. Warfare (including scalping) in the Mojave manner is of course no longer practiced. But the Mojave still hold old-style funerals. Mourning ceremonies have also been held in recent times, in honor of two Mojave soldiers killed in Europe in World War II, and after the death of Chief Pete Lambert in 1947.

[1] "Dreams, then, are the foundation of Mojave life; and dreams throughout are cast in mythological mold" (Kroeber 1925: 755).

[2] *Avikwame* is a peak in the Newberry Mountains to the north of Needles, California, at the extreme southern tip of Nevada.

[3] Ibid., 771.

[4] Devereux (1961: 18) mentions "non-specialist shamans" among the Mojave.

[5] Mojave shamans were usually men, although female shamans have also been reported (Drucker: 158; Spier 1933: 282; Devereux 1961: 88). And Bourke (1889: 175) stated that "The Mojaves have women doctors, who are born with the gift...

[6] My principal Mojave informants, with the approximate years of their births, were the following: Pete Lambert, 1866, Mrs. Abraham Lincoln, 1869, Lute Wilson, 1879, and Tom Black, 1884. Their statements will be identified in the text with their respective initials.

[7] "The object . . . has none of the characteristics of the usual material object. The belief is that an unspecified poison has been consumed under the almost hypnotic influence of a malevolent spirit. It is a poisonous essence, only vaguely material, which lies at the root of the disease. The doctor affects to suck out the blood that has been poisoned in this way and so relieve the victim" (Forde: 200f).

[8] "*Sumach achim*—those were bad dreams. A person might get in trouble or in a hole in sleep. The soul might leave and go somewhere else without anybody knowing what happens" (AL).

[9] Wallace 1953: 200f.

[10] Forde (p. 184) has reported spirit possession for the Yuma: "In witchcraft… both in the bewitchment and the curing, the spirit is believed to enter into the doctor and true possession occurs". Kroeber (1957: 226) described instances in which a Mojave clairvoyant's body was possessed in a trance by the spirits of mountains.

[11] Devereux 1961: 387ff.

[12] According to Fathauer (1951-2: 605), "...the Mohave believe that some people turned into owls after death... Owls were dangerous omens; an owl crying near the house at twilight meant a death in the family."

[13] Fathauer 1951-2: 605.

[14] Fathauer (1954: 98) in fact regards the scalper as the leader of the warriors.

[15] The Mojave cremated their dead on funeral pyres and threw the property of the deceased into the flames. The house of the dead person was also burned. In Mojave belief the ghost might come back to get his property if the mourners neglected to transmit it to him via the cremation fire.

[16] I have elsewhere published an account of the Mojave mourning ceremony (Stewart 1947a).

[17] Informants described the non-shamanistic functions of the *kohota* as follows: "He's the man who had a large house. Gives parties. Plants lots of crops. When the crop was fit to eat, he'd call all the Indians to come and eat. He was not a chief or *kwanami*. Everyone likes him. He's like a good Christian. He's quiet and doesn't talk dirty. He's like a missionary. He gives dances and eats. People introduce themselves at these times. There was more than one *kohota*. They lived at Topock, Needles, Fort Mojave, and in other directions. Different *kohotas* would give parties at different times. (PL).

"The *kohota* made speeches. He's like a preacher. He'd always have big pottery, big round pots and baskets, everything big. When there was a celebration, everyone came. He made speeches. He taught the children to believe, and not to fight or steal. He gives parties. When anyone comes, he'll feed him and be friendly to him. The people bring him crops to honor him" (LW).

[18] "He takes care of the clothing and the bad dreams of the *kwanamis* when they come back" (TB). "The warriors never died from 'screwworms' in their wounds. The *sumach kohota* knows all about that, and other things, too" (AL).

[19] Forde (p. 197) suggests that the *kwoxot* of the Yuma tribe may have practiced weather control: "Rainmaking, as a practice involving supernatural power, was associated with curing. It was formerly a prerogative of the *kwoxot*" None of my informants mentioned rainmaking as a capability of the Mojave kohota.

[20] Devereux :1956: 23. Devereux had a number of shamans among his informants on his field trips to the Mojave during the 1930s and 1940s. In 1961 he stated that (p. 35): "The initial treatment is almost always administered by a shaman. Only if shamanistic treatments conspicuously fail to help the patient is the sufferer hospitalized."

Chapter Four

❖

Early History

Photo courtesy of Mohave County Historical Society

Precarious Foothold On the Wild Frontier

By Dennis G. Casebier

Precarious Foothold on the Wild Frontier

Major William Hoffman's Colorado Expedition completely overpowered the Mojaves and, although the bulk of the command stayed only a few days, Hoffman established Fort Mojave in the midst of the Mojave Villages. He took nine of their principal people as hostages to insure the good conduct of the remainder of the tribe. These nine were incarcerated at Fort Yuma, many miles from Mojave country. After the departure of the bulk of Hoffman's command in late April, 1859, the garrison consisted of the two companies of the 6th Infantry and a detachment of the 3rd Artillery.

There were those, perhaps more familiar with the history of the Mojaves and their relationship with white men, who were sorely disappointed over the results of Hoffman's expedition and who felt the Indians were merely biding their time. In May, a long article appeared in a Los Angeles newspaper chronicling the past misdeeds of the Mojaves, citing what appeared to be deceit and duplicity in the past, and predicting disastrous results from them in the future. The writer lamented:

> To us it was a source of regret that the rules and customs of civilized warfare should have turned the muzzles of the rifles of Col. Hoffman's command to the desert air, instead of [into] the breasts of such deceitful murderers. That the foul murderers of our fellow citizens, their wives and their children, should have been spared, simply because they came crouching and supplicating, as they have ever done, even towards those whom they meant to most foully murder at the first unguarded moment, was most unfortunate.

Shortly after Hoffman left, five men belonging to Beale's Wagon Road party, that were traveling the twenty-three miles between Piute Creek and Fort Mojave, were attacked by about thirty Piutes. Captain Armistead took one of his companies of infantry and marched promptly to Piute Creek.

One of Beale's men was missing and never found. Armistead saw no Indians. He learned a lesson that would be crystal clear to many Army officers who would serve in the desert country after him—there was no point marching infantry after the Piutes. They would melt into the mountains and disappear as quickly and thoroughly and quietly as the water from a summer rain on the desert. Infantry had utility only to act as guards at permanent posts or if they were mounted or riding in wagons or marching as escorts. Even then, they could only provide protection and not be used aggressively in the field.

Armistead went to work at Mojave. Buildings and shelters were erected by the troops for protection from the elements. The style of construction at this early date was not too different than that used by the Indians themselves. Sticks and logs from the few trees in the river bottom were placed upright in the ground and chinked with mud. Roofs were fashioned in the same manner. Sunshades were

DENNIS G. CASEBIER COLLECTION

Two fishermen drift unknowingly across the historic spot where the Fort Mojave ferry crossed the treacherous "Rio Colorado of the West." The fort was situated on the mesa on the opposite side. Its site is marked today by crumbling foundations and sidewalks. Picture taken from the west (Nevada) side of the river looking east into Arizona. Photo by Dennis G. Casebier.

constructed of the same material. These were badly needed as summer, with its intense heat, was approaching rapidly.

The first commanding officer was optimistic about his situation. He projected an air of optimism about the site, the buildings and other improvements being constructed, and even about the Indians. In mid-June he wrote:

"The Mohaves are the best behaved Indians I have ever seen. They are the only Indians, I have ever seen, that I think might be civilized. As they live, almost exclusively, from what they can raise from the soil they can be easily controlled. They number, I think, about five hundred warriors. At certain seasons of the year, after gathering their crops, wheat and corn, they can concentrate. The Whalupi [Hualpai] and Payutes are more numerous, but from the nature of their country, they can not concentrate in any numbers."

Unknown to Armistead, trouble was brewing at Fort Yuma. Nine of the principal Mojaves had been taken to Yuma as hostages. They were being held in the guardhouse. This was a new experience for these Mojaves. Incarceration of that type was something with which they were completely unfamiliar and they were unable to cope with it. In their own culture, when they took prisoners (which was frequently) they were treated as slaves and given the run of the camp. If these "prisoners" escaped, they were relentlessly tracked down, brought back alive, and tortured to death as a lesson to the other "prisoners." This served as a graphic object lesson for the other prisoners and it made a decision to escape a rather desperate matter and a choice that the slaves seldom opted for.

CAMEL TRAIN IN NEVADA
From Harper's Weekly of June 30, 1877.
Courtesy Dennis Casebier

On June 21, 1859, the hostages sent to Yuma by Hoffman escaped. It appears they had the impression they were to be imprisoned at Yuma for only thirty days to begin with. The chief among them kept a string attached to his leg, and each day he tied a knot in the string. After there were thirty knots in the string, and it appeared they would not be released, the Indians became discouraged.

On the day indicated, while the Indians were out of their cells for their daily exercise, they broke loose. The old chief sacrificed himself by seizing the guard's gun. The others broke and ran. The chief was bayoneted and then shot through the head. The entire garrison was soon in pursuit of the fugitives. When the shooting had stopped, five of the nine Indians were dead. The remaining four escaped.

This incident left both sides in an uncertain position. The idea behind keeping the hostages was that, if the tribe misbehaved, the hostages would be punished. But was this provision designed to work in reverse? If the hostages misbehaved, should Captain Armistead at Fort Mojave punish the tribe? The answer to this he did not know. He wrote to headquarters for instructions. Meanwhile, he informed the tribe that they must give up the prisoners that had escaped. The Indians never complied with this demand.

A correspondent to a San Francisco newspaper at about this time described the effects the escape had on Fort Mojave:

"The news of the escape of the hostages and the killing of old Kiarook and five more, has been received here through the Indians. Since the arrival of Irataba, who brought the news, the Mojaves have been very shy; only two or three have been in for the last few days; formerly they would come in crowds. Since the overflow quite a large camp of them has been located about a mile below us; but as soon as the news came they all stampeded at 12 o'clock at night. What their intentions are remain to be seen."

To this point, very few trips had been made under the "Central Overland Mail" contract connecting Stockton, California, and Kansas City, Missouri. The excuse cited by the contractors was hostility of the Mojave Indians. Now, with Fort Mojave established, the contractors were making one last effort to carry out the terms of their contract. They had a mail station on the river about two miles below Fort Mojave.

On July 20 and 21 the Mojaves stole stock from the mail station and finally attacked it outright. The employee of the mail company fled to the fort for protection. Then, a few days later, a routine guard patrol from the post was fired on. This was war again!

Armistead attempted to precipitate an engagement with the Mojaves, but they eluded his troops. On August 5, he successfully drew them into a battle and they were defeated. The contest was fought at a point about twelve miles below Fort Mojave on the east side of the river. Armistead had achieved a night march with twenty-five men, reaching the site of one of the largest rancherias on the river during the night of August 4-5. (In those days, the term rancheria was used to describe small gatherings of Indian dwellings.)

In the morning he surprised three Indians working in a field. One of these Indians was killed, thereby initiating the fight. Soon hundreds of Indians were involved. After a time, Armistead's twenty-five men were reinforced by twenty-five more under Lt. E. G. Marshall. The arrival of this added detachment was in accordance with Armistead's plan. The Mojaves fought bravely but were soundly defeated. Armistead counted twenty-three dead on the field. Other estimates indicate the number killed may have been much larger. Armistead had three men slightly wounded and none killed.

No overtures for a peace conference were made by either side. Armistead was determined to continue hostilities until the Mojaves were "satisfied." For several weeks after the battle, he sent out patrols hunting Indians, burning rancherias, and destroying crops.

When Armistead's reports reached headquarters in San Francisco, the Department Commander became concerned for the safety of the garrison. Part of the dragoons at Fort Tejon were put under orders to march to his relief. Also, Company "E" 6th Infantry, then stationed at Camp Prentiss at the mouth of Cajon Pass, was alerted to prepare for the march. However, the Mojave War was over before that Company could be sent to the scene of action.

By August 31, the Mojaves had had enough. In the battle of August 5, they had tested their mettle against Army troops in a pitched battle for the first time. The result was, for them, a complete disaster. Then, in the weeks that followed, they were given a sample of another type of warfare that white men could direct against their homes and crops. It was the end of the war and, perhaps unknown to the Mojaves, it was the end of their nation. Armistead's report of his meeting with the Mojave peace commission on August 31 was brief:

> "I have the honor to inform you that I have, at their earnest solicitation, made peace this day, with the Mojaves.

> "I think they are sincere. They wanted a good whipping, which they got. They appear to be perfectly satisfied.

> "All the terms that I could demand of them were that they should behave themselves, and give up the bend in the river, where the mules are herded and never come on it.

> "I have done what I thought right, and if it only meets the approval of the commanding general, I shall be very much gratified.

> "We shall be out of everything in the commissary department by the end of next month, September."

It was all over for the Mojaves. They would fight no more. Fort Mojave would watch over them for many years, but there would never again be an uprising or disturbance by them as an organized people. In the years ahead, Fort Mojave's biggest problems would come from the Hualpai Indians to the east. But we're getting ahead of ourselves.

The immediate major threat to Fort Mojave now was obtaining supplies. Hoffman had stated the fort could not be supplied by way of the Mojave Road and that it would be necessary to carry supplies of all kinds to the fort by river steamer. The steamers on the Colorado River at the time had operated mostly between Yuma and the mouth of the river. Now when they tried to operate above Yuma they were found to be somewhat underpowered and they ran too deeply in the water. But they struggled with the problem.

The steamer *General Jesup* had accompanied Hoffman's command to the crossing in April. Then, the *Colorado* arrived at the fort with more supplies on May 12. By late August, the fort was running low on supplies, the new steamer *Cocopah* was known to be headed upriver, but it was not known whether or not it would arrive in time.

The Quartermaster in Los Angeles, Capt. Winfield Scott Hancock, put together a small train, consisting of two wagons, a small herd of beef cattle, and a pack train. The wagons were to be taken through nearly empty to insure they could negotiate the road. They were to be left at Mojave for use of the post. The expedition was considered an experiment to determine if Fort Mojave could be supplied by pack train.

The train went through with no problems at all. Not only was it practical to send pack trains, Hancock's wagon master and Hancock himself became convinced that the road might be practical for trains of heavily loaded wagons.

Meanwhile, the *Cocopah* arrived at Fort Mojave on September 1 with a load of supplies. It left again for Yuma on September 3 with Captain Armistead on board, en route for Los Angeles.

By October the fort had consumed the supplies that had been brought by the *Cocopah* in September. They were in a dire strait again. It had been discussed that at a certain date it would be necessary to abandon the fort and march the troops toward San Bernardino while consuming their last supplies.

On October 21, Captain Hancock started a train of ten 8-mule wagons over the Mojave Road with supplies for the fort. The train reached Mojave on November 5 with no delays or problems en route, thereby demonstrating the practicability of the Mojave Road to support heavy freight or any other kind of traffic. Suddenly the fort was no longer dependent upon the unreliable steamers and there was a regular flow of freight traffic to the fort over the Mojave Road.

Soon Fort Mojave settled down to a phase of construction and improvement. It attracted a few citizens that commenced development around them, and a small amount of prospecting took place in the mountains adjacent to the post. Steamers came and went. They brought supplies for construction of post buildings. The soldiers worked on the buildings. The commanding officers complained to headquarters about their isolated condition, the need for extra rations, the need for more wagons, and other supplies. These things were sent.

Wagon trains passed back and forth over the Mojave Road. Beale's Wagon Road parties continued with their work. Messengers made regular runs between Fort Mojave and Los Angeles. Camels were still seen on the Mojave Road performing messenger duties and carrying supplies for road-working parties. Consistent with Captain Armistead's projection, the Mojaves were "satisfied" and remained peaceful.

By early 1861 a creditable collection of buildings had been erected. Fort Mojave had become a viable place. An interesting chapter of history was enacted in that year when a Boundary Commission came out to attempt the first reconnaissance of the California-Nevada boundary.

First, Lt. Joseph Christmas Ives, U. S. Army Topographical Engineers, had determined the initial point—just a few miles below Fort Mojave where the 35th Parallel of North Latitude strikes the Colorado River. An observatory had been set up and sufficient sightings made to cause an "initial point" to be established and monumented.

The boundary survey party left the "astronomical station" on the Colorado River on February 13, 1861. Little of lasting value, so far as determining the location of the California-Nevada line is concerned, was accomplished by this commission. But there were some colorful sidelights: First, they took three camels with them and this, of course, adds uniqueness and charm to their undertaking. Second, they crossed Death Valley. Third, it was a topographical reconnaissance through this country just as the white men were beginning to penetrate it. They bumped into early activities (such as at Fort Mojave) while it was still a wilderness and a rugged frontier environment.

Meanwhile, events were taking place in the southern states that would completely change everything for the Army for the next four years. People everywhere anxiously watched events, even at isolated Fort Mojave—first President Lincoln's election, then secession, then a Confederate Constitution. Finally, on April 12, 1861, the shore batteries under command of Gen. Pierre G. T. Beauregard, opened fire on Fort Sumter in the harbor at Charleston, SC. The Civil War had begun. The Mojaves, and all the other Indians on the isolated frontier, were suddenly unimportant.

In the weeks and months that followed Sumter, United States troops were pulled out of Indian Country and sent East. Many brave and faithful soldiers had to make that terrible decision—to fight for the Gray or the Blue. Each struggled with it in his own way, each made a decision.

In common with many other frontier forts, Fort Mojave was hurriedly ordered abandoned and the troops, with such government property as could be carried, were directed to march overland to New San Diego. They left the post on the 28 and 29 of May, 1861. The commanding officer, Capt. Granville Owen Haller, reported his movements in a letter dated on the Mojave Road at Soda Springs, May 24, 1861:

> I have the honor to report that a U. S. Wagon train from Los Angeles Cala arrived at Fort Mojave N.M.T. at noon on the 27 inst. and that Fort Mojave was abandoned on the 28th agreeably to Special Orders No. 88 (Dept. of the Pacific) Current Series. All the public property & stores were brought away with the garrison.

> The command and train has been divided into two columns for the first six marches on account of the scarcity of water, the leading column consists of "I" Company 6th Infantry and marched on the morning of the 28th inst. The rear column consists of "I" Company 4th Infantry which marched on the 29th. The former was commanded by myself, the latter by 1st Lt. F. H. Bates 4th Infantry A.A.Q.M. the next officer in rank.

> Enclosed herewith I have the honor to transmit a return of the Garrison of Fort Mojave at the time of its being abandoned. The troops are en route to Los Angeles Cala pursuant to orders above cited.

> It is very gratifying to be able to announce that the Indians around Fort Mojave exhibited a very friendly disposition coming in by hundreds to see the troops off. The Chiefs have declared themselves friendly to the whites, and that they may pass through their country, and have promised to see that their people do not destroy the buildings of Fort Mojave.

As the troops left, the country was not the same unknown wilderness they had marched into two years earlier. Many soldiers and civilians had been introduced to the area. Active prospecting and mining operations were underway at El Dorado Canyon, near the Colorado River some fifty miles above the fort.

Interestingly, although all the soldiers left, the white men didn't completely abandon the fort. One man, a frontiersman named William Furlong (frequently called "Buck Skin Bill"), who had worked for the Army at the fort in various ways, stayed on with the Indians. He would be there when the California Volunteers returned in 1863.

The Mojave Expedition of 1858-59

by Leslie Gene Hunter

In October of 1858, Californians were shocked by the news that Mojave Indians had attacked a wagon train traveling the recently opened Beale Road in western New Mexico. An outraged public demanded that the government chastise the Indians and insure the safety of emigrants. In response to these demands, military authorities in California dispatched a column of 600 men under Lieutenant Colonel William Hoffman from Fort Yuma to reduce the Mojave threat. After a short decisive campaign, the Indians capitulated, and a military post—Fort Mohave— was established on the Colorado River to protect the overland route. Although small in scale, the Mojave campaign mirrored the problems the army encountered in fighting Indians in remote desert reaches. It also marked the end of Mojave resistance to an expanding white civilization intent on possessing the land.[1]

In the 1850s from 2,500 to 3,000 Mojave Indians (tribal name, *Aha Macave* or *Amacave*, meaning the people who live along the water) inhabited small, scattered villages along the banks of the Colorado River in Arizona and California. Tall, athletic, and physically robust, they were fierce warriors who practiced war more for gain and individual distinction than as a matter of revenge or necessity. Believing themselves inherently and racially distinct from other peoples, they avoided social intercourse with neighboring tribes and even some kindred Yuman-speaking peoples. Surrounded by formidable desert country, they remained virtually isolated from contact with westering Americans for generations.[2]

In 1858, however, the Mojaves suddenly found themselves on a new federal highway across the Southwest. In that year Edward F. Beale surveyed a government wagon road along the thirty-fifth parallel from the Rio Grande to the Colorado River and reported that it was the shortest and best route for the movement of settlers, troops, and mail from the Santa Fe Trail to California. As the road crossed the Colorado in the vicinity of the Mojave villages, the Indians soon faced increasing contact with emigrant parties. Conflict was inevitable.[3]

The first sizable party to use the road was a westbound group which had organized at Council Grove, Missouri. Containing some 200 persons, the emigrant train, led by Leonard J. Rose and driving over 400 head of livestock, reached the Colorado on August 27. The families had encountered problems one hundred miles east of the river when Indians stole a horse and a mule, but they had gotten the animals back by handing out presents to the poachers. The emigrants then divided into several parties to prevent their stock from exhausting the limited water at the springs along the route. At the Colorado, the whites found the Mojaves friendly. The Indians inquired about the size of the train, its destination, and sold melons and corn to the travelers. But the number of Indians quickly increased, and they became insolent, driving off several head of cattle, which they butchered and ate within sight of the train. Despite this ominous situation, the emigrants again distributed presents and began building a raft to cross the river.[4]

On the evening of August 30, three hundred Mojaves attacked the Rose party, killing eight, wounding thirteen others, and making off with most of the stock. Fearing for their lives, the survivors loaded a wagon and carriage with provisions, collected nineteen cattle and eleven horses and retreated east during the night to the second train. The reunited families in turn fell back to a third party who provided them much-needed supplies. When news of the incident reached the Rio Grande, Major Electus Backus, commanding a garrison at Albuquerque, dispatched two wagons of provisions with a military escort to meet the emigrants and escort them to the New Mexico settlements.[5]

The report of the attack on the Rose party appeared in the Santa Fe *Weekly Gazette* on October 16, 1858, and was widely reprinted in the California press. The *Sacramento Union* urged that immediate measures be taken to prevent further atrocities. Rumors also circulated that the Mojaves had attacked a party of the Stockton Mail Transport Company at the Colorado. The *San Francisco Herald* demanded that the government adopt comprehensive measures for "a final and complete solution of the whole difficulty" to insure permanent security for the frontier settlements.[6]

When Brevet Brigadier General Newman S. Clarke, commanding the Department of California, learned of the attack on the Rose party, he ordered that a post be established near Beale's Crossing on the Colorado to protect the overland mail and travel on the new road. He selected Brevet Lieutenant Colonel William Hoffman, a distinguished veteran of thirty years' service on the western frontier, to perform this task.[7]

On December 4, 1858, General Clarke handed instructions to Colonel Hoffman, who recently had reached Benicia Barracks, California, with his regiment, the Sixth Infantry, from Fort Bridger. Hoffman would send one infantry company to construct a temporary depot near Martin's Ranch at the Cajon Pass in the San Bernardino Mountains. Here supplies sufficient for four companies to operate four months in the field would be collected. With wagons moving food and forage to the ranch, Hoffman would take a dragoon detachment to the Colorado and select a site for a post near the crossing of Beale's Road. From the depot, four companies would be moved east to build and garrison the new installation.[8]

With two experienced guides, Joseph Reddeford Walker and William Goodyear, Hoffman left Benicia Barracks on December 18, and met an escort of fifty men of the First Dragoons at Martin's Ranch on Christmas Day. Designating the new depot Camp Banning, Hoffman and the dragoon detachment departed the next day, heading northeast, and soon picked up a trail along the banks of the dry Mojave River. As he crossed the desert, Hoffman quickly realized that the barren terrain would complicate a campaign against the Mojaves and hinder the construction and supply of a fort. The sandy soil taxed the animals' strength, and water and grazing were scarce. Small cottonwoods provided a satisfactory fuel supply, but were unsuitable for construction. He found small pools at intervals along the streambed of the Mojave River, but the water soon disappeared into the sand. After passing Soda, Marl, and Rock

Springs, the detachment on January 7 reached the Colorado River, two hundred and twenty-three miles from Martin's Ranch.[9]

As they descended from the river bluff nine miles west of the river, the soldiers saw columns of smoke rising at distant intervals along the river. As no sign of Indians was seen, Hoffman ignored the signals and encamped two miles from the river at Beaver Lake, a slough which formed a horseshoe along whose banks the Mojaves farmed. Soon a dozen or more well-armed Paiutes approached, and announced that they were camped in the vicinity. The Mojaves were farther away and would visit the soldiers the next morning. At sunset, Hoffman ordered the Indians to leave, warning them not to approach his camp at night or his sentinels would open fire.[10]

Hoffman was anxious to examine the bottomland above and below the river crossing, and at dawn on the eighth, he moved down toward the Colorado. In the distance, he saw bands of twenty to thirty Mojaves watching his progress. The Indians were painted, well-armed, and naked, except for a loincloth. As the morning was severely cold, Hoffman concluded that "something extraordinary" must have induced them to expose themselves in such weather. As they descended into the river bottom, he suddenly realized that his soldiers could be trapped between the bluffs and the river in the thick undergrowth. He halted his men and retraced his march, then sought to explore the valley above his camp. Encountering difficult terrain again, the detachment returned to Beaver Lake and bivouacked.[11]

Soon after the soldiers reached Beaver Lake, Mojave warriors entered the camp. Although angered by the presence of the troops, a spokesman told Hoffman that they would allow the intruders to pass through their country. He also said that the Mojave chief would visit the next morning, whereupon Hoffman warned that the chief should bring only twelve or fifteen warriors with him. At sundown the Mojaves were expelled from camp. The soldiers, however, spent a sleepless night, as Indians prowled around the perimeter of the bivouac, occasionally discharging arrows into the camp.[12]

Hoffman ordered reveille sounded at four o'clock on the morning of January 9. He had pushed the reconnaissance as far as he had intended. To remain in the valley one more day with his small force could mean a collision with the Mojave nation. The departure of the detachment, however, was not without incident. As the men packed their gear, some three hundred Mojaves gathered a short distance away. They taunted and mimicked the soldiers, imitating the commands being given. "If I had allowed this insolence to pass unnoticed," Hoffman later reported to Clarke, "they would have hooted us out of the valley with shouts of derision." He decided to attack. Dispatching the wagon, pack mules, and a six-man escort on the return route, Hoffman ordered his dragoons to dismount, take position and open fire. With a few rounds, the troopers drove the Mojaves back into the brush, leaving an estimated ten to twenty dead or wounded warriors behind. The command then hastily mounted and set off in pursuit of the train. A large group of Mojaves attempted to follow them, but a few shots from the dragoons' carbines discouraged them. On the morning of January 19, the party reached Camp Banning.[13]

Hoffman's efforts to locate a site on the Colorado had been unsuccessful. Although he had found a valley with fine grass and timber and a healthy climate near Cajon Pass, at the head of the west fork of the Mojave River, the location was two hundred miles west of the Colorado River and out of range for troop movement against the Indians. It would also be expensive to build a road to supply a post there. A fort site farther east at Beale's Crossing, Hoffman believed, was even less desirable. Not only would such a post be costly to supply via the river, but the intense heat of the climate, lack of forage, and an absence of wood for construction rendered the locale virtually uninhabitable for troops. Moreover, Hoffman frankly doubted that the new wagon route would ever develop into a regular highway.[14]

Californians had followed Hoffman's reconnaissance with interest. The *San Francisco Herald* editorialized that a comprehensive solution was needed to insure "repose and security" for the western settlements. An expedition to quell a single disturbance was too limited in scope, the problem was too "deep-seated" to be solved by "mild means," and the tribes were too savage to learn from a single campaign against them. "The only alternative is unconditional submission or extermination," the *Herald* stated. Prolonged and costly campaigns had been avoided in the past when Indians were surrounded by whites and unable to find refuge, or

when an overwhelming force was sent against them and they had no choice but instant submission. When the results of Hoffman's operation became known, California newspapers demanded strong follow-up measures. "They have got to be whipped, and with a moderate force, it can easily be done, for they live in an open country, where dragoons can get at them," the San Joaquin *Republican* advised.[15]

In late January of 1859, Hoffman submitted a detailed account of his reconnaissance to General Clarke. The desert rendered the northern route to the Colorado "wholly impassable" for wagons or for a large body of troops, he said. However, an expedition against the Mojaves could ascend the Colorado River from a base at Fort Yuma. The troops could march north along the river, carrying supplies on pack mules or camels, and draw further from a steamboat serving as a floating depot. Only through such an undertaking could the Mojaves be subdued and a post established to protect the Beale Road.[16]

General Clarke adopted Hoffman's recommendations and immediately ordered seven companies of the Sixth Infantry, a dragoon detachment, and two mountain howitzers be readied for the Mojave campaign. Of these, the four companies at Benicia Barracks would be shipped by water to the mouth of the Colorado, where they would be transported on river steamers to Fort Yuma. He instructed Hoffman to lead his column to Beale's Crossing and there locate a post. He would demand a promise from the Mojaves that they would never again attack emigrants or interfere with the construction of posts and roads in their country. He also would seize the chiefs who had led the attack on his party and hold them as "hostages for their future conduct." If the Indians refused to cooperate, Hoffman was instructed to "tell them you will lay waste their fields and that the troops to be stationed on the River will not permit them hereafter to cultivate their lands in peace." Clarke personally supervised preparations for the operation and directed Hoffman to employ Joseph Walker again as guide.[17]

On February 10, 1859, companies C, F, H, and I of the Sixth Infantry, accompanied by the full regimental band, marched to the San Francisco wharves and boarded the transport *Uncle Sam*. On the upper deck were sixty packers and two hundred mules who were to be landed in San Diego. From San Diego, Joseph Hooker, a California militia colonel later famous in the Civil War, would drive the mules across the desert to Fort Yuma for Hoffman's use. Colonel John K. F. Mansfield, Inspector General of the Army, also accompanied the expedition to Fort Yuma in order to test the practicality of the seaward supply route. With loading operations complete, Hoffman and his staff came aboard and the *Uncle Sam* sailed at eight o'clock the following morning.[18]

A few hours out of San Francisco, the heavily laden transport encountered a violent gale. By eleven o'clock at night, it was almost impossible to keep the ship's head to the wind and sea. Soldiers lightened the vessel by throwing overboard tons of barley and coal, marine tackle, and their own weapons and baggage. Only a sudden subsiding of the wind spared the two hundred mules and the other property on board. Finally out of danger, the ship turned about and on the morning of February 12, returned to San Francisco.

While carpenters repaired the damage to the *Uncle Sam*, Colonel Hoffman, somewhat shaken by his experience, "very respectfully" suggested to General Clarke that the freight on board was more than the ship could safely carry at sea. Another severe storm might make it necessary to throw cargo overboard, further delaying, if not canceling, the expedition. Hoffman felt his opinion was "confirmed by the opinions of many experienced and disinterested nautical men," and proposed that another vessel transport half of the mules to San Diego. But despite his objections, the *Uncle Sam*, inspected and pronounced seaworthy, sailed again on February 16 with both troops and mules on board.[19]

The second voyage passed uneventfully, and the ship anchored at San Diego two days later. The next morning two hundred "unhappy mules" were pushed overboard and swam ashore. Additional soldiers, Company G, Sixth Infantry, under Captain William S. Ketchum, came aboard, and at dawn the ship sailed for the Gulf of California. Completing its voyage around the Baja peninsula, the *Uncle Sam* reached the head of the gulf on the twenty-sixth.[20]

While the transport lay at anchor, a disagreement arose over landing procedures for the infantry. The captain of the *Uncle Sam* refused to risk his vessel in the shallow waters at Robinson's Landing, some thirty or forty miles away, and

proposed disembarking the troops in the ship's boats. Considering the captain's plan dangerous, Hoffman dispatched an officer to Robinson's Landing, where the U.S. schooner *Monterey* was unloading cargo. He requested that the Monterey transport his men and supplies to the mouth of the Colorado River, where the river steamers *Colorado* and *General Jesup* could carry the troops to Fort Yuma. With the assistance of the *Monterey* the transfer was made, and the soldiers began arriving at Fort Yuma on March 14.[21]

Hoffman now plotted the logistics of his expedition. Hooker had delivered the mule train to the fort after a trying march during which the animals, unused to carrying packs, had required "the unremitted attention of 48 men night and day." Hoffman estimated that the mules and the steamers *General Jesup* and *Colorado* together could transport sufficient provisions upriver to supply the command for fifty days. But there would be no supplies available for the new post, and the river captains could not guarantee that their boats could descend the river and return to Beale's Crossing before provisions ran out. Based upon careful calculations, Hoffman finally decided that steamers and mules possibly could carry two months provisions for the new post, in addition to the fifty days' rations for the expedition. For supplies after June, the garrison must depend on a new boat expected on the river in two or three months. To help prevent starvation at the post, a herd of beef would be driven north with the column. The cattle would have to range far and wide to find forage, and the danger existed that they would be lost or stolen.[22]

To his dismay, Hoffman learned that the dragoons had been detached from his expedition. The loss of the mounted troops, he wrote Clarke, crippled his command so severely that he could not operate in case the Mojaves combined with adjacent tribes. Clarke replied that Hoffman worried needlessly. The colonel doubtless would encounter difficulties, but Secretary of War John B. Floyd had ordered that a post be established "on the 35th parallel & Colorado." Hoffman had already personally inspected the upper route via Martin's Ranch and had pronounced it impractical. Now his force was on the southern route to Beale's Crossing. No obstacles which "time and labor can remove," Clarke said, should prevent the accomplishment of the undertaking.[23]

Hoffman protested to Clarke that he had been misunderstood. He was not trying to raise obstacles to the expedition, but rather to anticipate all eventualities. He clearly understood his orders. If the Mojaves declined to fight, and also refused to surrender the chiefs responsible for the Beaver Lake attack (plus hostages to insure future good conduct), his soldiers were "to lay waste their fields." Beyond destroying crops, the army was "not permitted to make war" upon the Indians.[24]

On March 26 Hoffman's Mojave expedition, accompanied by Indian Agent H. P. Heintzelman, marched out of Fort Yuma, heading north along the west bank of the Colorado. For the moment, the supply ship remained behind. The *General Jesup* drew only two and one-half feet of water, and the seasonal shallowness of the river prevented the steamer from passing over the sandbars upriver at that time. Because of this, each soldier carried a knapsack filled with forty days' rations, hopefully sufficient to last until the steamer could catch up with them. Despite spring weather the heat and dust seemed unbearable. The men soon began lightening their packs by discarding extra clothing. On April 5 Hoffman's dusty column of six hundred men crossed to the east bank of the Colorado and trudged on north.[25]

Newspapers followed the Mojave expedition with interest. A correspondent at Fort Yuma assured his readers that Hoffman would wage "a war of extermination on these savages" unless they agreed to his terms. After years of atrocities, it was time the Mojaves learned the power of the government. The *San Francisco Herald* noted that Hoffman was not marching simply to hold the Indians in check, but possessed the men and means to teach "those treacherous reptiles a lesson that will insure the unmolested transit of Americans through the country upon which they reside, while the sound of the word American shall continue to tingle in their ears."[26]

Hoffman's column reached Bill Williams Fork of the Colorado in six days. The problem of supply loomed constantly. Because the river route was almost destitute of grazing, the animals began to fail. By April 13 Hoffman doubted that one-fourth of the mules had the strength to return to Fort Yuma. If the river rose and steamboats could bring supplies, there would be no difficulty; however, rising water also could flood the river bottom through which his trail passed, preventing soldiers from returning to Yuma by land.[27]

General Clarke had doubts about establishing a post at Beale's Crossing. He advised Hoffman that after chastising the Indians, he should make a camp there for only two companies, and ignore all orders for building a fort, as instructions from Washington might yet defer the "permanent occupation of the point." In fact, Clarke already had written to the War Department expressing doubts concerning the practicality of constructing a post on Beale's route. In his reply, Secretary of War Floyd stated that after reviewing the evidence, he remained convinced that a post must be established. Clarke relayed this information to Hoffman, reminding him that his original orders would be carried out.[28]

Hoffman's troops reached Beale's Crossing on April 21 and camped. He crossed the river to the west bank and again found it unsuitable for a post. The bottomland was subject to floods and the sandy soil produced no grass. A post on high ground would put the men a mile or two west of the river and make them dependent upon Beaver Lake for water. On the east bank of the river, however, the bottomland extended several miles downstream, furnishing more grass than at any place along the route from Fort Yuma, plus an unusual quantity of cottonwood. But when the river rose, it would be difficult to communicate with the west bank. Although he could find no suitable site for a ferry landing, and the location was outside the jurisdiction of the Department of California, Hoffman decided to establish the post on the east bank of the river.[29]

Hoffman turned next to the Mojave problem. On April 22, the day after he arrived, two Mojave delegations came into camp and professed a desire for peace. They said they had always held the greatest friendship for the white man, and would declare their friendship in the presence of the troops. Hoffman reminded the Indians that they had committed numerous depredations on parties crossing their land during the past two years, and said that he had come to their land to prevent future incidents. The Mojaves had initiated the hostilities, and if they desired to fight, his soldiers would retaliate until the Indians "were tired of it." Hoffman told them that they must submit unconditionally to the terms he would dictate. He would discuss these terms the next morning at a council in his camp. If the Mojaves truly desired peace they would attend the meeting called for 10 a.m. The Indians must be punctual, or "they would not be received."[30]

Colonel Hoffman doubted the Mojaves would appear, but nevertheless made preparations for the council. Conferring with his officers that evening, he stated that if the Mojaves came in he would keep them in camp until a satisfactory settlement was reached. The Mojaves deserved a "severe chastisement" for their many offenses, and he firmly believed that a settlement with them would be more lasting if preceded by a military defeat. He was reluctant, therefore, "to encourage them to submit without a trial of their ability to resist." On the other hand, if the Mojaves agreed to his terms "it would be conclusive proof that they felt that they were wholly at my mercy, and would give every assurance that their fear of punishment which alone controls Indians, would prevent their ever again placing themselves in a similar jeopardy." Hoffman, therefore, made arrangements "to meet any emergency."[31]

At mid-morning on April 23, over four hundred Mojaves gathered outside the camp. When an officer went out to escort them in without their weapons, many Indians feared a trap and turned back. The chiefs, however, persuaded two hundred and fifty warriors to assemble at the council site. Wary of a possible fight, some of the Mojaves carried short clubs concealed under their belts. Sergeant Eugene Bandel recorded that "our arms, rifles, and cannons were loaded; and in addition, the Indians were surrounded by soldiers of the artillery company, with loaded revolvers (six-shooters), and were not permitted to leave the camp until the conference was over." Some distance away, one hundred and fifty Indians, armed with stone-tipped arrows and clubs, intently watched the proceedings.[32]

When all was ready, Hoffman opened the conference. He spoke through three interpreters: Captain Seth M. Barton, and Jose and Pasqual, two Yuma chiefs accompanying Agent Heintzelman. Hoffman spoke in English, Barton translated this into Spanish, and one of the Indians translated the Spanish into the Yuma language, and the second into Mojave. Hoffman sternly declared that the Mojaves had the choice of war or peace. If they wanted peace, they must submit to his demands; they had no say so in the matter. This blunt statement caused grumbling among the Mojaves and the Indian interpreters became alarmed. After some difficulty in restoring order, Hoffman listed his demands. He would tolerate no Mojave opposition to the establishment of posts and roads in their country, or attacks on passing emigrant trains. To guarantee future good conduct, he asked for one hostage from each of the six bands, plus three hostages from the group that had attacked the Rose party. In addition, Hoffman wanted the chief who had menaced his camp at Beaver Lake. His request for a hostage from each tribe was misinterpreted and every chief, except one, stepped forward. When the misunderstanding was clarified, the Indians taken hostage included Cainook, or Cairook, the leader of the band that had threatened Hoffman's party.[33]

Once the demands were made known, the Indians seemed relieved. The chiefs said that Hoffman could do as he pleased with the land, but they asked to "be permitted to live in it." With this declaration, Hoffman softened somewhat. He explained that the hostages would be taken to Fort Yuma and returned at General Clarke's pleasure. He believed the chiefs sincerely desired peace. Previously, the Indians had seen only small parties of white men; but his large expedition had surprised them and filled them with dread. Hopefully, the show of force would prevent the Mojaves from again entertaining thoughts of hostilities. In his report, Hoffman described the Mojaves' demeanor as "that of a subdued people asking for mercy."[34]

After constructing a post—originally designated Camp Colorado but several days later renamed Fort Mojave—on the east bank of the river, Hoffman made preparations to leave. Two companies boarded the *General Jesup* for Fort Yuma, while Hoffman himself took command of four companies destined to march westward for Cajon Pass. He left Brevet Major Lewis Armistead to command a garrison of seven officers and one hundred and sixty-five men of Companies F and I and Lieutenant John Tipton's detachment of the Third Artillery. On April 26 Hoffman crossed the river and headed west and the steamer started downriver.[35]

Living conditions at Fort Mojave were

difficult. Armistead's men were poorly provisioned, lacked tents and tarpaulins, and had little clothing and bedding. The "fort" consisted of quarters, storehouses, kitchens, a guardhouse, and a hospital. The buildings were "large brush sheds," enclosed with a basket-work of young willows, and covered with a thatched roof designed to exclude the sun and allow the free circulation of air. Even with the floors kept constantly wet, temperatures inside the buildings occasionally rose to 120 degrees. The soldiers' fare included half-rations of flour, beans, and rice, supplemented with beans and meal the Mojaves brought to the post to trade for shirts and blankets.[36]

Four days after Hoffman's departure, Beale's road party approached the crossing from the east. Observing the river from a mountain summit, and failing to detect the presence of soldiers, Beale decided to descend upon the Mojaves and give them "a turn." Early on the morning of April 30, thirty-five men in "fighting trim," carrying rifles, knives, and revolvers, reached the river. After quenching their thirsts, the hunters began prowling through the thick brush along the riverbanks, firing at every Indian seen. Three hours later, a detail of soldiers appeared and informed Beale that troops were encamped a few miles below and that Colonel Hoffman had made a treaty with the Indians. Beale called in his men and they encamped at the post, before resuming their westward journey.[37]

In the meantime, Hoffman was moving slowly across the desert to his depot at Martin's Ranch. As water was limited the companies traveled on alternate days. The grass along the route was dead, and the forty mules with each company subsisted on three or four small bags of barley carried with each train. Fortunately, cool weather prevailed during the two-week march, sparing the troops much hardship. But Hoffman's experiences on this march confirmed his opinion that only small numbers of soldiers burdened with feed for their stock could cross the desert to the Colorado River. Members of his command also voiced great displeasure over the route. Captain Richard B. Garnett submitted a critical report of the journey, and Sergeant Bandel hoped he would "never again see the deserts between the Rocky Mountains and Sierra Nevada," resolving to become a civilian when his enlistment expired.[38]

In his report Colonel Hoffman praised his officers and men for the cheerfulness with which they had endured the privations and hardships of the campaign. General Clarke expressed his satisfaction to Hoffman that "the submission of the River tribes is complete as is the *success of your expedition*." He was pleased that a show of force had been enough to achieve the objectives of the expedition without bloodshed. When Clarke's report reached Washington, General-in-Chief Winfield Scott concurred in the praise bestowed on Hoffman and his men.[39]

Newspaper reaction to the expedition was mixed. The *San Francisco Herald* approved of Hoffman's conduct, but wished that he had found an opportunity to chastise the Indians. However, it applauded his having conquered a peace from the Mojaves without the loss of life. Other newspapers were critical of the expedition. The *Weekly Bulletin*, which had urged Hoffman to "thrash them [the Mojaves] first, and treat afterwards," declared that "our anticipations of the practical failure of the expedition are unfortunately realized." Hoffman had concluded a peace without punishing the Indians, and the Bulletin predicted that the treaty would prove "utterly worthless." The *San Joaquin Republican* called Hoffman's peace a "Humbug."[40]

The nine hostages taken by Colonel Hoffman were confined at Fort Yuma. According to Mojave tradition, while the soldiers were eating at noon one day, the captive Mojaves tried to escape; seven were successful but two were shot. Three swam to the Arizona side of the river, while the other four fled along the California shore. Eventually, the seven Mojaves were reunited and made their way back to their villages. Information about the escape reached Major Armistead at Fort Mojave by a Yuma Indian, who also reported that the Mojaves did not want to fight. Armistead requested instructions from General Clarke.[41]

Clarke did not know what effect the escape would have on the river tribes, but he instructed Armistead to take a firm stand and demand the resurrender of the hostages. However, at Clarke's headquarters at Benicia, the assistant adjutant general, Brevet Major William W. Mackall, advised against taking Indian hostages for indefinite periods and prohibited further seizures. He also stated that the escape of the hostages could not be made the grounds for hostilities against the

Indians: escape was "what was to be expected if an opportunity offered."[42]

The Mojaves continued to cause trouble. They destroyed a garden at Fort Mojave, attacked a mail party and drove it into the fort, and killed a herder. Lieutenant Elisha G. Marshall led a scout, but was unable to locate the Indians and an ambush failed. Armistead again asked for instructions. General Clarke responded that the post was established to protect the mail and emigrants, and Armistead should demand that the offenders be delivered to him for punishment. "If not, you must inflict such punishment on the tribes as will determine the nation to submission in the future," he added. Destroying Indian crops was another matter. Hunger drove men, women, and children to desperation and compelled them to maraud to live. Armistead should exhaust 'every means of bringing the Mojaves to terms before ordering crop destruction.[43]

Armistead decided to take action. On August 2, Lieutenant Montgomery Bryant crossed the river with twenty men and destroyed an Indian farm. Two days later Armistead led twenty-five men of Company F on a scout and surprised an Indian band at a lagoon fifteen miles below the fort where the mules were herded. The next morning, Lieutenant Marshall followed with twenty-five picked men of Company I to reconnoiter in the same direction. At dawn on the fifth, Armistead surprised three Indians planting beans and killed one of them. Gunfire and the yells of the two fleeing Indians aroused other Mojaves, and in a short time a large number of Indians surrounded Armistead's command. The fight had been in progress for thirty or forty minutes when Lieutenant Marshall, who had also heard the firing, arrived and attacked the Indians in the rear, driving them from the field. Although the Mojaves regrouped and attacked the combined parties, they were soon dispersed again. Exhausted, the soldiers gathered under the shade of the mesquite and rested for two hours.[44]

On the return march to the fort, the soldiers had traveled only a short distance when large numbers of Mojaves struck the column. Some came within ten yards of the soldiers, but their crude weapons were no match for rifled muskets. After a half hour, Armistead ordered his men to charge and the Mojaves were completely routed. Armistead returned to the fort with three men wounded. Twenty-three Mojave warriors were counted dead; it was estimated that fifty to sixty were actually killed. An old Mojave woman later recalled that "the whites were using firearms and killed off nearly half of the Mojave men who were in that battle."[45]

The Indians sent a spokesman to the fort and asked for peace. On August 31 Armistead granted the request, but insisted that the Mojaves behave themselves and never go again to the bend of the river where the garrison kept its mule herd. The major subsequently asserted: "They wanted a good whipping, which they got. They appear to be perfectly satisfied." On September 3 Armistead turned over the command of Fort Mojave to Lieutenant Levi C. Bootes and left on the steamer *Cocopa* for Fort Yuma. Five days later, Bootes posted an order stating that "the war with the Mojave Indians" was over.[46]

The Hoffman expedition of 1859 had played a critical role in reducing the Mojave threat to travel to California along the thirty-fifth parallel. The Mojaves never again attacked parties of travelers or resisted the authority of the federal government. In the spring of 1862 when gold was discovered in the Colorado River region, and groups of prospectors swarmed into the area, some of the Yuman tribes, particularly the Yavapais and Walapais, clashed with these intruders, but the Mojaves did not become hostile. The government effort to chastise the Mojaves and secure travel along the Beale Road had been successful to the extent that the Mojaves committed no further depredations. The fort the army established to guard the river crossing was a permanent symbol of the white man's power. Yet Hoffman's expedition to insure emigrant safety on the Beale Road was somewhat premature. Not until after the Civil War did the route become a regular overland highway, and over twenty years passed before railroad crews laid a ribbon of steel to tie the region to the outside world. By that time the Mojave campaign of 1859, an expensive, disagreeable operation, merited only passing mention in the annals of Southwestern history.

Footnotes:

[1] *Sacramento Union* (California), November 11, 1858.

[2] A. L. Kroeber, "Preliminary Sketch of the Mohave Indians," *American Anthropologist*, IV (April-June 1902), 276-79; Arthur Woodward, "Irataba—Chief of the Mohave," *Plateau*, XXV (January 1953), 66. Hubert Howe Bancroft, *History of Arizona and New Mexico 1530-1888* (San Francisco: The History Company, 1889), 545; A. L. Kroeber, *Handbook of the Indians of California* (Washington, 1925), 727-28; Lorraine M. Sherer, *The Clan System of the Fort Mojave Indians* (Los Angeles: Historical Society of Southern California, 1965), 8.

[3] "Wagon Road—Fort Smith to Colorado River," *House Executive Document* [HED] 42, 36 Congress, 1 Session (Serial 1048), 7-8. See also Dennis G. Casebier, *The Mojave Road* (Norco, California: Tales of the Mojave Road Publishing Company, 1975), 29-53, 81; and Casebier (ed.), *The Mojave Road in Newspapers* (Norco, California: Tales of the Mojave Road Publishing Company, 1976), *passim*. The isolation of the Yuma Indians south of the Mojaves already had been destroyed by the opening of the southern road to the California gold fields. After several incidents involving Indians and emigrants, federal troops were dispatched to keep the road open. In 1850 Brevet Major Samuel P. Heintzelman established Camp (later Fort) Yuma on the crossing of the lower Colorado River. H. B. Wharfield, *Fort Yuma on the Colorado River* (El Cajon, California: n.p., 1968), 35-50.

[4] L. J. Rose letter in St. Louis *Missouri Republican*, November 28 1858; *ibid.*, December 6, 1858. John Udell, *John Udell, Journal Kept During a Trip Across the Plains....* (Los Angeles: N. A. Kovack, 1946), 2, 4, 28-29, 33-38, 40-45.

[5] The eight deaths included a family which was traveling several miles behind the Rose group and was trying to catch up. Udell, Journal, 44-58; A. L. Kroeber & C. B. Kroeber, *A Mohave War Reminiscence, 1854-1880* (U. of California Press, 1973), 11-14. Stockton Weekly *San Joaquin Republican* (California), November 13, 1858; San Francisco *Weekly Bulletin* (California), March 12, 1859; San Francisco Herald (California), November 8, 1858; St. Louis *Missouri Republican*, November 28, 1858; January 30, 1859.

[6] *Sacramento Union*, November 11, 1858; Stockton *San Joaquin Republican*, January 29, 1859; San Francisco *Weekly Bulletin*, February 12, March 12, 1859; San Francisco *National* (California), November 25, 1858; *San Francisco Herald*, January 12, 1859.

[7] Newman S. Clarke to Samuel Cooper, January 3, 1859, Letters Received, Adjutant General's Office [LRAGO], Records of the Adjutant General's Office [RAGO], Record Group [RG] 94, National Archives [NA]. Francis B. Heitman, *Historical Register and Dictionary of the United States Army* (New ed., 2 vols., U. of Illinois Press, 1965), I, 535.

[8] William W. Mackall to William Hoffman, December 4, 31, 1858; to James H. Carleton, December 4, 1858, Letters Sent, Department of the Pacific [LSDP], Records of United States Army Continental Commands, 1821-1920 [RUSACC], RG 393, NA. Post Returns, Camp near Benicia Barracks, November 1858, Returns from U.S. Military Posts, 1800-I916 [RMP], Microcopy 617, Roll 102, RG 94, NA. On instructions from Secretary of War John B. Floyd, dated December 1, 1858, Clarke modified Hoffman's projected garrison on the Colorado from four to two companies. Clarke to Cooper, January 3, 1859, LRAGO, RAGO. Selected correspondence of the Mojave expedition is in the "Report of the Secretary of War [SW], 1859," *Senate Executive Document* [SED] 2, 36 Gong., 1 Sess. (Serial 1024), II, 387-422.

[9] Post Returns, Camp near Benicia Barracks, November 1858; Camp at Benicia Depot, December 1858, RMP, M 617, Roll 102. Hoffman to Mackall, January 27, 1859; to Edward D. Townsend, December 8, 1858, LRAGO, RAGO. Mackall to. Hoffman, December 4, 1858; to Franklin D. Callender, December 13, 1858; to Carleton, December 4, 1858; to Thomas Swords, February 1, 1858, LSDP, RUSACC. Eugene Bandel, *Frontier Life in the Army*, 1854-1861 (Glendale, California: The Arthur H. Clark Company, 1932), 248-51.

[10] Hoffman to Mackall, January 27, 1859, LRAGO, RAGO.

[11] Hoffman to Mackall, January 16, 27, 1859, LRAGO, RAGO. Stockton *San Joaquin Republican*, January 29, 1859.

[12] Hoffman to Mackall, January 16, 27, 1859, LRAGO, RAGO.

[13] Hoffman to Mackall, January 16, 19, 27, 1859, LRAGO, RAGO. Stockton *San Joaquin Republican*, January 29, February 5, 1859; *San Francisco Herald*, January 24, 26, 1859; St. Louis *Missouri Republican*, February 24, 1859. Bandel, *Frontier Life*, 256-57; Kroeber, *Handbook of the Indians of California*, 751. An account by the second guide, William E. Goodyear, published several years later, was full of melodramatics with the battle lasting up to two hours and over sixty Mojaves being killed. John S. C. Abbott, *Christopher Carson, Familiarly Known as Kit Carson* (New York, 1873), 313-21. A Mojave Indian reminiscence over forty years later, which was remarkably clear in details, concluded that three Indians were wounded, one in the knee, one in the upper thigh, and one in the ear lobe - but none were killed. Kroeber & Kroeber, *A Mohave War Reminiscence*, 20.

[14] Hoffman to Mackall, January 16, 19, 27, 1859, LRAGO, RAGO. Bandel, Frontier Life, 258. In his *Mojave Road*, 83-87; and *Fort Pah-Ute, California* (Norco, California: Tales of the Mojave Road Publishing Company, 1974), 73-75, Casebier believes Hoffman was negative toward the Mojave Road from the beginning, and is critical of Hoffman's handling of the expedition. Contemporaries were also negative about the route. P[eter] R. Brady to Edwin A. Rigg, March 4, 1862, in *War of the Rebellion: A Compilation of the Official Records of the Union and Confederate Armies* (128 vols., Washington, 1880-1901), Series I, Volume L, Part 1, 911-12. Travelers over the road were divided in opinion about its suitability. San Francisco *Alta California*, June 11, July 19, 1859; Los Angeles *Southern Vineyard*, July 15, 1859; and Los Angeles *Star*, October 1, 1859, all cited in Casebier (ed.), *Mojave Road in Newspapers*, 14-15, 21, 23, 25.

[15] *San Francisco Herald*, January 12, 24-27, February 3, 1859; Stockton *San Joaquin Republican*, January 29, 1859; San Francisco *Weekly Bulletin*, February 12, March 12, 1859. Bandel, *Frontier Life*, 251-52.

[16] Hoffman to Mackall, January 27, 1859, LRAGO, RAGO. Bandel, *Frontier Life*, 258.

[17] Mackall to Hoffman, January 27, 31, February 1, 1859; to William S. Ketchum, January 28, 31, 1859; to George Nauman, January 28, 1859; to Charles S. Merchant, January 28, 1859; to John Tipton, February 1, 1859; Clarke to Lorenzo Thomas, January 28, 29, 1859, LSDP, RUSACC.

[18] Stockton *San Joaquin Republican* and San Francisco *Weekly Bulletin*, February 12, 1859; *San Francisco Herald*, February 10, 27, 1859. Mackall to Nauman, February 11, 1859; to Ketchum, January 31, 1859, LSDP, RUSACC. J. K. F. Mansfield to Irvin McDowell, February 4, 10, 1859, Letters Received, Headquarters of the Army [LRHA], Records of the Head-quarters of the Army [RHA]), RG 108, NA. Joseph Hooker resigned from the army on February 21, 1853, and operated a rancho near Sonoma, California. He helped promote John B. Weller for governor, and was appointed superintendent of federal military roads in Oregon. Early in 1859 he was made a colonel in the California militia, and apparently secured a contract to furnish mules for the Hoffman expedition. Walter H. Hebert, *Fighting Joe Hooker* (Indianapolis: Bobbs-Merrill, 1944), 38, 40-42.

[19] *San Francisco Herald*, February 13, 17, 27, 1859. Hoffman to Mackall, February 15, 1858 [1859], Letters Received, Department of California [LRDC], RUSACC. Bandel, *Frontier Life*, 264. The Stockton *San Joaquin Republican*, February 19, 1859, gave an inflated account of the gale.

[20] *San Francisco Herald*, February 27, 1859. Hoffman to Mackall, February 19, March 1, 1859, LRDC, RUSACC. Mackall to Nauman, February 11, 1859, LSDP, RUSACC.

[21] Hoffman to Mackall, March 1, 15, 1859, LRDC, RUSACC. *San Francisco Herald*, April 7, 1859.

[22] Joseph Hooker to Mackall, March 8, 1859; Hoffman to Mackall, March 16, 19, 25, 1859, LRDC, RUSACC.

[23] Hoffman to Mackall, March 16, 25, May 18, 1859, LRDC, RUSACC. Mackall to Hoffman, March 21, April 24, 1859, LSDP, RUSACC. There seemed little probability, however, that the tribes would unite against Hoffman's expedition. The river tribes hesitated to join the Mojaves. When they saw the size of Hoffman's force, they immediately professed friendship for the United States. Also, Indian Agent H. P. Heintzelman had traveled among the friendly tribes of the area

and had distributed goods among the Pima and Maricopa tribes to assure them of the government's good intentions. Finally, Joe Walker learned that the Mojaves themselves were divided; some wanted to allow the soldiers to enter their country while others opposed the intrusion. Many Mojaves were fleeing down the river in crude tule rafts. *San Francisco Herald*, April 7, 1859. Bandel, *Frontier Life*, 268-71. H. P. Heintzelman to James W. Denver, February 12, 1859, Letters Received, California Superintendency; Denver to Heintzelman, December 9, 1858, Letters Sent, California Superintendency, Records of the Bureau of Indian Affairs, RG 75, NA.

[24]Hoffman to Mackall, March 25, 27, 1859, LRDC, RUSACC. Mansfield to McDowell, March 26, 1859, LRHA, RHA. *San Francisco Herald*, April 7, 1859.

[25]Hoffman to Mackall, April 2, 3, 1859, LRDC, RUSACC; Mansfield to McDowell, March 26, 1859, LRHA, RHA. San Francisco *Weekly Bulletin*, May 21, 1859. Bandel, *Frontier Life*, 268-71.

[26]*San Francisco Herald*, April 27, May 5, 1859; San Francisco *Weekly Bulletin*, April 23, 1859.

[27]Hoffman to Mackall, April 11, 13, 21, 1859, LRDC, RUSACC.

[28]Mackall to Hoffman, April 13, 24, 1859, LSDC, RUSACC. Clarke to Cooper, March 21, 1859, LRAGO, RAGO. Cooper to Clarke, April 13, 1859, Letters Sent, Adjutant General's Office [LSAGO], RAGO, RG 94, NA.

[29]Hoffman to Mackall, April 21, 1859, LRDC, RUSACC.

[30]Hoffman to Mackall, April 21, May 18, 1859, LRDC, RUSACC. *San Francisco Herald*, May 6, 1859.

[31]Hoffman to Mackall, April 21, May 18, 1859, LRDC, RUSACC.

[32]Bandel, *Frontier Life*, 272-74; Kroeber & Kroeber, *A Mohave War Reminiscence*, 21-23.

[33]Hoffman to Mackall, April 24, May 18, 1859, LRAGO, RAGO. The Mojaves said that the Rose party had been followed from the mountains by Walapai warriors, and that only seven Mojaves had taken part in the attack. They were now at war with the Walapais over difficulties growing out of that affair. Hoffman reported that statements from the emigrants corroborated the Indian account. Hoffman to Mackall, April 24, 1859, LRAGO, RAGO. Bandel, *Frontier Life*, 272-73. A Mojave oral account indicates that they went on the warpath, but against the Maricopas. The chronology is vague at best, and this seems to have been after Hoffman's council. George Devereaux, "Mohave Chieftainship in Action: A Narrative of the First Contacts of the Mohave Indians with the United States," *Plateau*, XXIII (January 1951), 38-39.

[34]Hoffman to Mackall, April 24, May 18, 1859, LRAGO, RAGO. See also Stockton *San Joaquin Republican*, May 14, 1859.

[35]Post Returns, Fort Mojave, April 1859, RMP, M 617, Roll 787. Bandel, *Frontier Life*, 274-77.

[36]"Report of SW," *SED* 2, 36 Cong., 1 Sess., II, 416-17.

[37]"Fort Smith to Colorado River," HED 42, 36 Cong., I Sess., 49-50. Udell, *Journal*, 73. Upon reaching Pah-Ute Creek, some twenty-seven miles west of the Colorado River, on May 4, Beale discovered that Hoffman's men had plundered some caches left behind by Samuel A. Bishop, who had come from California with provisions for Beale's road construction crew. An angry Beale left his party at the creek while he went ahead to Los Angeles to procure supplies. Gerald Eugene Thompson, "The Public Career of Edward Fitzgerald

Beale, 1845-1893" (Ph.D. dissertation, University of Arizona, 1978), 246-50. It is impossible to resolve the conflicting accounts about Bishop's caches. The most complete account is Casebier, *Fort Pah-Ute*, 86-106, 118-40. A general court-martial exonerated Hoffman and his men of improper conduct, but Secretary of War Floyd disapproved the court's findings. Mackall to Hoffman, December 15, 1859; February 8, 1860, and Clarke to Cooper, March 8, 1860, LSDP, RUSACC. Hoffman to Mackall, January 26, 1860, LRDC, RUSACC. Cooper to Clarke, March 30, 1860, LSAGO, RAGO.

[38]Hoffman to Mackall, May 19, 1859, LRAGO, RAGO. Richard B. Garnett to Mackall, June 13, 1859, LRDC, RUSACC. Bandel, *Frontier Life*, 277-78.

[39]Hoffman to Mackall, April 24, 1859; Clarke to Thomas, May 2, 17, 1859, LRAGO, RAGO. Mackall to Hoffman, May 4, 1859, LSDP, RUSACC.

[40]*San Francisco Herald*, May 8, 1859, San Francisco Weekly Bulletin, April 16, May 14, 1859; Stockton *Weekly San Joaquin Republican*, June 4, 1859.

[41]"Report of SW," SED 2, 36 Cong., 1 Sess., II, 414-16; Devereaux, "Mohave Chieftainship," *Plateau*, XXIII, 43; Woodward, "Irataba," *ibid.*, XXV, 59-60. Kroeber & Kroeber, *A Mohave War Reminiscence*, 24-27, 67-68. See also San Francisco *Bulletin*, July 1, 1859, in Casebier (ed.), *Mojave Road in Newspapers*, 17-20.

[42]Mackall to Lewis A. Armistead, June 30, 1859, Letters Received, Fort Mojave [LRFM], RUSACC.

[43]Post Returns, Fort Mojave, July 1859, RMP, M 617, Roll 787. Kroeber & Kroeber, *A Mohave War Reminiscence*, 27-28. Clarke to Cooper, October 31, 1859, LRAGO, RAGO. Mackall to Armistead, August 3, 1859, LRFM, RUSACC.

[44]Post Returns, Fort Mojave, August 1859, RMP, M 617, Roll 787. Clarke to Cooper, October 31, 1859; Armistead to Mackall, August 6, 1859, LRAGO, RAGO. Stockton *Weekly San Joaquin Republican*, August 27, 1859.

[45]Armistead to Mackall, August 6, 16, 1859, LRAGO, RAGO. Stockton *Weekly San Joaquin Republican*, August 27, 1859, Post Returns, Fort Mojave, August 1859, RMP, M 617, Roll 787. Kroeber & Kroeber, *A Mohave War Reminiscence*, 30. Devereaux, "Mohave Chieftainship," *Plateau*, XXIII, 38-40.

[46]Mackall to Armistead, August 22, 1859, LRFM, RUSACC. Post Returns, Fort Mojave, August, September 1859, RMP, M 617, Roll 787. "Report of SW," SED 2, 36 Cong., 1 Sess., II, 421. Orders 76, September 8, 1859, Fort Mojave Orderbook, RUSACC. Mackall to Commanding Officer, Fort Yuma, November 7, 1859, LRFM, RUSACC. Kroeber & Kroeber, *A Mohave War Reminiscence*, 32-33. Captain Richard B. Garnett, Sixth Infantry, commanded Fort Mojave from October 1859 to September 1860. With the outbreak of the Civil War, the garrison abandoned the post. On May 19, 1863, Companies B and I, Fourth California Volunteers, reoccupied Fort Mojave. Following the war, regulars were stationed at the post until it was abandoned and transferred to the Bureau of Indian Affairs in 1890. The Indian Office abandoned Mojave in 1935, and in 1942 the remaining buildings were demolished. Philip J. Avillo, Jr., "Fort Mojave: Outpost on the Upper Colorado," *Journal of Arizona History*, XI (Summer 1970), 77-100. Ray Brandes, *Frontier Military Posts of Arizona* (Globe, Arizona: Dale Stuart King, 1960), 56-58.

Mohave Warfare[1]

by Kenneth M. Stewart

The Mohave indians of the Colorado River valley are by reputation a warlike tribe, although my informants insisted that the people as a whole were pacifically inclined. It was asserted that, while war was disliked by a majority of the Mohave, battle was the dominant concern of the kwanamis ("brave men"), who were responsible for the recurrent hostilities and over whom there was no effective control. Whether or not the mass of the population was averse to warfare, it is clear that the frequent warring expeditions were primarily the result of the existence among the Mohave of a distinct class of warriors with whom warfare was an obsession, who were set apart from other men by the nature of their dreams, and who were continually eager to join a war party to exercise the military powers conferred upon them by the spirits in those dreams. The Mohave were constant aggressors, and since they seldom plundered, economic motivation for war was inconsiderable. Prisoners were taken, but were a secondary objective in battle. Nor was territorial aggrandizement normally the reason for a military campaign, though it impelled the Mohave to drive the Halchidhoma out of what is now the Colorado River Indian Reservation.[2]

The Mohave, in alliance with the Yuma, made a number of incursions into Maricopa territory, the Pima on occasion coming to the aid of the Maricopa. Similarly, the Yuma were at chronic enmity with the Cocopa, and they repeatedly called upon the Mohave to join them in expeditions against the latter tribe. The Halchidhoma are remembered as "Maricopa" who were driven out of the Parker region by the concerted efforts of Yuma and Mohave, but my informants knew nothing of hostilities with the Kohuana or Halyikwamp[3]. There was no fighting with the Cahuilla or other Southern California Shoshonean, and the Kamia, Diegueño, Akwa'ala, and Kiliwa were regarded as distant, rather unimportant tribes who were not enemies of the Mohave.

Relations with the Yuman tribes of Upland Arizona were on the whole friendly, with trade and some intermarriage. The Mohave never fought the Havasupai or Yavapai,[4] and conflict with the Walapai was limited to a few minor encounters.[5] The Shoshonean Chemehuevi were friends until after the establishment of Fort Mohave, when on several occasions they attacked the Mohave. The Paiute, likewise, were normally not enemies, but they joined the Chemehuevi in these forays, and there were isolated skirmishes between Mohave and Paiute in earlier times.[6]

The following narrative of fighting with the Chemehuevi was told by Pete Lambert.

I heard of only two fights with the Chemthuevi. When the Whites were at Fort Mohave they gave the Mohave and Chemehuevi liquor. Before that time the Mohave and Chemehuevi were relations and friends. But then they started to kill one another in drunken fights. The Chemehuevi lost quite a few men that way, and they got sore at the Mohave. A bunch of Chemehuevi warriors came down early in the morning and killed several Mohave near Fort Mohave, and then the Chemehuevi ran to Sand Hill. The Mohave chased them and killed quite a few Chemehuevi at Sand Hill.

The other war with the Chemehuevi was also when the American troop was already here (1867). The Mormons in Nevada wanted some Mohave women for wives, so they gave guns to about fifty Ute [?], Paiute, and Chemehuevi, and told them to go down and kidnap some Mohave girls for them. They came through up at Forty Nine Road, the old military road up above Ghost Mountain (Avikwame). They went through on the south side of the big wash by Hardyville. Then they came to a place called Moss Mine (Kawacuthomb). A lot of Mohave were gathered to fight over a piece of land at a place called Sand Hill (Anikockwamb). So there were lots of Mohave there. They were camped and big dances were going on, singing nearly all night and day. At daylight the enemy attacked. Most of the Mohave were unarmed; so the Chernehuevi shot their guns and killed quite a few.

They were old-time guns, and shot rocks, not lead. They never cleaned the barrels, and they shot so fast that the guns were not working so good. So they started to run. An unarmed Mohave kwanami ran after the Chemehuevi leader, and the Chemehuevi shot him through the shoulder, but he went right on. He grabbed the Chemehnevi by the hair and threw him down and broke his neck and killed him.

One man lost several relatives in the battle, and that made him reckless for revenge; so he chased after the retreating Chemehuevi all by himself. He caught up with them, and he killed five Chemehuevi by himself, and then the others killed him. When they killed him, they cut him into pieces, and set up poles and strung his flesh out.

While the fight was going on in the morning, the Mohave sent a messenger south to Topock for reinforcements. The Kwanamis coming up from Topock did not go to the battlefield, but cut across the mesa to head off the Chemehuevi, and they got up to Hardyville about noon. Meanwhile the Chemehuevi kept on going, but they were exhausted from lack of food or sleep. Some of them fell down and died. The Mohave from Topock gave up the pursuit, or they could have caught and killed them all. The Chemehuevi crossed over to Nevada at a place called Avidunyor, a place where there are high cliffs with Indian designs on the rocks and a lot of bed-rock mortars.

After that the soldiers gave the Mohave a gun apiece to protect themselves. They never fought the Chemehuevi again.

The wasauwic ("all the warriors") was an informal association of the kwanamis. Kwanamis, of whom there were forty or fifty in the tribe, were men who had received the proper dreams (sumac ahot) for power in war,[7] and they constituted an amorphous warrior class. They were men of prestige, perhaps outranking even the tribal chief in this respect. The kwanamis were not the only men who went to war, since a war party of forty might include as few as six or seven kwanamis; but men who had unlucky dreams (sumac acim) remained at home and served as guards during the absence of the warriors.

The dreams of a kwanami began at birth, or even while the unborn child was still in his mother's womb. In his dreams spirits appeared to him, conferring power, instructing him in proper modes of fighting, and teaching him how to avoid injury in combat. The kwanami dreamed of the hawk, a predatory bird whom he would later emulate in battle; and he dreamed of going through dust, which signified that he would come through war unscathed. He dreamed of fighting and killing such ferocious animals as mountain lions and bears. In dreams he seized the animals by the legs and split them in two.

Kwanamis were unlike other Mohave. Their mode of living was Spartan. They were relatively insensible to cold and heat and were unconcerned about going four or five days without food They ate little, taking only one meal a day, and they ate alone. They were uninterested in women and sex, few of them marrying until they had grown too old for combat. A kwanami did not farm, although he might hunt or fish, and he spent most of his time reclining in a secluded spot while meditating on the subject of warfare. The kwanamis are described as even-tempered, little given to levity, and silent but not bashful. They "looked tough," but they were not necessarily large men, because "a small man might be a better fighter than a big man." The people believed that the eye of the kwanami was like the morning star, enabling him to discern the enemy in the distance. A kwanami was totally indifferent to death; his thinking was continually dominated by his supreme concern of battling the enemy.

In war the kwanamis competed among themselves to kill the first enemy. Certain honors accrued to the man who was the first to kill, though I am not sure that the emoluments were of a tangible nature. Mrs. Lincoln stated that only kwanamis who had killed first were entitled to wear eagle feathers.

Two or three men in the tribe ranked as head kwanamis or war chiefs, for whom there was no name other than kwanami. Like other kwanamis, they theoretically attained their positions through proper dreaming. Each war party was conducted by a head kwanami, whose powers were minimal and not clearly formulated, although he was not responsible to the tribal chief. The head kwanami acted as a leader and officer on the war party, and when the party approached an enemy camp he stopped the warriors and gave them instructions relative to the attack. The tribal chief was not a kwanami and did not go to war.

Since boys learned what they needed to know in dreams, special training for war was regarded as superfluous. Boys between the ages of four and six were subjected to a series of tests or ordeals to determine whether or not they possessed sufficient fortitude to become kwanamis, which meant, in effect, to determine whether or not they were having the necessary dreams for power in war. A kwanami might push a boy into a bee's nest, or he might draw blood by sticking his fingernail into a boy's forehead. He might pinch the boy, or pull his ears, or lash him across the bare back with a switch. The boy who did not exhibit stoicism was not dreaming properly; but the boy who did not cry, but who fought back or merely stared unconcernedly at his tormenter, was the boy who would become a kwanami.[8]

Boys who passed the ordeals became humar kwanamis ("half-grown warriors"). Between the ages of eight and ten they were taught to use bows and arrows, and they went hunting for practice in marksmanship. For conditioning they ran long distances, but they neither practised dodging arrows, as did the Yuma boys,[9] nor did they engage in sham battles.

The "brave boy" carried a warrior's bow rather than a hunting bow, and he seldom joined the other boys in archery games, since he thought only of going out to kill the enemy. If a brave boy entered an archery contest, he would put his war bow aside and tell the other boys not to touch it, and he would use a hunting bow. He would participate only for a short while, and other boys did not like to play with him, "he was too rough."

Four arrows were conferred upon the brave boy in his dreams, and these were named in sequence, enemy arrow, brave arrow, doctor arrow, and unbrave arrow. The boy preserved them carefully and shot them at the enemy in the above order on his first war party.

Occasionally a brave boy would go on a war party when he had reached the age of thirteen or fifteen. Such boys are said to have been cleverer in battle than older men. Once they had been to war, they became possessed with the desire to go out and fight again. Pete Lambert said that these boys were continually "keyed-up" like race horses; they slept little and were constantly straining to go out and kill. The majority of boys, however, did not go on a war party until they were nineteen or twenty, when they became known as mahai kwanamis ("young warriors"). Fighting men were in their prime between the ages of twenty and thirty, and they continued to go to war until they were forty. Members of a war party were naked save for

breechclout and sandals. The long hair of the warriors was wrapped up and bound at the back of the head with rawhide. Just prior to the attack warriors applied war paint, delineating on their bodies red, black, and white designs identifying them as Mohave. The hair was painted red. Face paint was always black for war: usually the entire face was blackened, although sometimes a black stripe was painted across the eyes. Horses were not painted.

Eagle feathers were attached singly to the hair of men who had killed first in battle; the other warriors wore feather headdresses (hal kwe). The headdress had a four-ply netting foundation made from black-eyed bean fibers, and a cord was tied under the chin to hold it in place. Wing and tail feathers of the hawk radiated from a central knot, projecting vertically and hanging down at the sides.

Each warrior carried a gourd canteen, five to eight inches in diameter, with a fiber stopper. The canteen was wrapped with ropes of willow fiber. There were horizontal ropes at the top, bottom, and in the middle, four vertical ropes, and a loop at the top by means of which the canteen was attached to the warrior's belt.

The principle weapons of the Mohave were long self bows (otisa) and mallet headed "potato-masher" clubs (halyawhai), the latter being the more lethal. The club, carved from a single piece of green mesquite or screw-bean wood, was used to advantage in hand-to-hand combat. Its overall length was approximately one foot, although a stronger warrior might carry a club of greater size. The handle measured seven or eight inches in length and two and a quartet inches in diameter, and the length of the cylindrical head averaged four or five inches, with a diameter of four inches across the top surface. A slight hollow was sometimes burned in the upper surface, leaving sharp edges which were made sharper still by carving. The top surface was painted red, and the remainder of the head and the handle were black. A wrist loop of buckskin or willow bark fiber was passed through a hole three-eighths of an inch from the tip of the handle. Contrary to Yuma and Cocopa custom, the handle was not sharpened for stabbing.

The club was grasped near the cylinder rather than at the end of the handle, and it was usually smashed into the chin or face with an upward stroke. Occasionally the warrior struck downward at the enemy's temple. A warrior might seize an enemy by the hair and club him, then throwing the foe over his shoulder to men armed with heavy straight clubs (tokyeta), with which they cracked his skull.

Both hunting and war bows were plain self bows with a simple curve, and they were usually made of willow. Mesquite was sometimes used for war bows and was regarded as a superior material. The length of the bow varied with the height of the man who carried it, the ideal length being from the ground to the chin. Hunting bows were shorter than war bows, averaging from three and a half to four feet in length. The depth from string to belly averaged six inches, and the grip measured one inch by one and a half inches. Bowstrings were four ply, and were made of horse or deer sinew. Fiber bowstrings were sometimes used on hunting bows, but never on war bows. The hunting bow was unpainted, while war bows were painted black on each end and red in the middle. The tips of the war bow were sometimes wrapped in sinew.

Each man made his own bow by the following process. A length of green willow, after drying in the sun, was split lengthwise and worked with stone knives. Willow bark which had been soaked in water was wrapped around half of the bow, and the wrapped end was thrust into a damp pile of earth on top of which a fire had been built. The bow was left in the hot earth for thirty minutes, after which the procedure was repeated with the other half of the bow. Next, the bow was bent back and forth over the knee to give even leverage and to ensure flexibility, and this resulted in a curving of the ends of the bow. Immediately after flexing, the bow was strung.

The Mohave occasionally reinforced their war bows by tying deer sinew on the back of the bow at the grip.

Bows were unstrung when not in use, since the Mohave had little fear of an enemy attack, and the bows could be strung in a matter of seconds. Warriors strung their bows only when nearing enemy country.

Warriors normally stood erect while shooting, holding the bow vertically. Hunters sometimes held the bow in a horizontal position. The bow was held in the left hand and grasped in the middle, although there were some lefthanded and ambidextrous archers. The Mohave knew the secondary arrow release, but the primary release was usually employed.

Arrows (ipa) were of arrow-weed (*Pluchea*), although some use may also have been made of cane arrows: at least the latter were known for tribes to the south. Foreshafted arrows were denied, and Mohave arrows were invariably untipped. No arrow poison was used. The arrow was three-eighths of an inch in diameter and nearly three feet in length. The shaft was painted either red or black. War arrows were provided with three feathers; hunting arrows had four, and the arrows of children two feathers. The feathers of any kind of big bird, except the eagle or buzzard, were used, with those of the hawk and crane the most common. The feather was split in two with the teeth, the outer edges were trimmed, and the halves placed on the same arrow. No gum was used in fastening the feathers to the arrow; rather, sinew was wrapped around the top of the feather, brought down to the bottom, and tied. To identify the arrow as that of a Mohave, the shaft between the feathers was painted black on one side and red on the other.

Green arrow-weeds destined for use as arrows were pulled up by the roots and placed in the sun to dry. The arrow was then heated, the bark was scraped off with a stone knife, and the end was whittled to a sharp point. The point was moistened and put in hot ashes for hardening.

No arrow-straightener was used for arrow-weed arrows, which were straightened only once. The arrow was heated over a fire to soften it, and it was straightened with the hands and teeth, the maker sighting along the shaft to determine degree of straightness. Cane arrows were sometimes straightened on a plain, heated stone.[10] War arrows were not decorated with pyrographic designs, although boys would peel the bark off of green arrow-weeds, twine the bark around the arrow, and set it afire. The bark burned away, leaving a spiralling black design on the arrow.

The maximum flight of an arrow was two hundred yards, but no damage was inflicted at that distance. Arrow penetration varied from two to four inches, depending upon the distance from which the arrow was shot. The arrow was said to be painful if shot from about fifty yards, and at ten yards a direct hit on the heart could be fatal.

Warriors wore a deerhide bowguard on the wrist of the bow-hand; sometimes the guard extended halfway up the arm. The hide was split on the ends and tied. Bark bowguards, braided and tied at each end, were worn by hunters and were discarded after they had been worn a few times.

Quivers (kupet) were usually of the whole skin of a fox, with the hair on the outside and the tail at the top. Coyote and wildcat skins were also used, and Mrs Lincoln mentioned deerskin quivers. An arrow-weed stick served as a reinforcing rod, with a sinew cord attached to each end of the stick so that the quiver could be slung over the back. The quiver was three feet long and three or four inches across, and it contained fifteen or twenty arrows. In battle, in order that arrows might be readily plucked out, the quiver was sometimes put under the arm and held in place with a willow bark cloth wrapped around the torso.

The tokyeta, a heavy straight club of mesquite wood, approximately two feet in length and two inches thick, was used for cracking skulls.[11] Men with tokyetas followed the archers in battle formation, dispatching enemies who had been felled but not slain by warriors with halyawhai (the "potato-masher" club). Warriors wielded the tokyeta with one hand, beating the foe over the head until he died. The tokyeta was sometimes carried over the shoulder, suspended by a cord passing through a hole at the end of the club, and halyawhai-bearers might have as additional weapons tokyetas thrust through the belt

Two or three warriors in a party of forty or fifty might carry spears (otat). These were five foot lengths of mesquite wood, sharpened at both ends, with a single feather attached to each end. They were ordinarily borne by horsemen.

Archers carried circular shields (sakol) of horsehide or deerskin, about two feet in circumference. These were used to protect the heart only. Two forms seem to have been in use: one with a rim of mesquite or screwbean wood over which a hide was stretched, the other rimless, with two hide disks sewn together around the peripheries with sinew. Two holes were punched in the middle of the shield, about four inches apart, with a sinew thong through which the hand was passed to hold the shield. The shield was not feathered, but was painted solidly in red or black. The Mohave did not paint the shield in four

quarters as did the Maricopa and Cocopa.

Neither the sling nor the stone-headed club was used in battle. Occasionally a sharp bone or sharpened mesquite stick was used as a dagger, and stone knives (kemadj) were carried to battle but were seldom employed as weapons. The knife was a foot in length, unhafted, and sharpened on one edge only.

The Mohave lacked the curtain shield, and the strip of horsehide to protect the stomach was denied. Mrs Lincoln said that warriors sometimes braided the vines of black-eyed beans and wrapped them around their stomachs for protection.

The feathered pike (okwil) was a three or four foot length of mesquite or willow wood, pointed at both ends, with chicken-hawk feathers tied onto the shift in pairs. According to Lute Wilson, the usual number of feathers was forty.[12] Usually an okwil was adorned with white feathers only,[13] although occasionally one with black feathers was carried. The shaft of the okwil was painted either red or black.

The okwil functioned as a flag or standard, and no war party was without one. All informants insisted that there was ordinarily only one standard-bearer on a war party, although if several groups of warriors were attacking from different directions, each group would have an okwil. The okwil-bearer went into battle in front of the other warriors, going into the middle of the enemy and fighting with the pointed ends of the okwil. He carried no other weapons and no shield He had non-flight obligations, and if he were killed the okwil was immediately picked up by another kwanami. There was a tendency, but not a rigid rule, for the same man to carry the okwil on each war party. The okwil might be borne by any kwanami, but the bearer was normally a man who had dreamed about feathers and carrying the okwil.

The huktharhueta, which has not been reported for other Yuman tribes, was infrequently substituted for the okwil, and it had an identical function. Both types of standard were not carried on the same war party. A huktharhueta in Pete Lambert's possession is a three foot shaft of screw-bean wood, unpointed at the ends, with a single fox tail pendant from each end and one from the middle of the shaft.

There was a definite distinction between the small raiding party (hunyu), consisting of ten or twelve kwanamis, and the larger war party (kwanatme), which engaged in a pitched battle. Raiders went out whenever seized with the desire to fight. They departed secretly; there was no meeting or dance of incitement, nor were they obliged to ask the permission of the chief before leaving. They surprised outlying Maricopa camps, killed a few people, and ran away with corn, watermelons, and horses. The horses were killed on the way home; the meat was not eaten, but the hide was saved for sandals and bowstrings.

The war party, an undertaking of the tribe as a whole, had an average strength of forty or fifty men, although on rare occasions it comprised over a hundred warriors. A war party might go out once or twice a year, although usually the intervals between expeditions were longer.

War parties were invariably preceded by one or two scouts, who reconnoitered in the enemy country, locating trails, water holes, and hostile settlements. With his hair done up in a mud plaster as a disguise, a scout sometimes went among the Maricopa at night, even entering the houses and sitting among the enemy. The scout usually succeeded in slipping away before dawn undetected.

Several months often elapsed after the return of the scouts before a war party set out. A few days before the party was scheduled to leave the head kwanami would call a meeting, at which song cycles were sung, and at which warriors were given an opportunity to volunteer for the campaign. If the expedition was to be a joint undertaking with the Yuma, a messenger ran to a prearranged place near Parker, where he left for the Yuma messenger arrows on which were painted black and red signs designating the place and date of attack. Sometimes a knotted string identical with one retained by the Mohave was substituted for the painted arrows, the messenger carrying it all the way to Yuma. The war parties of both Yuma and Mohave untied a knot each morning, and a simultaneous attack was thus ensured on the morning when the last knot was untied.

A dance of incitement was sometimes held prior to the departure of a war party. (The statements of my informants on the subject were vague and contradictory.) The dance lasted for one day and one night; the women dancing around scalps taken in previous battles; the men singing to the accompaniment of the gourd rattle. After the dance the warriors departed, leaving the women weeping.

There was no prohibition on sexual intercourse before a war party, nor were there food restrictions, although the warriors ate little. They carried with them a mere handful of ground parched wheat, which they consumed over a period of approximately two weeks.

The journey to the Maricopa country required six days. The party was guided by a scout who had previously made a reconnaissance of the territory to be traversed. The warriors at first traveled by day, walking along quietly in a group, talking little, but "feeling no sad feelings." A piece of willow or grease-wood was chewed to keep the mouth from getting dry, and warriors could smoke if they wished. Nearing the country of the enemy, the warriors traveled by night and slept in concealment during the day. A sentry, posted about twenty yards from the sleeping warriors, investigated all noises, and he was said to be able to hear footsteps over a hundred yards away. It was an evil omen and a sign that the Mohave would lose the battle if an animal came into camp, but since kwanamis were indifferent to death the party did not turn back.

At home the people watched the sky at night for meteors; the direction in which a meteor fell foretold the winner of a battle. Those left behind were under no special restrictions, but it was deemed harmful to the warriors to think of them except on the day when it was known that they would have joined battle.

Some war parties included one or two women. Such women were from brave families; their fathers or brothers were kwanamis. They functioned chiefly as morale-builders,[14] and they ordinarily did not enter the fray, although they were sometimes provided with tokyetas for self-defense. A number of women accompanied the warriors when the Mohave drove the Halchidhoma out of the Parker region, entering the fight and finishing off wounded enemies with their tokyetas.

On each war party there was at least one shaman. A doctor for arrow wounds (ipa sumadj) was always included in a party. There was sometimes a rattlesnake bite doctor, and Lute Wilson mentioned a third specialist, a doctor for club wounds. En route the shaman made speeches to the warriors, relating his dreams, and admonishing them to conduct themselves with valor in battle. He attempted also to work magic against the enemy, trying to hypnotize them from a distance, so that they would go to sleep or fall unconscious. The rattlesnake doctor was able to locate drinking water.

The wounded were treated at the first night's encampment after the battle; the doctor singing and bathing the wounds. A rattlesnake shaman cured by singing and the laying on of hands, but neither he nor the wound doctor sucked or blew on the wound.

Informants without exception maintained that attacks were always by surprise; the enemy was never challenged or notified of an attack in advance. The Mohave crept up on an outlying enemy settlement under cover of darkness and fell upon the enemy at dawn, shrieking and whooping, with annihilation of the foe the aim. A man might escape and rouse other Maricopa settlements, in which case, if the Mohave advanced, they would find the foe drawn up in battle array, and a major engagement would commence.

Mohave warriors were divided in battle formation according to the weapons they bore. The bearer of the feathered pike went first, followed in that order by men with halyawhai, archers, and tokyeta-bearers. In some war parties from two to five horsemen, carrying bows and arrows or spears, rode on the flanks.[15] A general melée ensued once the fray began, and the formation became confused. Warriors were not segregated according to their physical size, nor were there special names for the bearers of different weapons.

Warriors were sometimes separated into three or four groups, approximately equal in numerical strength, each group attacking from a different direction.

The head kwanami at times acted as a challenger before a pitched battle, hurling insults and imprecations at the enemy as he paraded up and down before the warriors. Single combat by champions was denied by all informants.

The duration of a battle was variable: it might last for an hour or two, for half a day, or rarely, an entire day. Lute Wilson said that occasionally the warriors would continue fighting without intermission for two days and nights, until one side was annihilated or until an agreement to suspend hostilities was reached. The Mohave head kwanami would talk to the enemy "face to face," saying, "Now we are returning. You don't have to be afraid of us tonight," and the enemy would reply, "You can go home, and you don't have to be afraid of us chasing you. We won't fight any more

until the next time."

Pete Lambert estimated that in an average battle from five to seven Mohave were killed: fifteen dead was a great loss. Eight or ten Mohave might be wounded, some of them succumbing on the arduous return journey, but the majority recovered to fight again.

Time permitting, the dead were cremated on the field of battle, but frequently the bodies were left for the buzzards. A funeral was later held for the deceased; the houses and possessions of the dead warriors were burned and their horses slain. Mohave warriors feared the magical potency of an enemy scalp; if a man should touch it he would go insane and "holler in the night." Consequently, scalping was performed only by a special scalper, the ahwe somadj ("dream[er] of foes"), who was a shaman rather than a warrior, and who, provided he underwent purification, was unharmed by contact with the scalp. The ahwe somadj, who dreamed his power to scalp, also doctored warriors who had fallen ill due to contact with the enemy.

The scalper went into battle with the warriors and watched for an enemy with "nice, long, heavy hair." There was no preference for the scalp of an enemy war leader. When the scalper spied an enemy with a desirable head of hair, he would knock him down, break his neck, and cut off the head with a stone knife. He ran off with the head to a nearby gulch, where he might hide and scalp undisturbed while the battle was still raging. The scalper made an incision at the outer edge of each eyebrow with a sharp stick of greasewood, and he cut back under the ears. He then made a cut down the face from the bridge of the nose, and ripped off the scalp, which included the ears.[16] Only rarely did he go back into battle to obtain a second scalp. On the homeward journey the scalper would go off by himself at night and "tan" the scalp by rubbing in adobe.

The scalper fasted on the way home, and upon arrival he relinquished the trophy to its permanent keeper, the kohota (dance leader). Then, like the warriors, he purified himself by abstaining from meat and salt and bathing each morning for four days.

Not only enemy slayers but all members of a war party had to undergo purification, lest the maleficent influence of the enemy drive them insane. Those who had killed were not separated from the others on the return journey, but all the warriors slept little, drank little water, and fasted. When they reached home they immediately bathed in the river and the ablutions were repeated each morning for a period of either four or eight days. The four day period was ordinarily observed, but it was considered more efficacious to undergo purification for eight days. During this time the warriors abstained from meat and salt, and they ate only a little cornmeal mush. Those undergoing lustration were not separated from their families, since relatives were likewise obliged to observe the food restrictions and to bathe each morning.

Now and then a warrior would be taken ill on the homeward journey as a result of the evil influence of the enemy, and he was doctored by the ahwe somadj. But he was regarded as potentially dangerous to his companions while in this condition, and if he were unable to walk the other warriors would not carry him.

After the battle a swift runner (konawowem) was sent ahead to bring tidings of casualties and to tell of the return of the warriors. The kohota then scheduled the scalp dance, fixing a date a day or two after the anticipated arrival of the fighting men. Word was sent to all the Mohave, for the scalp dance was a time of rejoicing and celebration, and since many marriages resulted from meetings of young people on such occasions, the ceremony was regarded as beneficial to the fertility of the tribe.

The kohota dressed and painted the scalp, and mounted it on a long cotton-wood pole, which was planted in the ground for the dance. Four or five old scalps were brought out and prepared in like manner.[17] For four days and nights men sang song cycles and women danced around the scalps. Although old women played a major role in the scalp dance, the aged were not the sole participants, since even little boys, painted like warriors and wearing feathers, were permitted to dance. The warriors did not take part in the festivities, but retired to their dwellings.

Women wore eagle feathers in their hair and were painted like kwanamis, with black paint on the face and red paint on the hair. While dancing around the scalp, they mimicked the actions of warriors, yelling and screaming, running and dodging with weapons, and shooting arrows at the scalps. They reviled the scalps; they talked "face to face" like rival challengers. They narrated their war exploits, telling how they had killed and scalped.

Prisoners were required to be present at the scalp dance, but were neither compelled nor permitted to dance. They were not tortured, though they might be insulted and recipient of an occasional blow.

After the dance the scalps passed into the keeping of their permanent custodian, the kohota (also called kohot kusuman, or ahwe kusuman), who, like the scalper, was immune to the maleficent power of the scalp. The kohota had as many as fourteen or fifteen scalps sealed up with greasewood or arrow-weed gum in a large gourd or olla which he kept in a corner of his dwelling.

The scalp dance was repeated at harvest time, the person with the largest crop announcing a dance and feast. The kohota prepared the scalps, washing and brushing them, dyeing the hair with boiled mesquite bark, and plastering it with mud, after which he painted the scalps and set them up on poles. The dance was the same as that following a battle, again lasting for four days and nights. After the dance the kohota and his family once more purified themselves by bathing and abstaining from salt for four days.

The Mohave took numerous captives (ahweth-auk). These were young women and children, and rarely, adolescent boys; older people were never taken prisoner. Captives were seldom mistreated; and while boys were made slaves and forced to perform domestic tasks, the Mohave in time came to regard them as fellow tribesmen, and "thought more of them than their own sons." Upon reaching maturity the boys might marry Mohave girls, but a Mohave girl would never marry a youth who had grown up in an enemy tribe because "she was scared of him."

Prisoners were magically dangerous, and they underwent purification immediately upon arrival. A shaman washed them for four consecutive mornings with a mixture of soaproot and arrow-weed, and during this period the captives, like returning warriors, were not permitted to eat meat and salt.

Since it was feared that such relations would cause insanity, women were not violated by their captors. Rather, they were given to old men as wives, partly as an insult to the enemy, and partly because it was felt that the old men had only a little longer to live and were indifferent to death. A child resulting from such a union was regarded as a half-breed.

Unlike the Yuma, Cocopa, and Maricopa,

the Mohave did not sell prisoners to the Mexicans, and all informants denied that prisoners ever tried to escape, because "they were too well-treated."

Defensive warfare was little developed, since the Maricopa never came en masse to attack the Mohave, and only in later years were the Mohave raided by Chemehuevi. Sentries were rarely on guard in time of peace, but they were stationed out on the mesa while a war party was away.

To sum up, Mohave warfare was in the main the responsibility of the bellicose kwanamis, who derived their power in dreams. Warfare was an obsession with the kwanamis, and beginning in late adolescence they joined frequent warring expeditions in which the Mohave were allied with the Yuman against the Maricopa and Cocopa. Raiding parties of ten or twelve kwanamis went out at any time, but larger war parties were less frequent, and since they were tribal undertakings they involved somewhat more elaborate preparations. A war party sought to surprise enemy settlements, attacking in a battle formation in which warriors were segregated according to their weapons. The belief in the dangerous magical potency of the enemy, manifested by the presence in Mohave culture of the special scalper, the lustration of warriors, the purification of captives, and the special custodian of the scalp, was the dominant motif of all post-battle activities.[18]

RIVER YUMAN COMPARISONS

I have compiled below a list of warfare elements common to the four River Yuman tribes for which detailed information is available (Mohave, Yuma, Cocopa, and Maricopa), together with lists of elements reported for one or more but not all of these peoples. The total of forty-seven traits shared by these tribes is impressive, and convincingly attests to the homogeneity of the warfare complex among the River Yumans. Such differences between the tribes as occur are not of fundamental importance, representing preponderantly variations in subordinate details. For example, while the basic weapons are the same from tribe to tribe, the Maricopa alone had feather ornaments on their shields, and the Yuma and Cocopa sharpened the handles of their "potato-masher" clubs for stabbing, while the Mohave and Maricopa did not. River Yuman warfare is essentially a unified complex in all of

its phases.[19]

Elements common to Mohave, Cocopa, Maricopa, and Yuma. Frequent warfare; large numbers of warriors in war parties; tribe acts as a unit in war; long plain self bow with sinew bow string; untipped arrow-weed arrows; triple radial feathering; arrows straightened with hands and teeth; "potato-masher" clubs; heavy straight clubs (tokyeta); short spears or pikes; feathered pikes with non-fight obligations; circular hide shields; skin of fox or coyote (with tail) as quiver; breechlout and sandals as dress of warriors; black face paint; red paint on hair; feather headdress, radiating feathers on netting foundation; feathers tied in hair of warriors; long hair wrapped and bound at back of head; dreams for power in war; office of war chief; shaman accompanies war party; formal speeches at nightly camps of warriors; warriors eat little en route to battle (ground parched corn or wheat); warriors drink little en route to battle; divided armament, including clubbers and archers; pitched battles; raids; slain enemies scalped; few only scalped, prefer those with "nice long hair"; special scalper with power from dreams; skin of whole head as scalp, including ears; scalp feared as maleficent; scalper purifies self by fasting and bathing; warriors bathe after arrival home; food restrictions on enemy slayers; enemy slayers' families under restrictions; victory dance with scalp on pole; women dance at victory dance; victory dance repeated; scalps kept in sealed olla or gourd; scalps taken out and washed at intervals; special custodian for scalps; sentries sometimes posted; young women and children taken captive; captives purified; women captives "given to old men."

Elements common to all but one River Yuman tribe. Hide bow guard (not reported for Yuma); secondary arrow release (not Yuma); dance of incitement (not Yuma); women go on war party (not Maricopa); challengers (not reported for Cocopa); scalp kicked in air four times (not Maricopa); enemy slayers secluded (not Mohave); all returning warriors restricted, eat and drink little (this applies only to enemy slayers among the Maricopa); scalps kept in house of custodian (Cocopa kept outside dwelling in special structure); captive children sometimes sold to Mexicans (not Mohave) "potato-masher" club wielded with upward stroke (Maricopa struck downward at temple only).

Reported for Mohave and Yuma only. Shield

painted solidly in red or black; evil omen if animal comes into camp of outbound warriors.

Reported for Mohave and Maricopa only. Boys subjected to tests or ordeals to determine fortitude; warriors compete to kill first enemy; warriors attack in groups from several directions.

Reported for Mohave and Cocopa only. Bows sometimes reinforced with sinew at grip; old scalps danced with at dance of incitement; victory dance lasts four days and four nights.

Reported for Yuma and Maricopa only. Captives sometimes killed.

Reported for Yuma and Cocopa only. Handle of "potato-masher" club sharpened for stabbing; feast, "good time" for departing warriors; scalp dance on field of battle.

Reported for Maricopa and Cocopa only. Foreshafted arrows with stone points; "poisoned" arrow points; shield painted in four quarters; enemy starts march separately on return journey from battle.

Reported for Mohave only. Bows unstrung when not in use; quiver sometimes put under arm and held in place by bark cloth wrapped around torso; huktharhueta (shaft with pendent foxtails) as standard; snake bite doctor accompanies warriors; head of foe cut off to scalp at leisure; scalper doctors those ill due to contact with enemy; certain warriors armed only with plain straight clubs; suspension of hostilities by mutual agreement; women imitate actions of warriors in victory dance; four "dream arrows" of boy who has war dreams; existence of a warrior class and an informal association of warriors (wasauwic).

Reported for Yuma only. Mediterranean arrow release; boys practise dodging arrows; smoke signals to call people together; sham battles; warriors march in single file en route to battle.

Reported for Cocopa only. Grooved arrow straightener; faces of warriors sometimes painted all red or half red and half black; horses painted; special victory songs at victory dance; naked woman in victory dance; people take property of greatest warrior.

Reported for Maricopa only. Sinew-backed bow; feather pendants on shield; white paint on hair of warriors; single combat with lone remaining foe; prefer to scalp enemy alive; enemy slayers make selves vomit.

[1] This material was obtained on a field trip to the Mohave sponsored by the Department of Anthropology of the University of California in March and April, 1946. Informants were Chief Pete Lambert, 8O, at Needles, California, and Lute Wilson, 67, Tom Black, 62, and Mrs. Abraham Lincoln (whose grandfather was a war chief), 77, at Parker, Arizona.

[2] Mrs Lincoln: "It seems like the Mohave wanted Parker valley pretty bad. It was rich, and they wanted to get rid of the Maricopa, although they spoke a related language. I don't know why the Mohave did it--I guess they wanted to hog everything like the Whites."

[3] For accounts of Mohave hostilities with these peoples see Kroeber, *Handbook of the Indians of California*, pp. 799-802, and Spier, *Yuman Tribes of the Gila River*, pp. 11-18 and p. 42, vol. 3, 1947.

[4] Mohave warriors served as scouts with the United States Army against the Yavapai and Apache.

[5] When some American miners were killed by the Walapai in 1867, the Mohave war chief sent warriors to escort the Whites and to pacify the Walapai.

[6] Wilson: "Sometimes we didn't have much tobacco, and a man might go up around Mespa or Las Vegas and be killed by the Paiute. This led to a fight. Sometimes they came down here, and sometimes we went up there".

[7] Kroeber has characterised Mohave culture as a dream culture, in which all conspicuous success is dependent upon dreaming (*Handbook*, Chapter 51). The situation is neatly epitomised on page 754: "The Mohave adhere to a belief in dreams as the basis for everything in life, with an insistence equalled only by the Yurok devotion to the pursuit of wealth. Not only shamanistic power but most myths and songs, bravery and fortune in war, success with women or in gaming, every special ability are dreamed. Knowledge is not a thing to be learned, the Mohave declare, but to be acquired by each man according to his dreams. For 'luck' they say sumach ahot, 'good dreaming', and 'ill starred' is 'bad dreams'."

[8] Lambert: "From the start, when he was a boy, they knew he was a kwanami and was going to be a warrior when he got old enough to go out and fight. The Mohave knew that he was dreaming about war."

[9] Forde, *Ethnography of the Yuma Indians*, p. 173.

[10] Kroeber pictures a Mohave pottery arrow-straightener (*Handbook*, plate 49).

[11] A model of a Mohave tokyeya in the University of California Museum of Anthropology (UC-1-4316) is two feet long, tapering from a thickness of one inch at the grip to a thickness of two inches at the far end. The club is provided with a wrist loop, and the upper half of the club is painted red.

[12] A ceremonial specimen of an okwil seen at Needles was three feet in length and had thirteen pairs of black and white feathers.

[13] White crane feathers, which were believed efficacious in locating water, were sometimes attached to the okwil.

[14] Pete Lambert: "She eggs them on; gives some kind of a speech to never do this or that. Makes a noise like a preacher."

[15] The few horses possessed by the Mohave were well-trained, and were ridden in battle by their owners. Pete Lambert said that the horses knew just what to do in a battle; they knew the formations and could dodge arrows. If a warrior captured a woman he had merely to throw her over the horse's beck and the animal would gallop away.

[16] Wilson: "The ear is the hardest part, so he bites and trims it with his teeth."

[17] Pete Lambert insisted that the scalps were tied at intervals on a single pole, but the other informants said that each scalp was on a separate pole.

[18] The recent novel *Crazy Weather*, by Charles L. McNichols, contains interesting and accurate narratives of Mohave warfare, as well as engrossing portrayals of other aspects of the culture.

[19] This conclusion accords with Spier's finding that "…Maricopa culture and that of the Lower Colorado Yuman was in large part a single entity" (*Cultural Relations of the Gila River and Lower Colorado Tribes*, p. 8).

Fort Mojave

by Leonard B. Waitman

During the early part of the 1850's, the United States government was sending out parties to study certain suggested routes for a transcontinental railroad. One such route under consideration followed approximately along the 35th parallel from Arkansas west and had been surveyed by Lieutenant A. W. Whipple in 1854. It ran into the San Bernardino-Salt Lake Road at the Mojave River a few miles east of what is now the desert town of Daggett, thence to San Bernardino and Los Angeles via the Cajon Pass.

Shortly after Whipple's survey, a concerted effort was made to open a wagon road along this line.

In 1857, Congress appropriated money for such a road from Fort Defiance, in the Navajo country in northeastern Arizona, to the Colorado River. Edward F. Beale, a former navy lieutenant, was employed by the Secretary of War to head the undertaking. The point where his road reached the Colorado was the point where, later, Fort Mojave was established, and the crossing there was long known as Beale's Crossing. [1]

When Beale was starting on his undertaking to open the thirty-fifth parallel road across northern Arizona to the Colorado, he was ordered to make use of camels, and deliver them at Fort Tejon. He was entirely willing to try them and gave them a thorough test. His conclusion was summed up in his report when he dubbed them, despite numerous difficulties encountered during the testing, "the noblest brutes on earth."

The Beale road ran through the Mohave Indian country, and the Mohaves resented the coming of white men to their lands. Their attacks on emigrants and mail carriers grew so serious that the government decided to place a military force on the Colorado River for the protection of travelers. [2]

Lt. Colonel William Hoffman was sent by Washington to select a site for the fort. Hoffman was unimpressed by the area but the Army officials were convinced that the post should be on the Colorado River in Mohave Indian territory. Thus it was that Fort Mojave was established in 1858. From this site the troops, under Major Armistead, were able to control the depredations and defeat the hostiles on their own grounds whereupon they sued for peace. The army saw fit to keep the camp active to insure peace within the area until May of 1861 when it was abandoned.

During the first active period of the Fort it was a major undertaking to supply the garrison with the necessities of life. The Colorado River steamboats proved uncertain since navigation was difficult and at times impossible. It was during such a dire situation that a rather enterprising young Captain decided to take a calculated risk to relieve the Fort. Captain Winfield Scott Hancock sent a relief force of Banning's best desert teamsters to conduct ten, eight mule-team wagons with supplies over the desert route. The relief force reached the river post in sixteen days and reportedly found the road excellent, for a desert road. Hancock described the area as having sufficient wood, water, and grass along the way.

Captain Hancock's bold decision to ship supplies overland proved successful in several respects. Not only did he get the supplies to the Fort in a quicker period of time, but he also was able to reduce the cost of shipping by a substantial amount. Prior to his experiment, supplies were transhipped from San Francisco to the camp via the Colorado River. The new route from Los Angeles across the desert was much shorter and more certain. (San Bernardino freighters used this road along the Whipple survey later, not only in furnishing Fort Mojave with supplies, but also in hauling to the mining camps which later developed.)

It is one of the "ironies" of history that Major Armistead and Captain Hancock were to meet again on the field of battle.

The Major Armistead to whom Captain Hancock sent relief was one of the southerners who resigned his commission in the Union Army at the outbreak of the Civil War in order to join the Confederate forces, and he was the Confederate General Armistead who was mortally wounded in the terrible charge at Gettysburg. Captain Hancock was the Union Major General whose men faced Armistead. Thus it was that the very man he saved he had to destroy four years later on the opposite side of the continent.[3]

From 1858 to 1861, Fort Mojave acted as the eastern anchor to a line of forts and redoubts established along the major trails of the Mojave. In 1861, Fort Mojave was abandoned on the order of General Sumner when he took over command of military affairs in California at the outbreak of the Civil War. General Sumner felt he could use his troops along the river to better advantage elsewhere.

The need for troops arose again, however, when miners discovered gold on the eastern side of the Colorado near the fort. The fort was re-established in 1863 for the protection of these miners. Another factor was the closing of the southern routes into California by Confederate forces from Texas. Thus, it became desirable to have a mail route further north, and this renewed interest in the Beale wagon road, hence the need for the reoccupation of the camp.[4]

DESCRIPTION OF CAMP MOJAVE

For the best description of Camp Mojave, Circular #8 Arizona, p. 613. 67 U. 58 from the War Department Surgeon General's office, Washington, May 1, 1875, gives us the following.

This camp is situated on a gravel bluff on the east bank of the Colorado River, near the head of Mojave Valley, latitude, 350 28' West, altitude, 600' above the sea level, and 75' above the river.... '

The plateau on which Camp Mojave was founded extended north and south about forty miles, with an average width of ten to twelve miles. There were two reservations, each three miles square. The camp was built on the upper one. The lower reservation was on the low bottom land, about six miles south of the post, Part of it was subject to overflow; the soil was fertile, and was covered with coarse grass, cottonwood and mesquite trees with a dense undergrowth of willows and arrow-weed. With the exception of the above, the country was waste. The elevated plains were covered sparsely with a growth of greasewood bush, interspersed with varieties of cacti. Rabbits and quail were found in large numbers; ducks and geese abound in the slough and the river afforded an abundance of fish of the salmon species. Deer, mountain sheep, and antelope were found in the hills. The mountains on either side of the river were barren and destitute of timber. Only a few springs of water were found in the adjacent mountains, and the country may be described as a sterile plain, broken by arroyos or dry gulches.

The climate, as would be expected, was healthful, with mild winters. The summers, however, were extremely hot, especially during July and August when the winds of the desert were so heated as to scorch all that they touched. The nights were as hot as the days, which made it impossible to sleep. Thus, we read in circular 8 that the entire garrison slept outside, endeavoring to catch any faint breeze. Evidently this was common practice since the walls of the barracks became so heated as to make them unendurable.

The post itself consisted of two buildings located on the north side of the parade ground. One had a shingle roof, the other a dirt one. Both buildings had dirt floors. Each building was 90 x 35 x 16 feet and were well-ventilated under the eaves, and by windows and doors. The shingled roof building was occupied as a dormitory and was warmed by two open fireplaces and two stoves. The building afforded about 900 cubic feet of air space per man for average occupancy and was considered a very comfortable abode. As if to offer frosting on the cake, each man had a single iron bedstead rather than those of double deck wooden variety.

Just a few feet away from the barracks the next most important building was located - the army kitchen and mess-hall. This building was 80 x 35 feet and was intended for use by two companies at a sitting. It was the first building to be floored. The barracks office and storerooms were in the west end of the barracks. These were floored later, in 1874, and proved to be very comfortable. A small root-house or vegetable room was built in the rear of the mess-room and answered a much-needed purpose.

The ending of the Civil War and the re-establishment of the camp saw the addition of more buildings – but this time for married couples.

These were situated about 400 yards from the parade grounds and were of adobe. The buildings, prior to being taken over by the army, had been occupied by civilians and formed what was then part of Mojave City. The officers' quarters were situated on the south side of the parade grounds and comprised two buildings, adobe also, well-finished and roomy. One of these was occupied by the commanding officer and was built in 1873. It was 15 x 15 feet and divided into three rooms. The other adobe set was divided by an adobe partition having three rooms on each side. Each room in each of the buildings was 14 feet high, ceiled and floored, with two doors and four windows and was provided with an open fireplace. Another comfortable building, converted into four rooms 16 x 12 feet, was the stockade building. It, too, was floored and ceiled, with canvas and dirt. It also was occupied by the officers at the camp.

Aside, and almost by itself, was the guardhouse which was located on the east side of the parade ground. It was 20 x 35 x 12 feet and contained a guard room 20 x 20 feet and two cells 10 x 15 feet. It was well-ventilated by openings at the eaves, by windows and an open fireplace.

The post bakery, which was located on the north side of the parade ground, was in fine repair and is the only building on which we have no dimensions as to size.

Several storehouses dotted the east and north sides of the parade ground. These were well-built and had shingled roofs.

Another major building of vital importance to any army installation, the hospital, was finished in 1873, having been used in partial completion for several years before its ultimate consummation. It was a well-built structure and suited its purpose. The hospital was located 200 yards north of the barracks and faced south. It was of adobe, floored and ceiled, had a shingle roof and a ventilation system along the ridge of the entire length of the building. A porch ten feet wide surrounded the entire building. The west end of the building housed a ward 40 x 20 feet for eight beds. Next to this ward was a hall 5 feet wide running across the building, an isolation ward 10 x 20 feet adjoining the storeroom which was 9 x 20 feet. The east end of the building housed the dispensary which was 10 x 20 feet. The rooms were all 12 feet high. The entire building of regular and isolation wards

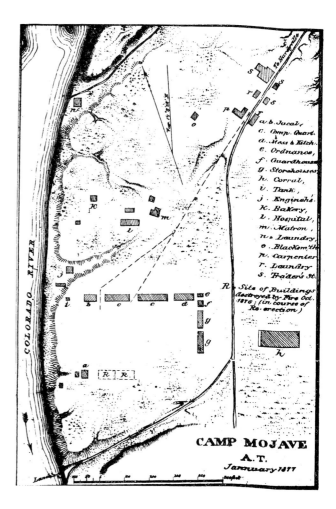

CAMP MOJAVE
A. T.
January 1877

were all amply furnished with windows and doors. Behind the main building was the hospital, kitchen, and mess-hall. The kitchen was 15 x 17 feet and the mess-hall was 15 x 12 feet.

These buildings were floored with boards but not ceiled. The entire building was shingled and was well-lighted and ventilated. It also contained several pieces of furniture. The morgue, "dead house," as it was called, was situated directly west of the main building, 160 feet distant. It, too, was of adobe and was shingled, being 10 feet square inside. The walls were 10 feet high. It was built over a pit, 15 feet deep, and had a ventilation shaft extending 4 feet above the ground. The dead house also contained a shower-bath and conveniences for bathing.

Several shade trees were scattered throughout the area and added greatly to the appearance of the fort.

The stable for the horses was a frame building open at the sides, shingled, with stalls for 52 animals, and situated in a corral with high adobe walls.

The post was amply supplied with water from the Colorado River by means of a six horsepower steam engine. The water was pumped into a 6000 gallon tank which supplied the entire area by pipes. Drainage was near perfect.

Most of the food for the camp was shipped in since no post gardens were cultivated. The troops had an abundance of potatoes, onions, cracked wheat, buckwheat, flour, and corn sent via San Francisco at first and later on via Los Angeles.

The means of communication varied from wagon trains, horseback, to steamers, from semi-weekly to monthly, depending on the speed of the carrier.

LIFE AT CAMP MOJAVE

Life at Fort Mojave was similar to that of other desert outposts of the era. Duties ranged from dull, boresome routine to exciting patrols and escort activities. The average enlisted man, however, found it often just outright monotonous. Duties for the desert soldier included menial chores such as cleaning the corrals or currying the horses.

Reveille sounded at the fort at five in the morning and breakfast was served at five-thirty. After breakfast, those who were sick reported for sick call, while those who were well reported for fatigue duty. This usually consisted of policing the area and straightening up the barracks. Other enlisted men were detailed to cut and haul wood for the kitchen. In addition, still other men were busy feeding horses, cleaning the stalls and engaged in endless odd jobs.

After the noon meal, the men usually had a couple of spare hours until work was resumed. Recall was blown at six-thirty and retreat sounded at sunset. Tattoo came at nine o'clock, followed by taps at nine-thirty.

When the men were not engaged in routine duties at the camp, they usually spent their time reading or hunting. Recreation was limited, and with time on their hands the desert G.I.'s were often warned about excessive drinking and rowdy brawling. Desertions were frequent and the guardhouse often did not accommodate the number of boarders.

Boredom within the camp was broken periodically with escort duties. In line with these duties, the men were assigned to protect travellers and the mails. Bullion from the mines was transported over the roads and the army furnished protection to insure safe delivery.

The men carried their own rations, seldom over seven days' supply, their guns, usually muzzle loaders, and a forage bag for each animal. The men were rationed to fifteen rounds of ammunition, and these were taken up by the non-commissioned officer in charge.

The toll on horses, mules, and equipment was tremendous, and report after report asks for the replacement of the above, sometimes to no avail. Fire power was later increased when the horse soldiers received Spencer rifles. Like all army personnel stationed at a desert outpost, the men of Camp Mojave griped more about the heat, food, and boredom than they did about the Indians.

Although unkempt in their appearance and rough in their manners, these desert horse soldiers proved to be a breed of their own. They were tough, rough, and willing to go as far as they were ordered, not without "bitching" like all army men before them, but willing to carry out their duties.

To the people traveling through the desert, these unpolished, gruff-looking individuals proved to be a godsend, a real blessing, for without them the history of the west might never have been written.

Today the staunch "Fort of Mojave" is a State Historical Landmark in Arizona, and well it might be, for with its final abandonment, a period of the romantic west came to an end. What finer tribute could there be to those heroes of the desert?

[1] 35th Congress, 1 sess., H. Ex. Doc. No., 124, Vol. XIII, Serial No. 959, Edward Fitzgerald Beale, Wagon Road from Fort Defiance to the Colorado.
[2] Beattie, George William and Helen Pruitt Beattie, *Heritage of the Valley*, Biobooks, Oakland, California, 1951., p. 322.
[3] *Ibid.*, p. 323-324.
[4] *Ibid.*, p. 326.
[5] Report of Acting Assistant Surgeons, F. S. Stirling and James B. Laurence, U.S. Army. Circular 8#, p. 613. 67 U. 58.

Chapter Five

❖

Language and Literature

Photo by Jeffrey L. Garton

Mohave Voice and Speech Mannerisms

by George Devereux

There is an extreme paucity of data pertaining to the management of the voice in non-Indo-European languages. Hence it may be of some interest to describe the vocal behavior of the Mohave Indians during conversations dealing with sexual topics. Since the Mohave discuss sexual matters, especially those not pertaining to the process of gestation, rather freely—being, in this respect, as in many others, different from their non-Yuman neighbors—the following data also shed some light on the overall vocal behavior of the Mohave. A detailed discussion of Mohave phonetics is not necessary in the present context, since this problem is adequately covered by Kroeber's monograph.

The Mohave are a talkative people, who admire skilled orators, witty conversationalists and expert swearers, though they have no liking for people who are merely coarse or verbally sadistic. Their enjoyment of talk is so great that one frequently finds oneself following with great interest the conversation between one's informant and interpreter, without being able to understand more than one word in a hundred, simply because they give the impression of being wholly absorbed by, and involved in, the act of communication.

It is, hence, not surprising that elaborate precautions should be taken to prevent the birth of mute children, by means of a meticulous compliance with the relevant taboos. Yet, the ability to speak is not thought of as a criterion of intelligence, since even fetuses about to be born, as well as twin infants and nursing babies are believed to be capable of understanding, and responding to, rational verbal admonitions, even though they are manifestly incapable of speech.

The Mohave of both sexes have pleasing voices, which they manage with consummate skill. They exploit to the utmost the musical and expressive potentialities inherent in a language possessing pitch, and transfer even to English some of the musical qualities of Mohave speech, without approximating the sing-song impression produced by Swedes.

Despite their skilful management of the voice, the Mohave do not seem to be *consciously* interested in sound-production. Thus, the date at which the male puberty rite occurs is not determined by the cracking of the adolescent's voice. Furthermore, unlike the kindred Yuma the Mohave deny that the laughter of women differs from that of men, except in its pitch, and perhaps also its volume.

It is also striking that, despite the intensity of the Mohave Indian's participation in the act of verbal communication, extreme forms of voice-production are rare or absent. In other words the Mohave are seldom shrill and do not whisper frequently. It is also significant that I have never met, or heard of, an individual possessing several 'voices', although in Western society certain latently homosexual and grandiose individuals frequently have three distinct 'voices': a basso boom, a shrill scream and an aggressive, low-pitched whisper. The avoidance of extremes of voice-production is especially conspicuous when a Mohave man quotes and imitates the speech of a woman or of a transvestite: The narrator does not change to falsetto but uses his normal voice, suggesting, rather than mimicking, nuances of female speech, even in imitating a male transvestite's use of the female expletive *peleley*.

Imperfections of Voice-Production and of Speech are obstacles to communication which are sometimes rooted in neurotic mechanisms and represent, among other things, an aggression toward, or a repudiation of, one's interlocutor.

(a) *Whispering*. Although the Mohave may whisper for reasons of discretion, I have never observed the type of whispering well known to psychiatrists, which is at once a reaction formation against the urge to scream at one's interlocutor, and a hostile act, which defeats the listener's desire to understand what the speaker allegedly `intends' to tell him.

(b) *Disregard for the Hearing Range* is relatively frequent among the Mohave, who sometimes continue to talk even after their erstwhile interlocutor has passed beyond the effective hearing range. This mannerism appears to be due to inertia, rather than to unconscious aggressions.

(c) *Mumbling.* Mohave informants, conversing with the interpreter about matters of which they are not quite certain, sometimes cease to speak in a manner which obviously subsumes an audience, and engage in a sort of musing pseudo-monologue, marked by a blurring of pronunciation, and sometimes also by a lowering of the pitch of the voice and a slowing down of the normal tempo of speech. The mumbleri̇s behavior gives one the impression that he is re-testing and re-appraising his knowledge by means of verbalization: He utters his sentences hesitantly, and seems to listen to his own voice, as though he were thinking "This doesn't sound quite right" or else "This does sound right, doesn't it?" I have never heard an informant use mumbling in a hostile or resistive manner.

(d) *Rhythm and Tempo.* The Mohave have a traditional staccato, strongly accented and rather rapid manner of delivering traditional memorized texts which are usually couched in brief sentences. This characteristic method of delivery is so completely a part of the recited text, that it is very difficult, even for the most willing informant, to slow down to the point where the text can be conveniently recorded. Although adhesions between a traditional text and its usual manner of delivery are, of course, to be expected in a non-literate society, they can be exploited for the purpose of resisting communication. Thus, when working with the rather timid and not overly willing old Nyahwera, in the presence of a shaman whom he feared, my interpreter and I found it impossible to induce him to utter slowly the archaic text of the `recitative' songs of the initiation ritual for transvestites. On the other hand my friends and willing informants Hivsu Tupoma and Ahma Humare always managed, after a few false starts, to dictate native texts at a speed which made it possible for me to record their recitations verbatim.

(e) *Text of Songs.* Everyone is familiar with the difficulty of reciting the text of a song without singing, at the same time, the musical part thereof. This difficulty is so genuine that, when Ahma Humare taught me his weylak curing songs I had to stop him from time to time to record certain half-heard words. In order to do so, I had to pronounce first what I *believed* the word to be, in order to enable him, to repeat it after me in the *correct* manner. Likewise, after recording an entire sentence, and after reading it back to him, Ahma Humare was usually able to ' repeat this sentence without singing it because, for the first time in his life, he had heard it recited without music. This observation underscores the significance of auditory factors in learning, in a non-literate society. The adhesion of the text to the music does not appear to be exploited for the purpose of inhibiting communication because of unconscious resistances and aggressions.

(f) *Pseudo-Communication* does not, properly speaking, belong in a study of voice-production, and is, hence, mentioned only because it also exemplifies defective communication. The shaman T.B., reputed to be a witch, managed to confuse completely both my very competent interpreter and myself. Not merely did he skip from topic to topic, not merely did he contradict himself periodically but even went so far as to utter what seemed to be long series of non-sequiturs. On re-reading the recorded conversation I am forcibly reminded of the ramblings of a moderately well-preserved schizophrenic, although there is no reason whatsoever to suspect T.B. of being a schizophrenic, or of having been in a dream-state induced by a conversation about the shamanistic and esoteric aspects of mental disease, as seen from the shamanistic point of view, since—significantly enough—his voice-production and speech mannerisms were not in the least unusual or deviant. In the end both my interpreter and myself independently reached the conclusion that T.B. was deliberately confusing us.

(g) *Suppression of Means of Communication.* The Mohave show a singular reluctance to speak English, unless they speak English well. On the other hand they do not seem to pretend not to understand it when, in reality, they do happen to know a little English. Thus old Mrs. Chach who knew only scraps of English, always made a genuine effort to understand what I said to her, or in her presence,—even to the point of laughing out loud even before some affectionate jibe of mine was interpreted to her—although, except on one occasion, she never attempted to utter a single English word. In 1938, however, when I visited her to bid her goodbye before leaving the reservation, after asking the interpreter to translate several of her affectionate parting remarks to me, she took my hands and with great warmth bade me 'Good-bye.' The formal English words were pronounced very hesitatingly, clearly indicating that she barely knew them. She probably used them only because she admittedly had a premonition that she would not see me again, and, hence, presumably wanted to speak to me directly at least once in her life. The shaman Hivsu Tupoma, one of my closest friends and most willing informants, readily admitted that he knew a few words of English, but insisted on using an interpreter. On one occasion, however, when, under the influence of alcohol he decided to speak to me of his acts of witchcraft, he saw me in private, and thus revealed that he spoke broken, though intelligible English. I know of no English-speaking Mohave who, because of his contempt for Whites or for some other reason, pretends not to speak that language, although e.g. Pueblo Indians are known to use this mode of evasion.

(h) *Temporary Mutism.* The Mohave Indian, who is not addicted to sulking, does not refuse to communicate by simply assuming an attitude of stolid silence, or by playing dumb, which is the traditional defense of less proud and less mercurial minority groups. On the other hand, although all young people speak English fairly well, shy youngsters, and especially young schoolgirls, sometimes become almost speechless with embarrassment. A little genuine friendliness generally suffices, however, to induce them to converse in a cheerful, easy and animated manner.

The Expression of Emotions is a notoriously elusive matter. The following observations may, hence, be of some interest.

(a) *Merriment:* When discussing scabrous matters, or when engaged in affectionately obscene banter, speech tends to speed up and to alternate with guffaws, though never with giggles, snickers and salacious whispers. The transition from speech to guffaw is a swift, though a gradual one, and many Mohave almost, though not quite, manage to laugh and to speak at the same time. The face becomes relaxed and the features expand into a mobile and infectious smile.

(b) *Embarrassment:* On rare occasions, especially when I had just begun to work with my octogenarian friend, Mrs. Chach, I was able to detect a certain amount of embarrassment in her speech. Once or twice she even clapped her hand before her mouth, a gesture also known to be used by embarrassed men. During one of our early interviews she repeatedly pronounced the word *modhar* (penis) as *modhar*, greatly exaggerating the length of both vowels. When I naively inquired whether this was an archaic or idiosyncratic manner of pronouncing the word in question, both Chach and my interpreter laughed and explained that the old lady was merely a trifle self-conscious. Her embarrassment also manifested itself in a slightly greater meticulousness in reproducing the regular pitches and stresses of ordinary pronunciation. This peculiarity of speech disappeared very rapidly, and, later on, when we exchanged affectionate insults Mrs. Chach gave me rapid-fire tit for tat, without the least trace of embarrassment. On a subsequent field-trip, on hearing her pronounced *hispan* (vagina) as *hispan*, I asked whether she again felt embarrassed. Both Chach and my interpreter guffawed and told me that her pronunciation was due solely to the absence of upper incisors. She even put her right index in her mouth to show me the gap in her teeth.

(c) *Solemnity and Reserve.* When discussing the serious side of sexuality, i.e. gestation, my informants' voices tended to become more resonant, and were a trifle lower pitched than usual. Pronunciation also tended to be unusually meticulous. At the same time they displayed a tendency to use short, clipped, 'preaching-style' sentences, and the characteristic staccato delivery of orators, or of persons narrating a major myth, which has already been described above. When speaking in this manner their faces bore a frown of concentrated attention.

Summary. The Mohave are expert speakers and conversationalists, who manage their voices with consummate skill and tasteful restraint. Gross abnormalities of speech-production and obstacles to communication were absent.

Spirit Mountain: An Anthology

by Leanne Hinton and Lucille J. Watahomigie

Introduction

In the deserts and along the waterways of the lower Colorado River, in the oak and pine forests, the canyons, plateaus, and mountains, the land sings through its people. When the song seems to be fading from living memories, it is time to write it down. In confining the song to markings on paper, there is a risk of freezing and paralyzing it, robbing it of vitality. In this collection of stories and songs from the Yuman Indian peoples, we have tried to preserve the song in ways that will turn the hearts of modern readers, as it turned the hearts of men and women before they began to forget. The song must continue as full of life as earth's own celebration.

Spirit Mountain represents the beginning. It rises from the desert floor at the Colorado River near what is now Davis Dam, capped by white granite bluffs, dwarfing other landmarks. At its base, inhabitants long since gone have left behind a rich legacy of petroglyphs as an account of human origins. Versions of the name Wi Kahme', "The Highest Mountain Range," are known to exist in Hualapai, Havasupai, Mojave, Diegueno, Maricopa, and Paipai. It is known as a sacred place to all the tribes. Yuman oral tradition names Spirit Mountain as the source of human emergence from the earth. Narratives describe the original unity of the Yuman peoples as well as the events which led to their dispersion over the land from Spirit Mountain.

The Yuman Tribes are so-named because they speak closely related languages. The Yuman communities represented in this volume are the Hualapai, Havasupai, Yavapai, Paipai, Diegueno, Mojave, Maricopa, and Quechan (Yuma). When people speak related languages, it means that they shared some history somewhere back in time. Thousands of years ago, the ancestors of modern Yuman peoples probably spoke a single language, and perhaps lived somewhat closer together. "Yuman," of course, is not a term that has ever been applied to this group of communities by

Photo by Victor Masayesva

themselves; but the people do recognize their kinship in some of their origin tales.

The first four languages mentioned above are closely enough related to be sub-grouped together as the "Pai" languages. Havasupai and Hualapai are so alike as to have only minor dialectal differences; Yavapai (which has several dialects) can also be understood quite easily by the Havasupai and the Hualapai; and Paipai is slightly but not fully intelligible to people speaking the other Pai languages. A second sub-grouping within the Yuman family is sometimes called the "River Tribes," consisting of the Mojave, Maricopa, and Quechan. Their languages are very similar to each other, and relatively different from the other Yuman languages. Diegueno enters into a subgroup with Cocopa (the latter not represented in this volume), sometimes called "Delta Yuman." Kiliwa (also not represented here) is a branch unto itself, showing major differences from the other Yuman languages, but still clearly belonging to the same family. These groupings are represented below as a "family tree."

When people who once lived together separate and lose contact with each other, their languages—imperceptibly slowly—begin to differ from each other. Given enough time, and little enough contact, the dialects can diverge so strongly that their speakers can no longer understand each other, and then they would have to be defined as separate languages. In this manner, the Yuman languages have diverged over the millennia.

The Yuman peoples have developed different ways of life from each other in response to the varying opportunities of their lands. Agriculture was and is practiced by all Yuman communities that had sufficient water, most extensively by the tribes living along the Colorado and Gila rivers, where large permanent settlements arose. The Havasupai also have large year-round water supply, and have an intricate canal system for irrigation. Smaller gardens were tended near springs and small watercourses by other Yuman peoples. In southern California, even where irrigation was not possible, wild and semi-domesticated grasses, seeds, bushes, and trees were planted by the Diegueños. Along the coast, seafood was collected regularly in the old days; and such coastal products as abalone and other seashells were traded along inland routes. Abalone shell has been found in archaeological sites as far away as Ohio, indicating the complexity of the trading networks in traditional America. Where the oak grows, the acorn was a staple. In the higher mountainous and plateau regions the pinon replaces the acorn as the staple. All Yuman peoples also practiced much hunting and gathering of wild foods. While all these traditional modes of living are still practiced by many individuals among the Yuman peoples, they have tended to become less easy to follow in modern times, as land and wild resources have been taken away. Newer ways of living, such as raising horses and cattle, and earning wages in order to buy food from stores, have come to be dominant.

Along with these different ways of life, the Yuman peoples developed different patterns of knowledge, different religious traditions, different stories and songs. Many of the same themes run through all the oral traditions of the Yuman territory, and indeed a considerably larger area than that. But every community also has many themes and many songs and tales entirely their own. This variety produces such a rich set of traditions that a book of this sort can hope only to touch the surface. We can, however, provide representative and authentic examples of this continuum of imaginative verbal expression.

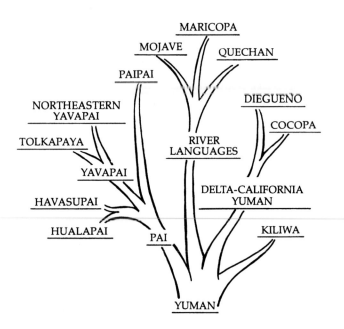

The Traditional Role of Oral Literature

Traditionally, oral literature was not merely a means of entertainment—not merely something to do because television had not yet been invented. Instead it was the means by which the generations transmitted cultural mores. All human activities are part of a universal scheme, and the wise person always knows the relationship of himself and his behavior to this universal pattern of nature. The traditional tales and songs helped people learn about the world and their place in it, how to behave toward other people, and how to lead a life harmonious with nature. It also taught people how to respect other species and how to respect the places on the land, by telling their own place in the pattern of the universe. Many of the tales have morals, but few of them actually say "such-and-such a behavior is wrong." Instead, they are designed to cause people to contemplate their own behavior, to understand something about the consequences of such behavior, and to give them insights that allow them to change their behavior when necessary. "Coyote Law," as some Yumans call it, is the law of the land—sometimes capricious and unreasonable like Coyote himself—but nevertheless, the way things are. The tales tell about Coyote Law.

Traditionally, most Yumans did not expect a large and attentive audience for singing and story telling. Most of the traditional songs and stories in this book were told to members of the family during a winter's night. Adults would often sit and listen well, but children would probably go off to play, or fall asleep. Yet they would hear bits and snatches over and over, and listen with greater and greater attention as they grew older—and in the end, would know enough to lead a wise life, and perhaps to begin telling the stories to their own children. Through these songs and tales, everything in their daily lives would be imbued with powerful significance. Every plant, every hill, every spring was the actual site of some historic or spiritual event in a tale, and the harvesting of a plant or arrival at some location would recall the rich set of events depicted in the tales. The associational framework attached to events in our daily lives now must be so pale by comparison!

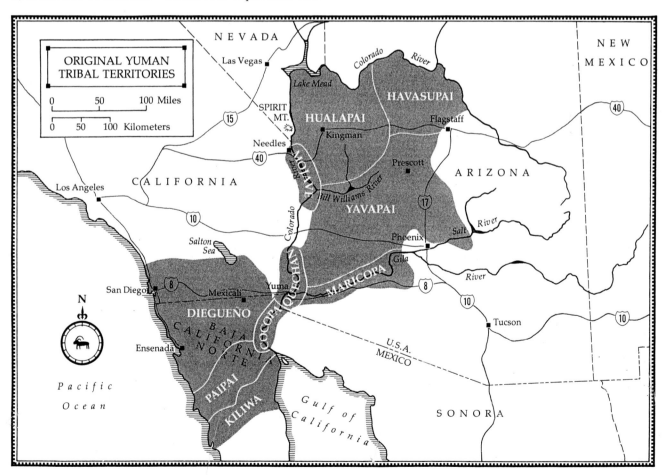

Transcription and Translation

Since Yuman languages were not traditionally written, once the decision has been made to write, the first task is to find a writing system. There are many different writing systems presented in this volume. Some are slightly modified versions of technical writing systems used for linguistic scholarship. Others are practical writing systems devised by native speakers, often Indian educators with the goal of designing a writing system that ensures readability by children in elementary grades. Some communities, such as the Hualapai and Havasuapai, have agreed upon official writing systems, now in wide use. Some other communities are still in the process of designing writing systems for their own use. Because of the complexity of the status of writing systems in Yuman communities, we have not tried to regularize the orthographies. We have generally left it up to each contributor to decide how he or she wishes to write the language.

Oral literature in many of its forms has sometimes been captured by scholars and written down as faithfully as possible to the spoken word. These scholarly transcriptions and translations of oral masterpieces are invaluable for linguistic and ethnographic research, and they form an important resource for people interested in these works for their artistic merit. And yet the artistic merit itself is not well portrayed in scholarly transcriptions. Lost are the intonation patterns, the gestures, the performance context, and the enormous background of cultural knowledge surrounding these performances. The format of presentations rarely allows easy reading. And their translations are, quite appropriately, based not on artistic goals, but rather on the goal of being as literal a translation as possible. The translation itself, then—that part of a presentation of Native American oral literature most frequently read—has little of the beauty and power of the original language.

Many poets and some linguists have made attempts to overcome this barrier by the development of free translations of Native American performances that attempt to create the same emotional impact on its English-speaking audience that the original might have on the Indian audience. Many of the results are artistic masterpieces. And yet they are sometimes so far removed from the original that no one can tell if they bear any resemblance at all to it.

There is also an audience left out by both these styles of translations: many of the American Indians themselves. Among the tribes whose works are represented in this book are many native speakers, with varying degrees of experience in reading their language, as well as people who do not know the traditional language but have some knowledge of the stories and songs. The arcane transcriptions and transliterations of linguistic scholarship are close to unreadable by native speakers of the languages so written. The artistic translations that are without the checks and balances of the presence of the original language leave a gap for people steeped in traditional culture. There is, then, a large audience who wants to read an English version of Indian oral literature which is moving and beautiful and true to the original—and at the same time wants to have before them the same piece in the native language, for the sound and the rhythm and for all those subtleties of meaning that no translation can hope to achieve with total success.

In this book, therefore, we have tried to combine approaches in the richest way possible. The literature is presented bilingually in the Indian languages and in English. In the case of Paipai, the presentation is trilingual—the third language being Spanish. We have attempted to present the book in an attractive and readable format; we have labored over translations to make them as true as possible to the literal text of the native languages, but also to give them something of the same flow and tone of the original performance. In some cases, contributors have added extra devices to preserve aspects of rhythm and intonation. Of course, there is a power in these tales that can never be transmitted through writing or translation. But the Sun Tracks Series has dedicated itself to continued improvement in the presentation of Native American literature and has provided us with the opportunity to attempt to put these Yuman stories and songs into a form that can communicate more of their feeling to readers.

The Yuman communities have always enjoyed the oral literature of their neighbors. Traditionally, there were always people in every community who had learned and could perform the songs and stories of other groups. Thus, by compiling the literature of various communities together, we are doing nothing that is new to Indian communities. And we hope people will enjoy these selections as they enjoyed them in the past—to delight in the retelling of stories they know, and to delight in the novelty of those they have never heard.

The Mojaves
Leanne Hinton

The home range of the Mojaves centered in the lower Colorado River valley and covered an extensive area within the present states of Arizona, California, and Nevada. This tribe has always had a strong sense of nationality, of identity as a unified tribe; therefore, settlements were small and often nonpermanent. Their location along the great Colorado River allowed extensive agriculture both in the days before contact and in the present. They were a large and powerful nation, whose access to water allowed the development of a permanency and high population density not available to the desert and mountain tribes that surrounded them. Their ability to produce an agricultural surplus made them important traders; trading and a sense of adventuresomeness led Mojaves hundreds of miles away on journeys, even as far as the California coast. They also had great military prowess in the old days, with excellent military techniques as well as superior weapons in the shape of long war bows and war clubs. Like other Yumans, the Mojaves had a strong clan system: clans were patrilineal and exogamous, with names referring to animals and natural phenomena. The Mojaves had hereditary chiefs descending in the male line. The chiefs who first confronted the American military men and settlers were remarked on by writers and historians as very strong, wise, and honorable leaders of the people. One chief, Irataba, gained national prominence in the troubled times of the late nineteenth century; he was probably the first Mojave to learn English, and in his own language was an unusually eloquent and persuasive speaker. His speeches were often attended by white men, who found themselves enormously moved by them even though they could not understand the language. Irataba traveled twice to Washington, D.C., where he had audience with President Lincoln, and was shown a review of American military troops (presumably to impress upon him that American military strength was too great to be worth fighting against). Irataba's pro-American stance made him a controversial figure, but Mojaves today view him as figuring among the great leaders of their history.

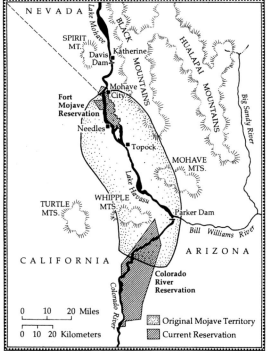

Anthropologists were greatly struck by the highly developed skills of the Mojaves in the oral arts, and much has been written by Kroeber and others on the songs, story-telling arts, and the importance of dreaming to the arts. The Mojaves believe that dreaming is the basis of all learning and experience. As Kroeber says, "Dreams... are the foundation of Mohave life; and dreams throughout are cast in mythological mold. There is no people whose activities are more shaped by this psychic state,... and none whose civilization is so completely, so deliberately, reflected in their myths" (Kroeber, 1953, p. 755). Songs and myths are believed to be given only in dreaming—a person may have heard the songs and stories many times from others, but it is only through dreams that final learning and spiritual authorization of their use takes place.

The Mojaves sing long song series at funerals and other ceremonies; in the late nineteenth and early twentieth century, these songs have spread to neighboring tribes as well, and the Mojave singers are often invited to lead the singing at wakes for members of other tribes. These song series, each of which takes anywhere from one to four full nights to sing, are depictions of sacred myths. Each song represents one point in the myth. The songs themselves are not stories, nor even usually intelligible to the lay listener; they are simply representative of some event, some character, some place, some sound, occurring in the myth.

Some of the short stories given here are from another realm of the rich Mojave cosmology, the Coyote Tales.

The Mojave Alphabet

Vowels

a	*marikan*, 'English'. Like the vowel in English f*a*ther.
aa	*nyahu'aak*, 'marry (of a man)'. Same quality as *a* but longer.
e	*ahwer*, 'fence in'. Like the vowel in English p*e*t or Spanish p*e*so.
ee	*ahwee*, 'smell'. Same quality as *e* but longer.
i	*akwiny*, 'go through, go over'. Like the vowel in p*i*t.
ii	*akwiich*, 'be tatooed'. Like the vowel in f*ee*d.
o	*'ahot*, 'good'. Like the vowel in p*o*ke.
oo	*hool*, 'five cents, a nickel'. Like the vowel in f*oa*l.
u	*hayuny*, 'cricket'. Like the vowel in f*oo*t.
uu	*upuuv*, 'enter (of more than one person)'. Like the vowel in f*oo*d.

Consonants

ch	*chuksa*, 'head'. As in *ch*eck.
d	*iido*, 'eye'. As in *th*ough.
h	*'aha*, 'water'. As in *h*at.
k	*kulho*, 'boat'. As in s*k*in.
kw	*kwiyer*, 'airplane'. As in *qu*it.
ky	*kyaanti*, 'candy'. As in than*k y*ou.
l	*lapalap*, 'flat'. As in *l*amb.
ly	*lyavii*, 'look alike'. As in mi*ll*ion.
m	*machay*, 'hungry'. As in *m*an.
ny	*'anya*, 'sun'. As in ca*ny*on.
p	*pay*, 'all'. As in s*p*ar.
k	*qampanyq*, 'bat'. Like *k* but with tongue farther back; no English equivalent.
qw	*'aqwaq*, 'deer'. Like *kw* but with tongue farther back; no English equivalent.
'	*anya*, 'sun'; *nyahu'aak*, 'marry (of a man).' Like the break in the middle of the English expression *uh-uh* (no).
r	*tharap*, 'five'. Flapped *r* as in Spanish pe*r*o.
s	*siviily*, 'feather'. As in *s*it.
t	*timma*, 'mesquite root'. As in s*t*ir.
th	*thampo*, 'bee'. As in *th*istle.
v	*vatay*, 'big'. As in *v*alue.
w	*iiwa*, 'heart'. As in *w*aste.
y	*iiya*, 'mouth'. As in *y*es.

Mojave Texts

Tharavayew

Nellie Brown, Narrator
Edited by Pamela Munro

"Tharavayew" is the Mojave story of the man in the moon and how he got there. It is a coyote story—Tharavayew is one of Coyote's Mojave names—presented here both in Mojave and in Mrs. Brown's free English translation. "Tharavayew" contains an extended conversation with no indication of change of speaker, a rarity in a Mojave tale. (For comparison, note the occurrence of "he says" in the English version—it takes us some thinking to unscramble all the "he"'s.)

Tharavayew huktharvch, hukthar Tharavayewche thuuvak im.

Ivesk vuuvak pi'pa kwa'atay halyuuvak vuuvakt i uma, "Hee, 'inyeche haly'a huviily 'ichips 'im, 'tahakyev'e," ikm.

Nyaa'iim i'iima pi'panych havuuv'ookt a'iim, "Kamadoomote."

"'Iduutahane 'iyemtahank 'tahakyevtane 'ichipsk imakly 'uupaame!"

"Macham mipuype nyamtakaveekmotm!"

"'Aa, 'iyemke 'ayuu tadiich 'ayuu 'chakama'awe."

Akyook iduum nyayuu apook akyook korly aadosk viidiik im, aadosk viiyamm ivesk viiyemm isaamk vuuv'oochm viidiik ichipspatk iich ichipsk iyem 'asenta havikm uuyoovm uunyaqk chakavar ipooyk.

Pi'panych havuuv'oochk im, "Iyemntike korly anyoompotk," iichm.

Anyoomkum isaamkum halyvuunuuchkte, "Haly'ahly ivak," iichtm 'a'aamm'o. Tamuunaly aados-hayk haly'ahly ivatk ivak.

'Anya vidam viivatk vii'iichtke, Tharavayewch.

There's a man, a coyote, a man, and his name is Tharavayew.

And he goes around bragging all the time, and he says, "You know what, fellows?" he says, "you know what I'm going to do?" he says. "Well, I think I can jump over that moon! I can jump it, and get on the other side."

"I'm afraid you can't," he says; "you'd better get something, so that you'll have something to eat."

"Oh, yes," he says, "I've already had some corn and some beans and some things in my bag," he says.

And he said he was going to jump, so everybody got out there, so he ran and jumped once or twice before he really did, you know, and then he jumped. And he never came back.

And then he still stays in that moon, they tell me. So they call him the man in the moon, Tharavayew.

Going to School for the First Time

Nellie Brown, Narrator
Edited by Pamela Munro

Hayikoly 'ahav 'ahipuktaahank, nyayu 'asuu-
pawa 'emottaahank, marikan chuukwarny 'asentm
'asuupawmotk, 'iiweek 'imuulyny aseechm pay
'asuupawmotk—havnya 'uuvaak. Huchqol nyan-
yaahavkum a'wemka uusma im a'wintm 'avaly
nyicham hayikonych a'wiim. Nyichqathk a'wiim,
'atayemk 'upaka'eechm, nyanyatanyuuchk, nya-
nomakm. Thanya'idiikiki, 'liwanych'alaytaahank.
Manyeechuvikm 'ahotm: 'atuunyuuchke. 'uupava
'iyuuk'iduum, 'ahottaahanke. Nyamathavtm 'iman-
ka ('anyamhanyoony 'iyuunypatka 'a'aamotntk,
'iimiivk vu'uwatka, hachorm 'idotk nyakapilym
'idotk—nyakapilym 'ithava nyany 'avutlyesk,
'amayk 'akach'iim, 'avahinmk thi'iyepmtk—'idotk
'iduum iduum), 'anyahamaruy marikan hani-
dal uu'wiichny nyany nyachamharuychm, 'anyamharuyk vu'uuvaatka. 'Anyamharuyk 'a'aamach
iduukte duukat 'anyamharuyka'eeka vu'uuvaak.
'Uhaymottaahanka'eeth pay 'anyamharuyk 'iduum.
Nyidawn nya'inak 'akalyhoqm makathk 'ichatk
vu' uuvaatk—vi'idiitk 'iduum. Huchgolch vaaduu-
nyapatk mo'wav natumakik upuuk vanyuun-
uuk. Kaaduuch 'ama pithahayk iduum iduume.
Nyaavachkuu'eekum ahwerk a'wiitaahanm—
vu'uunuuka'eek 'iduum. Imakly inakik huchqol
'ama aym; 'inyechvach idoth 'atayemchka chuuh-
wer imakny thu'uutpam—thinyith'iilym, nyi-
nytatavirk, nyanyatselk a'wekum—hav'atadiipk
'iduuchich iduum. Ayim marikanvny 'amasdeetaa-
hanm. Marikan thinya'aakny 'iyuu a'a'taymotntk
mat'ar nya'uwaak, duum *school* nya'ahavtm marikan thinya'aakny 'iyuuk 'iduuke. Kaaduuch 'ahot-
taahanm, do'itpataahanm. Kaaduuchiche marikan 'uhaymotm suupaw pay nyatara'uym, nya-
maayevk iduuntm. Kaaduuchich 'imatichev nyay-
tntk a'wetm—hav'idiitk 'iduum. Nyiwaamtaahan
one word im 'asenta havikm 'asuupawka'eek. Pi'pa
'anawah imuuly pay 'asamodiik ipetm—kaa'epk
vidany aseechuvaa?, 'aly'etk. Mah hav'idiitk 'idoptk
'iduum, 'iduuchm duum. Pi'pa 'ich suupawmot-
taahana 'alyaviik vi'ivak nya'iduuntm.

When I first went to school, not a thing did
I know, I didn't know one word of English, when
my own name was called, I didn't know it—that's
how I was. When it was evening the white lady
told the children to go to sleep and put them to
bed. She called us, we went in to sleep, she covered
us up, and she left us. I was lying there, and I was
sad. It was very nice: I was covered up, I had a bed,
it was very nice. In the morning I got up (I never
had shoes either, I was barefoot, in winter and
in summer-in summer I would break off pieces
of arrowweed, I would step on it, then move on
further—that's how I was), a government shoe was
put on me, and I was wearing shoes. I had never
had a shoe on before, but I was wearing shoes. I
didn't know how to wear shoes at all. When I had
a chance to sit down, I would pull them off and
put them down somewhere—that's how I grew up.
Most of the children were like that too when they
left their families and came to school. Some still
weren't weaned. When the parents had a chance
to come in, they had fenced the place in—that's
how we were. They sat outside and gave milk to
the children; even us, we'd go outside the fence—
they didn't want us to, she'd follow us, she'd beat
us—that's the way we were. We were scared of
every white person. When I was outside I didn't
see many white women, but at school I saw white
women. Some were real nice, some I really liked.
Even though they knew I couldn't talk English,
they took care of me, most of them were like that.
Some gave me medicine—that's how I was. At last
I learned one or two words. Sometimes I even
forgot my girlfriend's name—"now how did they
call her?" I thought. I was just like that, I was. I was
acting like someone who didn't know anything.

Coyote and Crane

Robert S. Martin, Narrator
Transcribed by Judith Crawford

Nyakw'ech 'aha kwa'uurly ivak.

'Achii satok istuum.

'Achiihaan a'wetk 'achii chahnap a'wetk istuum.

Ithook vuwaam isamk.

Hukthar chudoorm, iyuuk thuwaak.

"Kaa'we ke'eeyk a'wim va?" im.

Thinyuwaak, "tha'a'wetpat'e, 'inyech!" etk.

Thinyuwaak, iyemk 'a'iis takwerakwerk, ta'akyuulyk
    ta'ahaank uunuuk aaviirk.

Iyemk 'ahpily iyaak kamim, iihunyk tahpilym
    uunuuk nyaaviirk.

Kor 'aha kwa'uurly ivak, uudoorm vivak.

'Achii chaam iyuuk vivake.

"Achii inyto'och idotm iyuuk.

"Humer valytaaytaahaanch vidiit 'iyuuk 'a'wiis,
    duum 'ithootahaank 'atootahaank," etk,
    vivak iduum.

'Achiich viyaam nomaktk, vivakete, 'achiihaan
    kwavalyteetahaan vidiikum, iyuukum,
    "nyath ta'ahaan 'a'wiith," etk.

Kor uusaaptk, nyasachooqm, 'achiihaanch ithpeertk
    iduum.

Kor idaawptk aawemk a'wim.

'Ahpily ulhuyulhuymotm.

Hamahak aawemm, 'ahaly ipuyk.

Haly'anyoomtk, 'anyook uuwaalymotm.

Kor nyamaamk.

Crane sat on the river bank.

He speared fish with his beak and got them.

He got salmon and humpback fish.

He [Coyote] looked at him eating [fish], walking
    back and forth.

Coyote was spying on him and he saw him as he
    moved about there.

"How did he do it, poor thing?" he said.

As he was walking back and forth there, he said, "I
    can do that too!"

Then he walked around there, he went and
    sharpened a screwbean [branch], making it
    really long.

He went and fetched pitch and brought it back, and
    stuck it [screwbean branch] on his nose.

Now he sat on the river bank, waiting here.

He saw a lot of fish [go by] as he sat here.

He saw little fish [go by].

"Later I will see a very big one come this way and I
    will do [spear] it, then I'll really eat and be
    very full," he said, as he sat here.

A fish went by him and he let it go, and as he sat

here, a very big salmon came toward him,
    and he saw it, saying, "That's the one I'm
    going to get!"

By and by he speared it, and after he speared it [a
    second time], the salmon was too strong.

Then it took him.

He could not loosen the pitch [from his nose].

It took him down, and he drowned.

He disappeared, was gone, and never showed up
    any more.

Now that's all.

A Story From The Stones

by Luke Johnson

Preface

This story is about a couple from two different cultures who met around 1840 when there was a great migration to the west by easterners. The river crossings were at Yuma to the south, La Paz near Blyth, Parker and Needles to the north. This is a fictional romantic story where the couple's lives intertwined around the places, legends and stories of the Mojave People. Those legends invariably included rocks and stones. This tale tells how the *stories found in the stones* at Needles and Parker became guiding forces in the couple's lives. The following are the main characters of the story.

Hom-Hee-Vouch–Known as Hom who was born into the Oach Clan, the "Above the Earth Clan" where the birds fly. Hom chose the two tail feathers of the sparrow tail bird or two tassels hanging from his headband as his sign. Hom meets Dawn and becomes a prince among the Mojaves.

Marie Dawn–The Macav (Mojave) called her Dawn, like the morning sun. She and her family were traveling from Kentucky to California, crossing the great river at Parker where her parents were lost to the river. Hom's uncle and aunt adopted Dawn and it is here the two meet.

Homoak–Meaning the "third". This was their first son.

Maya–Their second child was a daughter who was lost to the pony soldier plague.

Nunie–Their third child, a daughter.

Katala–Selected Homoak at the spring maturity ceremony as her mate and lifetime companion.

The Land of Hom

The Northern band of Mojaves still lives in the Great River Basin of Needles. Their territory is in the Tri-State area. This is where Hom was born and where the great stone Maze is located on the high ground.

The Southern band of Mojaves still lives in the Great River Basin at Parker. This is where Hom meets Dawn and where the spring ceremony or maturity dance around the giant was held at the high ground.

From their first encounter with the white man in 1776 until the 1850's there were explorers and trappers who came to the land of Pipa-Aha-Macav. By the 1840's there began a great migration west through the land and the two cultures began to mix. Like the Bible with all its stories about morals that Father Francisco Garces brought to the People, so too, the Macav had stories and legends with values to guide their lives. The Sumach-a'hot Clan of the People had the ability to receive and interpret dreams or to place stories into the stones. This is a story about such a family that had the Sumach-a'hot ability and how the stones showed them the way.

It was noon and Hom-oseth, a young warrior of the Pipa-Aha-Macav, was at the river gorge where the rock formations are like "needles" pointing to the sky; when around the river bend came a strange watercraft. He had never seen a vessel such as this nor the fair white skin of the strangely dressed people with multicolored eyes. Hom-oseth saw them pointing at him and speaking in a strange tongue. He immediately ran through the brush along side the river towards the nearest settlement of the southern Macav the "Kavi-lythum" pausing silently to observe the strange people who had put ashore. A Sumach-a-hot medicine man in the past had given him his river stone that he now clutched in his hand and the Sumach-a-hot medicine man whispered in his ear, "Come to me." Excitedly Hom-oseth found the medicine man and told him of the strange people. The medicine man told Hom-oseth that Mata-vilya, the Great Spirit, had foretold the coming of the "white man", the Hy-go, and the time was finally here. "My son, go to the village of Hutto-pah in the central valley and tell the chief. Together we will meet our visitors." The Chief came and was in council with the elders of the village, when the villagers excitedly reported the "Hy-gos" were here in the village.

Hom-oseth, with the chief and Elders, approached the Hy-go. Hom-oseth observed a Pipa (Quechan) from the south was with the Hy-gos and the Pipa spoke the Macav language. The leader of the Hy-go spoke and the Pipa said, "What are you people called?" The chief spoke gesturing, "We are the Pipa-Aha-Macav, the People who live along the water. We have lived in this river valley from time immemorial and who are you?" Interpreting for the Hy-go, the Pipa spoke, "We are from beyond the great ocean to the east, we call ourselves—'Spanish'."

For the Europeans this was a time of invention, adventure and exploration. Adventurers like Christopher Columbus happened on the Americas looking for the East Indies in 1492. Up until now the Europeans had ventured into Central and South America and now turned their attention to exploring western North America. It was the practice of the Macav when strangers arrived in peace to invite them to eat, so the Chief said, "Come, let us eat." There was an exchange of gifts and Hom-oseth looked on with interest at the Hy-gos who were making strange marks in what the Pipa said was a book. "By this way the Hy-go tells his story over and over again. His eyes can read the written language." Hom-oseth asked to look at the book and asked, "What does this speak?" After the Hy-go read the words the Pipa said, "In this summer in the year of our Lord 1776, we have found the land of the Giants!" *Father Francisco Garces—*

So began the history of the Pipa-Aha-Macav and the Hy-go.

The Pipa-Aha-Macav (The People who live along the water) have lived on the lower Colorado River basin from time immemorial. The Great Spirit Mata-vilya created the People and the river basin with all the animals and vegetation for their use. The People respected their place on the earth, prospering and becoming like the sand on the river beach. They numbered some six thousand at the time of this story. The People were a peaceful tribe, intermingling with other people of the area and serving as messengers between the peoples. The river basin was the center of the earth and from it the trails went to the four directions of the earth. The trail that went west to the great sea became known as the Mojave Trail. Later in time many peoples would use this trail in their migration west. It was here in this river basin that the People would ferry all other peoples across the great river for it was a natural crossing. The crossing was on the southern end of the basin where the river narrowed and wound through rock canyons, where the mountains were shaped as "needles" pointing towards the sky and even to this day this area is called "The Needles." In their language the People knew the crossing as 'tu-pock' meaning to bridge or cross. It is here that the People came to know others coming from every part of the earth. It is here that this *Story from the Stones* begins.

With the spring came the untamed raging water each year and the People moved to the high ground to the southwest of the basin. Hom-Mata-Hee-Vouch and Got-su, grandfather and grandmother of little Hom-Hee-Vouch, arrived at the spring campsite. Hom looked forward to this time of playing with his cousins and friends. At this spring campsite there was a great stone maze that had existed for hundreds of years and all the children would play there, in and out, hide and seek! It was a great life, with the freedom to experience life, make new friends, and reestablish old friendships.

When the great river subsided the People would return to the river basin. For Hom this too was a great time because grandfather would take Hom to the river to see what strange rocks and stones the river brought that year. Grandfather would say, "Son, there is life in the stones and some of them came from faraway places and from strange peoples. Look at this one, see how round and smooth it is? A boy like you picked it up one day and kept it for awhile in his medicine pouch. He observed the stone with all its marking that told its story. The stone absorbed his spirit and now holds the story of his life. Finally he decided to give it back to Mother Earth, so he threw it back into the river watching it skip, skip, skip until it sank. Here, put it to your ear and listen carefully. Maybe it might tell you the boy's story." I would listen intently and sometimes I swear I could hear his voice, "Hom, listen to my story!"—Sometimes I would take the stone to the maze and find a secluded spot and hold the stone to my ear and think about the boy who owned this stone and would imagine what his life was like. Grandfather had started the family tradition of being "Sumach-a'hot" (a gifted one) by passing it on to little Hom.

One day as grandfather and I walked along the river, I saw a bright glint of light coming from a stone. I ran to it and picked it up shouting, "Grandfather, grandfather, what is it?" My grandfather said, "Son, today Mata-vilya has smiled on you, for he has brought you a "havasu-avi", a water blue stone. Look at it. It is a crystal clear stone; there are no markings on it. This stone has no story to tell. Such a stone was made for the owner to make his own marks in order to tell the stone his story. Make your marks full of meaning and may your life be as beautiful as this stone!" I took the stone and placed it in my medicine pouch next to my heart so it would capture my deepest thoughts. Sometimes I would sit in the maze while others played and they would call to me, "Hom, come and play with us!" "In a minute, in a minute," I would say. I was talking to my stone!

As time passed by my grandfather taught me the ways of the People: planting and harvesting, the making of tools, hunting animals for food and skins for clothing. From the gourd we made water caskets. We took the skin from the hind leg of the rabbit and made our medicine pouch and this now holds my havasu-avi, my river stone. From the skins we made strapping to hold our homes together and from the mesquite tree we fashioned our war club. This was the learning time in my life.

Once my grandfather took me to the Land of the Walapais, our cousins near the south end of the Grand Canyon. As we stood at the canyon's edge, grandfather said, "See the layers of Mother Earth. Today we are standing on her present layer. The story of her life is in the *layers of stone*. Mother Earth can look back on her life and see the subtle changes like that one over there and we can see the violent ones too like that lava layer there. My life has many layers that my mind often reflects back on, the peaceful ones and the ones that changed my life. Like Mother Earth we all have to accept change. Sometimes we plan for it; sometimes it changes us violently. Think about this stone canyon as changes that happen in your life. Recognize the change and act wisely." My young mind was racing to keep up with grandfather and what he was teaching me. Grandfather sensed my internal questioning and added, "Think of the layers you have experienced already. Your early days in your life have been formative years, listening, learning, and understanding the People's way. These are the thick layers of stone you will come to rely on for the rest of your life. Your lava layer was when you lost your parents to the river." Yes, I could see what grandfather was teaching.

I became aware of the changes happening in my life just like the layered stone canyon that tells Mother Earth of her history. My next layer of change came when I went through the spring ceremony where the young men were initiated into manhood by dancing around Goth, the giant slain by my peers hundreds of years ago. This was a maturity dance where boys became men and it was my turn to dance. So I took my stone and wondered what my life would be like as a man— who would I be, what would I be? I was born into the 'Oach Clan' the 'above the earth clan" where the birds have freedom from the constraints of the earth. It is the Chieftain Clan. Could I prove myself to be a prince, an elder, or a chief such as Chief Hom'o'she a' hot someday?

For now I chose the sparrow-tail bird and his two tail feathers hanging from the back of my head as my sign and everyone would know I was a free spirit like the sparrow-tail bird soaring to great heights in my thoughts and mind, planning and exploring life itself. I clutched my stone speaking to it saying, "Remember me in these days of my life and what I plan to do as a man." When my stone listened it would send a receptive message with a cool sensation where it was touching my body. There, I feel it. There was a cool refreshing feeling over my heart!

We are runners, messengers! To the four directions of the earth. It was summer and there were many people from the east needing to cross the great river and I was doing my part with the men. My grandfather came to me and asked:

"Son, the elders have asked for you to take a message to the family at the south river crossing."

"I will go," I responded.

"Good, I knew you would. Come, let us go to the river and make preparation."

As we walked to the river, my grandfather told me the story of the runners and how they would select a perfect river stone to place under their tongue as they ran across the desert. The stone would sustain them and they would not get thirsty. Then he said:

"You will need this stone. When you go past the place where the buzzards roost, they will look down on you to see how thirsty you are. Spit on the ground and show them you have a river stone, that you are fine, that you have a message, and that you are Aha-macav! You are a runner! They will leave you alone."

My grandfather always had a story to tell and in my minds eye, I could see those buzzards looking down at me from their rocky perch!

I was to leave with the setting sun; the best time to run across the desert was in the coolness of the night. The family to the south was about sixty miles as the Hy-go-wee (white people) would say. This was the southern band of the Pipa-Aha-Macav and there were about six thousand people who lived there.

This was also a natural river crossing. The moon was full, lighting the way for me and I could see the mountains in the distance. Grandfather said not to concentrate on them for vast distances can become discouraging; instead, "concentrate on each step you take, and choose your path wisely." Then he would relate it to life itself. My grandfather always had sayings about life. About half way through the canyon where the buzzards roost, I saw no buzzards. They were all asleep and not one perched his head up to see who was going by. In my mind I uttered this thought:

"I am Hom. Mata-vilya has blessed me as the sparrow tail. I too can glide by as a buzzard—unheard!"

As I approached the southern crossing (now known as Parker), the trail took me by a mound of rocks and stones purposefully placed there. I stopped and looked at this strange stone mound and wondered as to its purpose. I picked up a stone and immediately felt energy from the person who placed the stone there. I knew that she was in a great need of help! I could feel her urgency

in the stone! How could this stone be telling me this story? What is the meaning of this? I uttered a prayer to Mata-vilya:

"Oh Great Spirit, have you brought me a special message?"

As I meditated on this strange happening I was also rubbing my river stone and it came to me:

"This is the land of my uncle. He is a Sumach-a'hot, a gifted one. He would know of this mound of stones and maybe the meaning of the *story from this stone* that is speaking to me."

I looked to the north where the Great Spirit lives and felt my river stone and it was—Cool! Cool! Cool!

The sun was just coming up over Black Mountain; the sky was in hues of blues, reds, and yellows. The river was a silver path coming out of the canyon and broadening out into a large lake. I could smell all the life that lived on the river. I had the feeling of being home, as I observed the land of my uncle. I arrived at the campsite and the men were already ferrying the easterners across the river.

My aunt Meck-a-tha greeted me with open arms saying:

"Hom, how much you have grown, you are a very handsome young man. You look more and more like your father. Come and eat!"

I sat down to eat a dish of mesquite beans made into a mush and wild melon. I could feel my energy returning. I watched as my aunt scurried around, laughing and joking the way Macav ladies do. I clutched my stone, and whispered:

"How much I treasure my aunt and uncle. They are just like the parents I lost to the river."

"It's a natural thing," my grandfather would say, "to yearn for your parents, so we as your family are your parents now."

My stone felt cool. I interrupted my thoughts and asked my aunt:

"Auntie, when is uncle coming home?"

"He'll be home in a while."

"OK, I'll talk to him then. Wake me when he gets home."

As I drifted to sleep I thought of my run through the desert night, the buzzards roost and the stone mound. What does this mean? Why do I feel the owner of the stone is in urgent need of help? How could she speak to me *from the stone*?

As I drifted off to sleep I was thinking of how it would be nice to be Sumach-ahot, a gifted one and to know the meaning of the stone mound. I started to dream with the word---Sumach! Sumach! Sumach! Sumach! echoing on my lips!

She was gently caressing my hair saying: "Wake up son"---startled I sat up thinking it was my mother! "Your uncle is home and hungry. Come and have some wild tea with him."

My uncle was a tall noble man. He was an Oach and an elder and some day he would be chief over this band of southern Macav. I gave him the message:

"Thank you son, for making the trip."

We began to talk about the family to the north and he shared family news here at the southern crossing. I was thinking as he spoke on how the older men chased the children away as they talked about the families, and now he shares it with me. I am accepted as a man now. I clutched my stone and it was cool! The river was especially troublesome this year.

"It is already summer and we have not returned to our summer homes," uncle said, "but that doesn't stop the Hy-go-wee. They just keep coming."

"Uncle," I began, "as I approached the southern camp this morning, I came upon a mound of rocks and stones which caused me to pause and stop. I picked up a stone and I felt an urgent message in the stone. It spoke of hardship, sorrow and despair. How is it this stone from this mound can speak to me?"

My uncle began to tell me the story of the ancient ones and how they would place a stone on the mound telling their story as to why they passed by this way. It has become known as the *story mound*. Some of the stones have forgotten their story: they were never touched to tell their story. Sometimes easterners placed a stone there but there was no story in their stones because their spirit is a different belief.

"Son, sometimes the Great Spirit reaches out and touches an Easterner and gives that person the understanding of the People's way. I would say the stone you touched was an Easterner's stone because the People only left story stones that would build up the spirit of the next traveler. Even if it were a sad story, he would leave the story in a manner that would benefit the next traveler. Son, there are thousands of stones in the story mound, thousands of stories to be told and when a stone speaks we learn from it."

We talked at length about the story mound and my uncle told me some of the stories he knew:

"And who are the ones that can listen and talk to the stones?" uncle asked.

"The Sumach-ahot, the gifted ones," I answered.

"Yes, as you know some of the Sumach-Ahot have the gift of dreaming dreams and interpreting dreams and with our family it is knowing *stories from the stones*, speaking to and reading the stones."

Uncle asked, "Do you have a river stone for yourself?"

"Yes," and I showed him my havasu-avi that I found with grandfather, sharing the meaning of this special stone as told by grandfather.

"Grandfather has showed you well. You are a seer and a hearer for the People. The Great Spirit has given you a great gift. I can listen to my own stone and sometimes the stones of others. For you, you can hear the voice and the calling of others from the stones. Son, the Great Spirit has made you Sumach-Ahot! Someone has called out to you from the story mound and I think I know who it is."

"Old Lady!" This is how my uncle addresses my auntie, it is the People's way and there is no disrespect in it, "go get Dawn." Her name was Marie Dawn and the Macav have few R's in their language and could not say her name Marie so they called her "En-likee" meaning dawn. For this story we will call her Dawn. Dawn. I had never heard a Macav called by this name before. I heard my auntie and Dawn approaching, laughing and joking the way Macav ladies do and I was thinking that this southern family names their people very differently. "Uncle, how do you say her name?" "Dawn." As they met us uncle did the introducing. It is the way of the Macav.

"Dawn, this is my son Hom. Hom this is Dawn, she is from the east."

"Hey, Gootch Kamathu?" (A greeting such

as hello, welcome, how are you)

I reeled back in astonishment as Dawn extended her hand to mine and as she touched my hand my stone turned cool! I looked at my uncle in bewilderment. She was Hy-go-wee, a white person, and she could speak the People's tongue. How is it she could turn my stone cool? Many thoughts were racing through my mind. She was tall and of fair complexion. Her shoulders were narrow and she had a small waist. Her hair was reddish auburn and her eyes were circles of green and blue. As I gazed into her eyes, they seemed more of a blue hue but when she turned to talk to my auntie her eyes were green. When she turned back and looked at me, there they were blue/green again. What sort of person can change the color of their eyes?

She had a soft color to her skin that tanned to the sun. She was the most beautiful woman I had ever seen. My uncle began telling her story —About how she lost her parents to the river last season and she had been living with the family ever since. My aunt and uncle had become her caretakers; it is the Macav way. Dawn had learned the Macav way pretty good. Some things my uncle said she'd question, and through elaborate gesturing he would try to explain the Macav word or meaning. On one occasion I just blurted out in the Hy-go-wee tongue what the meaning was. Everyone's focus was now on me, especially my aunt and uncle.

"How is it you know the Hy-go-wee words?" my uncle said.

"I learned it from the easterners who were crossing the river."

After that Dawn and I began a fast conversation in a combination of Macav and Hy-go-wee. The heads of my aunt and uncle were just going back and forth and when we realized it we all started laughing. We talked all night. Now that I had met Dawn, I wanted to know more about her *story from the stones* that I had touched at the story mound. So I asked my uncle if I could stay with the family for a while. As I drifted to sleep, my mind kept echoing over and over again, I have to know this Dawn! Dawn! Dawn! Dawn!

So our journey in life began. Yes, grandfather was right; there came a new layer in my life, a change! One day Dawn asked me in the Macav tongue:

"Would you like to rub faces with me?"

The People had a saying that you can only get to know another person by rubbing faces, that is, by talking in depth about your life, and your dreams about life's meaning to which I answered, "Yes!" We found the best place to talk was along the riverbank and soon our conversation turned towards the river stones. Dawn asked,

"Uncle says that all the members of the clan have chosen a stone from the river for their own to listen and talk to and that I should find one for myself and to this stone I could tell what's in my heart. Do you have such a stone?"

"Yes"

"Can I see it?"

"Yes, here it is in my medicine pouch next to my heart."

I took my stone out and as she gazed at it her eyes sparkled green and she said:

"Uncle told me this is a very rare 'havasu-avi', a water blue stone. Look at what I found and chose as my river stone."

Out of her pouch she dropped into my hand a 'havasu-avi', a water blue river stone, just like mine! Her stone turned cool in my hand! She spoke of her origin saying,

"I am from a land we call Kentucky. (Hom had a difficult time saying Kentucky), and we find these stones there. We call them aqua marine stones. Hom, aqua means water in your tongue and marine is a water blue color. It has always been my favorite stone. It makes my hand cool and I was surprised to find one here in your river.

"My grandfather says the river brings all sorts of stones along with stories but for some stones like our havasu-avis, you have to make the story," Hom said

"Yes, I believe what your grandfather said. You see, I cried out to my stone for my lost family. I even tried to place it on the story mound but it said no, for me to choose another stone. So I chose another stone and placed my story there on the story mound. I could have returned to Kentucky but the stone would stop me. I would wonder why? Now I know, the story mound was waiting for you to find me. Hom, I love your family. They treat me as one of their own. My spirit is the same as you and your family's spirit. What tells me this is your gift of hearing the stones speak! You are Sumach-ahot! Hom, it was you who heard me cry out for an answer this summer. I will never forget how our stones brought us together!"

So began the companionship of Dawn and Hom. Together, they began to explore their "Stories from the Stones."

Summer grew old and finally uncle said the family could return to their ancestral home in the river valley. It had been the longest stay on the high ground the people could remember. Uncle said, "Mother Earth has taken extra time to cleanse the land herself this season, she has removed all the salt, the water will be sweet for us." For Dawn this was a new experience and she busied herself in helping the ladies pack and we started moving onto the eastern side of the river valley. Uncle said,

"Look, the river is here, last season it was way over there. We will make camp here. The river has left good soil for planting the winter squash." (The river cut a new channel every year.)

It was the custom of the People to let the children play. They had only one playtime in their life and they were left to explore it; there was plenty of time for chores later. So the women began setting up camp, our new home. Some of the men brought mesquite or cottonwood logs for the structural lumber of the huts. The young men brought willow and arrow weed for roof hatching or wall reinforcement and others located mud clay that was used for brick or wall plaster. Huts were made to keep out the cold. Most winters were mild. Powdery frost fell on the lower mountain ranges. It was known to snow in the valley one time in the memory of the People. For now, opened walled summer sheds were made. The families did the work collectively and it was here under the shed that the summer evenings were spent telling the stories of the ancient ones and more recent stories too.

One evening my uncle said:

"Dawn, would you like to tell us a story?"

Dawn looked at me, her eyes sparking green in the night camp fire. I gave her a nod and in the People's tongue she began. Even the children stopped playing to listen.

"My name is Brigitte. The People call me "Enlikee", Dawn, and I have become a Macav. I was once Hy-go-wee who came from a land called Kentucky. Like Hom, I have lost my parents to the river. Like Hom, Mata-vilya has given me the havasu-avi, the water blue stone, as my sign and like Hom, today you are my family!"

There was commotion among the family with soft whispering along with "ahh", an affirmative recognition that she was a Macav as she now claimed. I clutched my stone and it was cool. I looked at her and she was holding her stone too. She winked at me smiling and her eyes seemed green now. "Aha", I thought to myself, "That's it. When Dawn is happiest and at peace, after she has soared like the sparrow tail bird in her deepest thoughts, and has been given the sign by the Great Spirit, it shows in the green hue in her eyes! "

The family began to ask questions:

"Tell us, what sort of mud huts you make there? Do you have a river there?"

The questions were many and Dawn answered them one by one in a manner with respect to gender in which they were asked. Truly she had learned the way of the Macav. She had found peace. The stone she placed on the story mound has forgotten its story; she found a new story of life with the family of Hom. Finally uncle asked this question:

"To the south where the great river enters the sea, the Quechan (Yuma) runners have told that the pony soldiers have built a fort there (1851) and the iron horse is coming. Do you know of this?"

"In the land where I come from the pony soldiers and the iron horse are everywhere," Dawn said.

"Do you think they will come here?" uncle asked.

"Yes, this is a natural river crossing, they will build a 'tupock' and a fort here," advised Dawn.

"From time immemorial all the people have crossed the river here. The river belongs to all the People as it flows through all the people's lands. They have always crossed at the 'islands' in peace." Uncle explained.

Uncle looked at his people and felt their peace and he wondered if peace would continue when the pony soldiers came. He saw the children had fallen asleep so he said:

"We will continue this story again,"—"ahh, ahh"—the family agreed!"

As the next season approached Hom and Dawn would take long walks especially after the evening meal. It was a good time for body and spirit. One evening Hom said:

"Come and take a walk with me and observe the new moon. It is a good time to start a new way of life; then your spirit is in harmony with the universe."

"Yes, I will walk with you."

Dawn's heart reached out to Hom from the first day she met him. She sensed this when her stone turned cool. She asked Auntie about the family way of really walking with Hom. Auntie said, "It is the custom of the People for the young girls to select a prospective mate when the young men dance around Goth showing the family they are men and accept responsibility to the family. Hom came from the northern family to dance here with his family. Dawn, you should have seen him, he was a stellar sight among all the young men." Dawn could see Hom in her mind dancing the maturity dance. "I think Mata-vilya blinded all the girls; they did not see Hom. He (Auntie pointing to the sky) had other plans for him. Since your eyes are open to Hom and you are the one that has seen him, you can make your selection known to the family of elders the next time they gather." Hom was walking and talking about the family but Dawn's heart and mind was on what auntie had said. She clutched her stone and made a wish—

"Yes Hom, I want to walk with you"—her stone was cool in her hand and she blurted out into his conversation—"I can't wait until the next family meeting!" "What?"

"Oh, I mean I just want to finish my story."

"And what a story! Did you see the family? How can you top that?"

She whispered to her stone, "Just Wait! Wait! Wait! Wait!"

A few days later after the evening meal, the Elders came over to our summer shed and began talking about news brought by messengers from all over. Dawn squeezed her stone and wondered if she would have the opportunity to make her selection known at this time. Her stone turned cool. Uncle rose and said:

"There was a messenger from the east, and he says the pony soldiers and the iron horse are advancing west. It is their plan to cross the river to the south at the Quechans and with Hom's family to the north. There is talk they will cross here at our river valley. Brothers, you all know Dawn, 'Ahh, Ahh'! she lived in the east. Tell us child, what was it like to live with the pony soldiers? Did the people fight with the pony soldiers where you come from?"

In the custom of the People she made a gesture with her right hand extended from her heart to the Elders:

"Yes, the People fought the pony soldiers; the People were very brave but they could not fight against the pony soldiers' diseases. They became sick and died. Now they are prisoners in a faraway land. Be careful! Do not touch the pony soldiers."

Uncle said:

"When the pony soldiers come they will think we took you from your people." "No uncle, I will tell them what happened to my family and that you took me into your family and I belong to this family."

"I am told that the pony soldiers have skins that describe what belongs to them, and that you must have this skin of ownership. We have no skin that says you belong to us."

Standing up now, Dawn again gestures with respect to the Elders and says:

"We, the People, have the right of selection of our mate handed down through the generations at the spring maturity dance around Goth by all the eligible young men. Hom danced with his family around Goth and he was passed over. No one selected him and now, before my whole family I make known my selection of Hom to be my mate in life, to be my protector, to be the father of my children, the man I wish to belong to. This will be my skin to show I belong to this family."

There was utter silence—. Finally an Elder spoke questioning:

"Hom comes from the northern family and is a visitor here. He will be returning to his family soon."

Dawn spoke:

"Hom's grandfather is Hom-Mata-Hee-

Vouch and father to you, uncle."

Gesturing to uncle, Dawn spoke:

"I ask you Uncle, you are Hom's father now, and I respectfully ask you and my Elders for this selection right now. When Hom returns north I will go with him."

Another Elder spoke and said:

"Your children will have no clan."

Uncle rose and said:

"The children will get their clan from Hom the father as we all have received our clan from our fathers and they will have full rights to the clan."

There began an excited discussion about this matter by all.

Hom rose and spoke:

"My family, I exercise my right to speak to the Clan. I too have a say in this matter and I accept Dawn's selection of me as her mate. I was not spoken for at the spring ceremony five stones ago and Dawn and I are free spirits as the sparrow tail bird. Together we have soared to lofty heights in mind and thought. Truly I believe the Great Spirit has brought us together for he has given to both of us the water blue stones as our river stones! They were crystal clear when we found them and the only markings are the marks we have put there. Mata-vilya has given us a mandate to create a new life, to show us a new way."

Some of the women said:

"Let us see the stones."

Hom and Dawn gave up their stones to verbal 'ohhs and ahhs'. Many of the women had never seen such stones. Another spoke saying:

"Our stones speak to us, how does yours?"

Dawn spoke:

"My stone, when it hears favorably sends a message with a cool touch."

Immediately the woman holding the stone screamed in delight!

"It just turned cool!"

She gave it to another, and she too acknowledged the coolness. Everyone wanted to touch the stones and for many this was the first time a stone had spoken to them. The women looked at the Elders and spoke:

"Well, what are you going to do about this?"

The Elders looked at each other and spoke:

"We approve of course!"

Dawn's mind was blur thinking about the past two years and it seemed like a lifetime— seeing the stones in Kentucky, moving west, experiencing tragedy, somehow the river bringing the water blue stones to each of them, finding a new family and finding Hom! At last! Hom and Dawn knew each other and they were one. Hom became the caretaker of Dawn! As they drifted to sleep in each others arms, they said a prayer together—Mata-vilya, Thank you! Thank you! Thank you! Thank you!

This is the beginning of their life together. Like the canyon Hom saw as a child, there was a new layer starting in their life. The 'Stories from the Stones' continues concerning their joy and sorrows, their children, Hom becoming a prince, the wars with the pony soldiers—but that's another story!

It was towards the end of summer Hom and Dawn explored most of the river valley with Hom carefully telling the stories of his People. Their imagination carried them away so that they could experience the stories as if they were inside them. One evening Dawn said:

"Hom you have spoken about the 'Islands of Refuge' but we have never been there. Tell me a story about the islands."

Hom thought a minute and in his story fashion he began:

"There was a couple from an eastern tribe sent on a quest by their medicine man to go west to the great sea and return with washed sand from the beach which was to be used in a ceremony. Their journey would take them through this land where they were to cross the great river. In their land they had no such river as this. As they approached it they were in awe of the beauty of the gorge the river had cut through the colorful rock formations. They had no such rocks where they came from. This rock was as if Mother Earth belched it out in a heat of anger. The vegetation was spiny unlike the leafy trees of the homeland. This was all new. And the great river! Never had they seen so much water before."

They camped on the eastern side of the river and were told the best route to cross the river was at the "Islands of Refuge'. Here the river spread out several miles wide and would be at best waist deep and they would find the 'Islands of Refuge' halfway across the river. The islands were a high ground area that was always above the high water season and this is where all the people would camp in safety. The couple started their journey across the river at dawn, and were told it would take the better part of the day to reach the islands. They found the river shallow and meandering through the willow reed, mesquite and cotton wood trees. They saw all kinds of fish they had never seen before and in abundance was the humpback catfish (now extinct). They met other tribes headed east and would pause and share information on the best crossing areas. By late afternoon they reached the islands, which were great sand dunes covered by willow and sand grass on the surface.

There they met many peoples from strange places and speaking in many tongues. All the People believed they came from one common ancestry and held the common belief of a universal presence. They felt that they were stewards of the environment and which therefore bound them into a common brotherhood relationship. It was easy to speak the universal language of the hands. Sometimes there was a difference among the People and there were wars but here at the island, it was forbidden. There was a spirit of universal peace, People helping People. That night the People gathered and told their stories. One elder told of seeing the 'white man'! No one else other than this elder had seen a white man. The couple was shy and just listened and later the woman began poking her mate in the ribs indicating 'let's go to bed'. That night there was a tremendous roar coming from a distance, it was the river. A great flood unexpectedly came and the People were in fear for their safety,. but the islands held together. From time immemorial, these islands were indeed 'Islands of Refuge'; the People were safe! The People had to stay on the islands for several weeks waiting for the river to subside enough to begin crossing again. The couple came to the west side of the river where the young men danced around Goth at the spring maturity dance—but that's another story."

Dawn and Hom decided to go to see the 'Islands of Refuge' and she found that the islands were just as Hom described in his story. There were all kinds of people there, even the Hy-go-wees. Dawn bustled around talking to everyone with her hands. She talked to the Hy-go-wees from the east and they invited her to go west with them. She declined for in her mind she thought:

"I have no desire to go, I am a Macav and I
live here with my family. Thank you Mata-
vilya for you have given me refuge with the
People."

As they lay there that night they talked about all the people they met that day and how right their feeling of a universal oneness was among the peoples. Finally Hom said,

"Tomorrow we will cross to the west and
I will show you where the young men
do their spring dance of manhood and
maturity, where the giant Goth sleeps.
Then we will go to see my grandfather."

Dawn held Hom dearly and speaking to herself these words:

"Yes, we are finally going home and we
will see grandmother and grandfather."

Early the next day they met another couple and together they began crossing the great river to the west. Hom invited the couple to stay another night on the hill where Goth sleeps and there he told the story of a long time past when giants walked the earth and they were eating the People. The People were in great fear and the warriors would track Goth down and try to kill him without success. It was in the springtime of the year when the young men among the tribe went to the medicine man and asked how they could kill the giant. The medicine man told them that when Goth ate he would become sleepy and this would be the time to kill him.

"The reason why the men cannot kill Goth is
a heart matter; his heart is in his left knee!"

With this information the young men began looking for Goth and found him south of where he now sleeps. There he was lying on his back sound asleep.

The young men saw that his left knee was swollen; it was larger than the right knee, and it was pulsating! "Goth's heart was in his left knee!" Dawn and the couple's minds were caught up in the story. Hom continued:

"They crept up on Goth and in unison they
speared his left knee! In great pain and

bleeding, Goth rose up and began chasing the young men north and this is where he fell, never to eat the People again. See the red sand over there? His blood still stains the earth."

All the People heard the young men's story and gathered to look at the giant and in time the earth absorbed his body and left this impression of him we see to this day. The medicine men and the elders gathered and decided that the People would forevermore remember and celebrate the young men and the great deed they performed for the People.

So an annual celebration began based on these events. It would be in the springtime when the People left the flooded river valley and camped here at this high ground hill. The slaying of the giant occurred on the day the new moon was chasing the star (Venus). Now would be the time for initiating the young men into manhood by their dancing around Goth, retelling the story of the young men killing the giant with all the young girls giggling, laughing and pointing. It was the time for the young women to select their future mates. Hom said:

"See the circle they have etched into the ground? I too danced here five seasons ago."
"Did Dawn select you here at the dance?" asked the couple.

Dawn and Hom shared their stories from the stones, their havasu-avi stones and how Dawn selected Hom before the elders. Now Hom said:

"Tomorrow Dawn and I will be leaving you. We are to journey to the north to the Land of Hom to see my grandfather, Hom-Mata-Hee-Vouch. We will stop at the story mound to place a stone there telling all the People of our meeting you and we will say a blessing for you and your journey. Where you are going to the west there is another story mound. Find a stone and tell it your story and place it on the story mound. Come with us to the river and I will show you how to select a river stone, a story stone. Place this river stone under your tongue and as you cross the desert you will not get thirsty. The stone will absorb your thoughts, so talk to it, tell it your story."

The next day the couples parted and Dawn and Hom began their journey north to the Land of Hom. They reached the story mound by midday and found the stone Dawn had placed there last year. Together Dawn and Hom placed their hands on the stone and Dawn spoke to Mata-vilya saying—

"Thank you, Mata-vilya, for guiding me to hear this stone speak. And thank you, Mata-vilya, for guiding me to the People of Hom."
Together their prayer was—
"We thank you for our life together and ask that you bless our life and may it be remembered as a *story from the stones.*"

No longer did Dawn's stone speak of despair and the hard times; it had a new story to tell! Dawn now touched her river stone and it was cool. Mata-vilya had heard their prayers. Together they placed the stone back on the story mound and together they took a new stone and spoke of meeting the couple and said a blessing for them. Their journey north continued and by evening they arrived at the canyon where the buzzards roost, and decided to stay there for the night. By noon the next day they would be at the Land of Hom. Hom began telling Dawn about his family in the Land of Hom, the way of the People, and how to address oneself to the People. Hom told Dawn how the People also ferried all the white people across the Great River. Dawn asked:

"Are the pony soldiers there?"
"Yes" "Hom, be careful of the pony soldiers, do not touch them."
The next day they arrived at the Land of Hom.
As they approached the river valley Hom pointed out the mountains of the valley.
"See there? There is Spirit Mountain where Mata-vilya lives and there's Weeping Woman!"

Hom was enjoying telling Dawn all the stories of his people.

"One day I will take you to the stone maze and we will listen to the *stories from the stones* and I will show you how the stone maze speaks of the four seasons and counts the years."

By midday they arrived at Hom's family home. Hom's grandfather and grandmother were very happy to see Hom again, for he had been gone for six moon stones. Hom began telling his story of meeting Dawn and grandfather replied:

"We already know."

"How did you know?" asked Hom.

"Let's just say a little stone told me!" grandfather replied.

They talked endlessly into the night around the campfire telling their story. Grandfather was pleased that Hom had acquired the gift of Sumach-ahot, a gifted one, and was now able to hear the *stories from the stones*! This thought was in grandfather's mind:

"Sumach-ahot does not just happen. It is the result of years of gentle persuasion and teaching. This gift will guide him well. He will be a great prince and one day chief over the People."

The sun was setting lower and lower in the southern sky. The days were getting shorter and winter was coming. Hom and Dawn busied themselves with the People in getting ready for the cold weather. About this time Hom took Dawn to the maze telling her of his younger days of playing in the maze each spring when the People went to the high ground during the swelling of the river. He said:

"We will come here next spring with the People and you will see the children play."

"Hom, what is the maze for?" Dawn asked?

Hom spoke of the young children learning discipline and how they could play there but were not allowed to disturb the rows. The People placed *story stones* near the maze telling stories about happenings in their lives, their dreams and wishes. It would be sacrilegious to disturb the *story stones*.

Some of the elders would etch story lines and mounds to mark the years the People have been here. Hom continued:

"Look, we have been here for thousands of years. There are thousands of stories to be told in these stones. Then too, when the morning sun comes up and casts a light on a certain row it tells the elders what season has arrived. The maze is our calendar and history of the People and is not to be disturbed. See these stones? The women come here to see about their life cycle. They know the seasons by these four moon stones and that they are among the thirteen moonstones. They understand their body flows by the moonstones and when their flow stops they can tell the new life inside them is to arrive in nine moonstones."

Dawn thought a minute and told Hom:

"My flow stopped two moons ago."

Hom and Dawn were excited that they were in a family way. Using the moonstones they determined that their child would be born one moon short of the longest day of summer or the summer moonstone which is a good time of the year.

Hom said:

"My grandmother calls herself a survivor because she was born two months after the summer moonstone (August), and many young ones did not survive the heat. She did! She is a survivor! Come, let me show you my family."

Walking around the maze they came to a row of stones.

"These rows of stones are for each of my parents, Their row ended at forty-two stones. This is grandfather's row of seventy-eight stones. Right here, when our child is born, we will start a new row off my row to count his years."

Dawn thought to herself:

"The white people speak about the People as ignorant savages and here they have developed an elaborate calendar dating back centuries. They are an intelligent people living within the laws of the universe. Their minds are the same as my mind. They believe in the universal oneness among all peoples, and our child will be blessed with two cultures to draw from."

Dawn sat on Hom's lap and buried herself in his body. Together they just held each other, quietly reflecting on their new discovery. Hom said:

"We are a family. We will start a new row for you, Dawn. How many stones do we need?"

"Twenty-two stones," Dawn replied. Then she asked,

"Hom, the next time we go see uncle, can we bring my story stone from the story mound and make it a part of my row?"

"An excellent idea."

So a new layer in their life as a family began! Together they descended back to the river valley anxious to tell their grandparents the news. Grandfather had only one thing to say:

"He will be Hom Homoak (the third)."
Grandmother replied:
"How do you know it will be a boy child?"
Grandfather said:
"Let's just say a little stone told me."

Grandfather looked at Hom and winked. Dawn silently decided to also name him Andrew. She touched her stone and it was Cool! Cool! Cool! Cool!

Time went by slowly for Dawn and Hom who were both anxious for their first child. The ninth moonstone soon came and Dawn gave birth to Homoak. The entire village was abuzz wanting to see Homoak. He was a beautiful blend of Hom and Dawn, for now you could see the multicolored hue in his eyes like his mom. Life was unchanging for the next several years. There was planting, harvesting, fishing, going to the high ground in the spring, and attending to the family rows at the maze. Hom told Dawn this was so because the Great Spirit was unchanging. "Look at the night sky, at the stationary star to the north above Spirit Mountain where he lives. See his cup with the long handle below the star and how he positions it where he fills it up with all good things and then he turns it over and pours out all the blessings on his People. This has been repeating itself from time immemorial. We are a blessed People." But times were changing and the white man kept crossing the great river. This would soon affect their lives. During this time they had another child and they named her Maya.

As with most families Maya became very attached to her dad and Hom favored her. Hom had to sleep a certain way because Maya would snuggle up on Hom's back to sleep. Dawn, who cared for the whole family, gave special attention to Homoak. She was careful to instill the ways of the People in him because she knew he would be a great leader some day. Grandfather and grandmother had explained that there was a need for constant teaching for one to acquire the gift of Sumach-ahot. So this is what they did with Hom. In her moments of solitude she would talk to the Great Spirit asking for direction and answers came through the stones. Yes, even the Hy-go-wees like Dawn could become Sumach-ahot!

It was easy for Dawn to talk to the Great Spirit. She remembered back in the days when she was growing up and had many questions about life's purpose and was trying to find answers as to her future. It was her grandfather who had wisdom and instilled in her how the Great Spirit did not belong to any one people but to all the people, and that wherever she found herself he would manifest his presence to her.

"You see, the Great God is also a universal intelligence creating all life forms. He made us dependent on each other. You must have a great respect for all of his life forms for he has set into motion all the laws that life must follow. Know these laws and rules, for breaking them brings discipline. The Great God is a universal presence and watches and cares for all the life forms. To man he has given the power to reason on the law and to learn the principle behind the laws. Know this and you will find the direction to go and you will always know his presence."

Dawn had always followed her grandfather's advice and found the laws and principles practiced among the People of Hom. Truly, the Great God's intelligence and presence was here among the People. It was easy for Dawn to talk to Mata-vilya and she was at peace with the People. And today when she spoke to Mata-vilya, she told him of Homoak and all the good things she was doing to prepare him for his future as a leader of the People. She had a long range plan to prepare him to be a Sumach-ahot and to carry on the tradition of a "gifted one." For an assuring answer, she touched her havasu-avi water blue stone and it was—Cool! Cool! Cool! Cool!

Despite Dawn's warning to stay away from the pony soldiers, Hom became friends with them. She forbade Homoak and Maya to visit the pony soldiers with Hom. It became a contentious difference between them. One evening, despite Dawn's feelings, Hom left the family to visit the pony soldiers. When he arrived at the Fort he saw a strange commotion. The pony soldiers were burning all their belongings! Hom went straight to his friend, Paul's tent, to ask about this strange happening. He found Paul shivering under a blanket. Hom reached down and pulled at the blanket awakening Paul. Paul awoke, saw Hom and screamed:
"Hom, get away from me, don't touch me. I'm sick with the plague!"

✳ ✦ ✳ ✦ ✧ ✦ ✳ ✦ ✳ ✦ ✳ ✦ ✧ ✦ ✧ ✦ ✳ ✦ ✧ ✦ ✳ ✦ ✳

Hom backed away after seeing the red spots and splotches on Paul's body. Paul explained that for some unknown reason the pony soldiers would become sick with the plague and that it was a highly contagious sickness.

Hom's feelings were mixed, and not fully understanding what Paul said, he went back to his village. His mind was on Dawn's warning not to touch the pony soldiers and to stay away from them. He immediately told Dawn what he had just experienced. Dawn screamed, waking the children.

"Hom, come with me, quickly!"

Dawn took Hom to the campfire stripping him and herself of their clothing and threw them into the fire! In tears and with great emotional sobbing she grabbed Hom's hands placing them in hers and thrusting them through the fire!

"Fire, it's the only way to kill the plague!"

Despite the great pain, Dawn's mind turned towards the children,

"Hom, the children!"

They ran to the grandparents lodge waking them. Dawn told them,

"Quickly, make a hole in the back of our
lodge and take the children out that way.
Do not pass them where Hom stood!"

Grandfather approached the lodge and saw Maya standing at the doorway, but it was too late! Grandfather made a hole in the back and took Homoak out that way. Dawn saw Maya, grabbed her and took her to the campfire. She considered passing Maya through the fire, but instead removed Maya's clothing and tossed them into the fire. Then she bathed and bathed her in cactus soap! Grandfather spoke to Hom about this happening and said:

"We have to burn your lodge now!" They
burned it that night.

The village elders called a meeting and Dawn was the focus. She had an understanding of this Hy-go-wee sickness and explained what she knew. It was called smallpox, a deadly disease to the People! The People burned all their belongings and moved to the high ground even though it was the wrong time of the year. It was too late; many of the people began to come down with the sickness and died. In great anxiety Dawn watched her family. One morning Hom awoke with Maya shivering on his back. She had the

sickness; there was nothing they could do but pray. Hom prayed for her survival but his prayer felt guilty remembering Dawn's warning to, "stay away from the pony soldiers. Do not touch the pony soldiers!" Dawn prayed and her prayer felt guilty; she should have explained the principle behind her request. She should have checked the stone for Maya's safety; she only concentrated on Homoak! With great sadness together they faced the inevitable. Finally Maya spoke:

"I see Mata-vilya!", and she died.

As was the custom of the People, the child was cremated and the sky was filled with smoke from all the people dying. The cremation lasted parts of three days where the family openly, vocally and emotionally expressed their feelings and their remorse over their child. Dawn and Hom never spoke of this happening again. It was the way of the People. Their grief had been expelled at the cremation ceremony. There was no blaming to be done.

Dawn explained the principle behind her request to—

"Stay away from the pony soldiers. Do not
touch them" this way.

Truly it is the People of the land that are the true caretakers of Mother Earth. They wisely use what Mother Earth has given them for sustenance and living. The Hy-go-wee from across the great sea pollutes and rapes the land with no consciousness of Mother Earth and by not following the universal laws they have created all sorts of communicable diseases such as smallpox, typhoid and tuberculosis. Before the Hy-go-wees came the People had no such diseases so your body is unable to defend against it." Eventually the scars on their bodies and heart healed with time. Dawn found herself more and more with the desire to just sit on Hom's lap burying herself in his body, feeling his warmth and uttering a soft mmmm! For assurance she began touching her stone more often reassuring herself that her family was—Safe! Safe! Safe! Safe!

(The original band of People that arrived centuries ago eventually numbered some six thousand at the time of this story [1850] living in what is now known as the Mohave Valley. When I was a young man in 1950 we had dwindled down to 350 tribal members. We were close to extinction because of acquired diseases brought

by the Europeans. Today [2007] we number 1200)

Thirty-two stones into their lives came another child. She was fair with multi-colored eyes like her mom and depending on the light they looked brown or green. They named her Nunie. Together they took Homoak and Nunie to the maze and Hom holding Nunie high in the sky uttered this prayer—

"Mata-vilya, we thank you for this child. Together this family of the People will teach her to be one of the People, to learn to feel *the stories in the stones*, the principle behind the laws, the way of the People, the way of Mother Earth"

Young Homoak had learned the way well for he brought a special river stone for his sister and said,—

"I have brought a special stone for my sister and when she is not around you, I will be her protector and her caregiver, I will teach her the way!"

Homoak then placed a selected stone against his family row to start the story of Nunie! And what a tale—*but that's another story!* Homoak then said,

"I have found this river stone and I have made a medicine pouch for my sister. I wish to place it around her neck for protection."

Dawn stood there with tears of joy in her eyes. Her family was safe for now and reassuringly she felt her river stone and it was—Cool! Cool! Cool! Cool!

Dawn had learned the power of the stones; she too had attained Sumach-ahot, leading her in the way. She came to rely on the stones and was always aware of the stones' response to life's layers and shifting changes. Again and again Dawn would check the stones when her family had to deal with the pony soldiers and again and again the stones kept harm away from them. Now their row became thirty-nine stones each when these stories came about. Hom became a prince in the tribe, for he had acquired much knowledge and understanding with the stones and he became a wise man leading the people in the way. Together Hom and Dawn would spend many evenings under the stars talking about their family and about the universal thought process of selecting life's choices. These she had learned from her grandfather and Hom applied it to his family in everyday life. Dawn had learned her place among the People and never stepped over the bounds of authority in the way of the People. Hom understood this and together they learned universal love where their love was unconditional, without demands, without selfishness, full of understanding, communication, and commitment that would decide life's choices for the good of the family. The Northern Tribe of the Macav came to rely on Hom as Prince for all the People's needs.

Homoak would become seventeen stones by the coming of spring and families were moving to the high ground, to the Maze. Hom and Dawn listened to Homoak and his decision to accept responsibility in the tribe, to become a man among the People!

"This year I will become seventeen stones and I am ready for the initiation (maturity) ceremony and I wish to do this with my uncle's family to the south at the site of Goth."

Dawn's mind flashed back and saw when she first found her river stone, how she found Hom, their first summer together at the south site, the stories told by Hom and now their son Homoak was ready for the ceremony. She clutched her river stone thinking about the past seventeen stones of the gentle persuasive teaching of Homoak and spoke what she was saying in her heart—
"Yes, my son, you are ready."

Hom, too, thought about all the happenings that occurred to the south. He could see Dawn, a very pretty twenty-two year old green/blue eyed easterner, he had just met. He thought about his urgent need to know this person named Dawn; he turned toward Dawn and looked at her. She was no longer a pretty girl; she had become a beautiful Macav woman. As he stood there and stared at her she turned and looked into his soul with those beautiful multi-colored hued eyes and his thought was this, "She is not only beautiful, she is gorgeous." As she smiled at him he observed her skin color, her eyes, the flaming red/auburn hair against the evening sun and her beautiful mind; all this made her a beautiful, gorgeous woman! Hom now looked at Homoak, who had become a tall bronzed young man with a beautiful mind and placed his hands on his shoulders and spoke what was in his heart, "Yes my son, you are ready!" Together they clutched their river stones.

Nunie gleefully spoke:

"Mommy! Mommy! Look! I'm a messenger!"

"Oh Nunie, it's just a story."

"No Mommy, see that buzzard over there?"

Nunie spat on the ground and showed the buzzard her river stone and said:

"I am fine, I am not thirsty! Go away Mr. Buzzard! I am a messenger from the family of Hom!"

Hom beamed with joy! Dawn muttered to herself—

"Once a Macav, always a Macav."

Hom showed the kids the Turtle Mountains and told the story of the Guata-hun-nees (Spanish) who buried their gold there and lost their way. To this day no one has ever found it. He pointed out Lizard Back Mountain and said the Mojave Trail passes to the east side of it. They would camp there that night.

They arrived at the stone story mound late in the afternoon and made camp. Nunie ran around checking everything out, but she did not move the stones because she knew they were other people's stories. Nunie asked her dad if she could place a stone for her story on the mound; so they began searching for just the right stone and after finding it, Nunie spoke to it and placed it on the story mound. After a light meal, Hom began randomly picking stones from the story mound and told the *stories from the stones!* Nunie asked:

"Mommy, where is your stone?"

The family began looking and touching the stones. It was Homoak who found his mother's story stone. Together they all touched the stone and it was Homoak who felt the energy from the stone and the energy finally caused him to speak:

"I have seen things in your lives I never knew before."

Hom was pleased that Homoak would now hear these stories: he, too, now was Sumach-ahot, having the gift of knowing the *stories from the stones.* Dawn said:

"We will take my stone and place it on the story mound near the family row at the Maze."

Evening was approaching and Hom would be able to tell the stories from the sky.

Hom raised his arms in prayer to Mata-vilya and uttered a prayer for his family asking that this journey would be added to the *story stones.* Dawn clutched her river stone and it was cool. Homoak had been here before with his father and found his original *story stone* and added these words to it -

"Remember these days of my life and what I plan to do as a man."

Hom thought and remembered—

"I said the very same thing as I approached my manhood initiation."

Hom touched his stone and it was cool; Homoak's story stone accepted his plea. As the evening progressed and the sky turned yellow, fiery red, and a darkening blue hue, Hom pointed to the sky and said:

"Look, the new moon. See how the evening star is chasing the new moon; tomorrow the new moon will be chasing the evening star which is the ceremonial sign."

Dawn could see the perfect silhouette of Hom shadowed against the ever darkening evening sky and she approached him putting her arms around him and gently cried for she knew that their life had come full circle and they were still deeply in love with each other. All these years they learned that there had to be a recommitment to each other and continual expanding and exploring of their universal love for each other. Hom asked Dawn, "Sing us story song," and Dawn nodded and began—

I am the person I am today,
I have come a long, long way.
From the land of my grandfather,
Who was oh so gentle and kind,
Always nurturing and expanding my mind.
Grandfather would often say,
Listen, observe the universe around you,
To all the truths found in the laws,
And from this you will learn life's cause
Which is to know universal love so you too
Can share life's meaning with the one you love.
It was in the Land of Hom
I found you my sweet Macav
And it is with you my dear, sweet dear,
I will love year after year.

Hom knew that Dawn loved music that was a different style from the bird songs of the People. He came across a musical instrument the Hy-go-wees call a mandolin. It was with this mandolin that Dawn played and sang story songs to Hom and her children. Dawn fashioned her story songs as a teaching tool where the children would learn life's ways and the Hy-go-wee language. She taught the instrument to Homoak who became a musician like his mother. Hom taught the bird songs of the People, but Homoak's love of music was for his mother's songs. He would gather his friends and play the mandolin while others played the gourds or the long drums. Their music improved when they acquired a skin drum from an eastern tribe at the 'Islands of Refuge'. There was a new sound of music in the Land of Hom made by Homoak and his friends. It was under this setting that the family sat around the *story mound* under the new moon. Dawn had just played the mandolin and sang her song to Hom accompanied by Homoak and his friends. Now Hom said, "I too wish to tell a story song, Homoak. You and mom play along."—

The People follow the universal way,
This ancient way is still followed today.
Listen to the drumbeat! Repeat, repeat, repeat.
It sounds like my heart beat, beat, beat, beat.
This is life in the universe,
Full of meaning and verse.
Feel my heart rhythm; it's seventy plus two.
With each beat it says, I love you.
Listen to the mandolins melodious sound,
It was here at the Story Mound
You spoke to the stone and you I found.
And here today,
Let me say,
It is you my dear,
I too will love year after year!

Together Hom and Dawn placed their hands on their havasu-avis, their water blue stones, and they were cool. They embraced each other with their eyes gently speaking to each other a silent, "I love you!" Nunie spoke saying:

"Oh, Mommy, Daddy!"

She giggled, not at what they said but about the way they were acting.

"Daddy, daddy, tell us another story," and Hom began.

Dawn looked up at the new moon in the western sky as if it were looking over the people and especially over her family. She thought to herself saying:

"Thank you Mata-vilya. Yes, you are the protector over the Land of Hom and my family. Thank you for teaching us universal love and bless our son as he approaches a new layer in his life,"

And as she looked at their family she saw this universal—Peace! Peace! Peace! Peace!

There were other families camping at the story mound and they were asking, "Who is this family?" An elder among one of the families spoke:

"This is Hom-Hee-Vouch, Prince of the Northern Macav people and this is Dawn his wife and these are their children."

Hom and Dawn rose and said:

"This is our son Homoak. We are going to the ceremony at the site of Goth where he is to become a man tomorrow."

Nunie rose and said:

"I am Nunie, I am a messenger from the Land of Hom!"

Everyone laughed!

A young maiden rose and said:

"I am Katala and I too am going to the ceremony at the site of Goth to see Homoak dance."

Dawn and Hom turned to see who spoke. Katala continued:

"I am from the Nu-wev People, the Looking for Fish (Ache-Mo-Wev in the Mojave tongue) Clan, and I will select Homoak as my mate."

The Nu-wev People are a sub-group of the Shoshone who were mountain hunters ranging from the Tehachapi Mountains to Banning, California (today) and this band migrated to the great river preferring fish as their diet. They coexisted with the Macav in the land of Hom. Later in time when the Hy-go-wee came he began to change the people's names. We said, we are the Macav and from this it became Mojave or Mohave to the White man. Nu-wev became Chemehuevi and even personal names soon became anglicized. Look for Fish became the Fisher family. Today many of the families here have a mixed culture of Mojave and Chemehuevi and the writer of this story is a product of this inter-mingling.

Dawn nudged Hom and whispered, "She is a Chemehuevi." Dawn noticed her light brown hair, which was very fine, not coarse and black like the Mojave. Katala was slender and her skin was of fair complexion; these are traits of her people. Katala looked at Homoak, and Dawn could see that knowing gleam in Katala's eye as their eyes met.

Dawn now looked at Homoak, her baby, standing tall looking back at Katala. Their eyes fixed on one another. Dawn reached for her river stone. It was cool! Dawn thought about Homoak as a baby, a child, a young boy and now on the threshold of the maturity ceremony and the *selection process!* My, how time had flown by. The families met, and there was an exchange of family talk, a rubbing of faces, it was a good evening.

The next day the families arrived at the ceremonial site of Goth. Homoak spent the morning catching up on the happenings with his family and friends. Dawn and Nunie readied Homoak's ceremonial dress. In Dawn's mind she reflected back on how she selected Hom before the elders, and now she was going to see how the selection ceremony was actually conducted. Hom visited with his uncle and caught up on the latest news. The Fishers were busy with Katala's ceremonial dress and Katala was preparing her selection speech to the elders. She was excited!

The evening hour had come with a fiery red glow in the sky that blended upward with yellow, violet and blue tones. The new moon (it is known as the crescent moon but the Mojave called it the new moon) could be seen as a sliver of new life in the sky. Everyone had gathered around waiting for the evening star to appear so the ceremony could begin. It was the children that would announce the first glitter of the evening star. They waited and waited and it was Nunie that shouted out, "There, there it is, below the new moon!" Hom was chosen as the story teller (he was the best) and he began telling the story of the—"giant and he was eating Mojaves,"—and at the end of the story Hom spoke saying—"and to this day, the people gather here each spring to celebrate the slaying of the giant by the young men and to initiate them as men among the people with full rights and responsibilities to their families.

Hom continued:
"Let the dance begin! Let the gourds sound, begin singing the bird songs and Maidens, you may look to see who is your choice and the one you wish to dance with for the rest of your life! Maidens, choose your dancer!"

By now it was dusk and in a great arc the young men began to dance in a great circle around Goth following the ancient path of their peers etched into the earth. Dawn walked up to Hom and stood by him and together they observed Homoak dance and they felt very proud. As was the custom of the people, maidens waited until the moment their prospective mate passed by the elders. They would then dart out and take their young man's hand bringing him before the elders making their request and many would do so in poetic form.

Dawn and Hom watched as Homoak was dancing and approaching the elders and saw Katala quickly darting and placing her hand in Homoak's hand and bringing him before the elders. She said:
"Elders of the People, I am Katala from the Ache-Mo-Wev people, I have come to this ceremony to exercise my right and selection of my mate in life and I choose Hom-Homoak-Hee-Vouch, known as Homoak among the Northern Mojave People"

It was the custom of the elders to ask questions of the couple, which they did. The Elders recognized Homoak as the son of Hom, the Prince of the Northern Mojaves and asked if she recognized this and the responsibilities that go with this position? Katala surveyed the entire ceremony. The young men were dancing and some of the maidens were waiting for their prospective mates to come around and were full of laughter enjoying the celebration. Katala's attention now turned toward Homoak; she observed him and his family and gazed into his eyes and silently her eyes spoke:
"Yes Homoak, it is you I want as my care-taker."

Note: I have heard the story told as above and in the earlier renditions that the young men danced naked and this is why the maidens were pointing, laughing and giggling. This celebration has not been practiced for one hundred and fifty years. Though this was the most important annual celebration of the People, it was viewed as heathen and pagan and forcibly stopped.

Katala now gestured with her right arm, extending it from her heart to the Elders to show respect for their way, and spoke to Homoak, the Elders and for all to hear—
See the new moon in the sky,
For sometime you have been in my eye.
I see only you my darling Macav man,
The sunshine has made you tan,

It is you I wish to share my love,
See all the dancing Macav,
Tonight I place my river stone in your pouch,
For all here to see our stones respond with touch.
For the rest of my life I seek your protection
This is for all to hear, you are my selection!

Homoak nodded to Katala and extended his arm to show respect and now standing before the Elders, spoke these words for all to hear—

I too see the new moon,
Though I speak, in my heart I sing this tune
Listen to the sound of the mandolin string,
How it makes a melodious sound.
It was under this spell that you I found.
Music has brought us together this spring.
The new moon is a part of the universal way,
It's been here a long time, and it's here to stay.
For as long as the moon shall rise,
We shall listen to the elders old and wise
By this universal way, we make life's choice.
With this ceremony begins our life of rejoice.
Welcome to my family and in celebration,
Be known to all, you too are my selection!

Hom was holding Dawn and together they watched as the Elders nodded and Katala joined Homoak to dance around Goth. In their minds eye the past eighteen stones passed them by. Yes, they could see all of life's layer thus far in their lives. Dawn with a tear in her eye clutched her river stone. It was very cool. She turned to Hom and said:

"Life's circle has been completed. There is a new layer of life and life starts again."

She looked at the new moon and knew all was well in her—Universe! Universe! Universe! Universe!

So it came to pass that the family of Hom returned to the Land of Hom and their days of living were full of life in the Mojave way. The following story occurred in the twenty-second stone of their life as a family....

The pony soldiers and the iron horse did come to the Land of Hom. No longer were the Mojave needed to ferry the white man across the great river since a 'tu-pock', a bridge, was built and dissention grew between both people. Hom was a negotiator for the elders since he spoke the white man's language fluently, and he was also an elder now. Some of the Mojaves began drinking the white man's "fire water", which caused uncontrolled emotions between the two sides with the Mojave often being incarcerated. Trouble came to the Land of Hom; no longer was there peace in the universe. Hom tried to apply universal law, but there was a new group of pony soldiers who had other intentions.

The Mojaves became very angry over the mistreatment of the People by the pony soldiers towards the people. Eventually it came about that a drunken pony soldier tried to assault Katala, which called for war. Homoak spoke for the group saying:

"There has been peace in the Land of Hom for many years and now the peace has been broken. There are new pony soldiers here that have no respect for the People. We shall teach them a lesson of respect!"

The young warriors cheered! The Elders had already decided there would be no war and that the negotiation process was the best course to follow. They reasoned with the young warriors about this decision.

Homoak again spoke for the young warriors saying:

"With great respect for the War Chief, he has forgotten how to go to war! My brothers and I have chosen Thut-a-thun (Thunder) as our leader to war against the pony soldiers so they will again gain respect for the Mojave!"

Hom and the Elders could not stop the young warriors and they began raiding the Pony soldiers in a hit and run tactic used by the People. The Mojave weapons of war were the bow and arrow, and the war club. The Mojave arrows were without stone arrowheads, which sometimes worked and sometimes didn't. If the stone arrowhead merely wounded you, the warrior could fight another day. Instead, the Mojave watched the creatures of the earth and noticed they used their enzymes to paralyze their victims. So they used sharpened and fire hardened arrow shafts and painted the tips with a concoction of ground up insect enzymes, and it always worked!

The war club was made from the branch of the mesquite tree cut to the desired length by the warrior. Now it was rounded, tiered and stepped down from about five inches in diameter at the blunt end to three inches; and then to the desired handle grip sized to fit the warrior with a tethered strap to his wrist. This club was used to literally club their opponent to death; it was the weapon of choice. The Mojave male averaging six foot six in height with his war club was a fearsome warrior to all the peoples around. On one such raid Hom was at the pony soldiers' fort when the young Mojave warriors attacked and a pony soldier was clubbed to death. The Commander charged Hom with instigating the raid. Despite protests of his innocence, Hom was arrested and removed from the Land of Hom. The Elders and Dawn tried to intervene but without success. Hom was taken to an eastern prison, just where nobody knew. That was the custom of the pony soldiers at the time. Indian prisoners in the west were taken east and eastern Indians were taken west. This was done to break their spirit.

Dawn approached the Elders and requested that she go east to look for her husband, Hom. The Elders denied her request. In her grief, she rose and speaking to the Elders, she said:

"I have been here among the People for twenty-two stones and you have accepted me in the ceremonies with the People and now my husband is gone. My duty as one of the People is to listen to you, my Elders, as I have always done. But now my other culture as Hy-go-wee directs me to go and look for Hom. I have prepared myself for the journey."

An elder spoke:

"Dawn, yes, you are one of the People and a leader among the women and we all respect you. In the twenty-two stones you have been here, have you not noticed a new attitude among the white man where their lust for the yellow stone and sand has blinded them? They will not understand you searching for Hom, one of the People, let alone that you belong to the People, that you are one of the People."

Dawn was blinded with her loss of Hom and restated her intentions to search for him. As she left the Elders she reached for her river stone. *It did not turn cool!*

"Oh no," she thought, "What have I done?"

She explained to the children what she intended to do. Then she dressed herself in Hy-go-wee clothes and boarded the iron horse going east. A white man said there was a prison in Tucson in the Arizona Territory, so she went there. Hom was not there and the Elders were right; the white people could not understand her search for a Mojave, let alone being married to one. The pony soldiers behaved abusively towards her as she tried to seek information. This was when she learned about breaking the spirit of the people and that Hom had been taken to an eastern prison. For many of the people across the continent this forced movement came to be called "the trail of tears." Constantly she felt her river stone and it no longer provided that comforting cool sensation. She remembered that the Elders had not approved of her journey.

So she decided to go back to the Land of Hom to obtain a blessing from the Elders before continuing her search. As she approached the river valley she could see all the mountains she knew, "There's Spirit Mountain and there's Weeping Woman Mountain and I know how she feels!"

Her thoughts turned to how the People must have felt when they returned from a long journey back to the Land of Hom and saw all the familiar mountains and smelled all the valley odors of the mesquite, the willow, the great river. They knew they were finally—Home! Home! Home! Home! Dawn was home!

Dawn's immediate family and especially Nunie were overcome with joy at seeing her again and everyone began asking questions,

"Mommy, did you find dad?" asked Nunie

"When is he coming home?" asked Homoak.

"We have to work on that," Dawn said.

"What do we have to do?" Grandfather asked.

So began the plan for the return of Hom, Prince and Elder of the Northern Mojaves. First there was a celebration by the People for the safe return of Dawn and after the evening feast the Elders called upon Dawn to explain her journey. She concluded her story by saying—"and they took Hom to an eastern prison."

This time Dawn did not state her plan but allowed the Elders to discuss among themselves on the action that should be taken. After much deliberation and after checking their special river stones, the Elders turned towards Dawn and said:

"It is our decision that you return to your Land of Kentucky and to your grandfather and he will show you the system obtaining Hom's release. The remainder of this celebration will be a blessing ceremony for your protection and the success of your journey. Let the celebration begin!"

Dawn asked for a moment to herself and she climbed a nearby hill and noticed in the night sky that the cup under the stationary star was upside down. The last time she saw it, it was filling up. She remembered Hom's story of how Mata-vilya fills up the cup with blessings and when full turns the cup over to pour out all his blessing on the People! She thought back on her grief and how it prompted her to act on her own and how her stone would not support her efforts. Quickly now she felt her havasu-avi, her water blue river stone and it was—Cool! Cool! Cool! Cool! Her emotions were overwhelming!

The Elders gave their final blessing and Dawn said goodbye to her family. Homoak and Nunie gave their mom a special river stone and Homoak said:

"It is for your protection and for a safe return with our dad."

Dawn thought:

"This is the right way, it is the way of the People."

She boarded the iron horse and began her journey east. The pony soldiers and the people in general were blinded to Dawn and she experienced no problems, nor did she draw attention to herself. This was difficult to do because at some stops she saw the plight of the people. Once they were a proud people and now they were reduced to being a subservient people. Her heart went out to the people but there was nothing she could do for now. Her mission was to find Hom! Through casual conversation Dawn found out that there was a prison for the people near her home in Kentucky. At forty-two stones, Dawn had been gone for some twenty-two years and did not know about the well being of her family. Her family had emigrated from Germany a century ago, traveling from New York through America and finally settling in Kentucky.

With wonderment in her heart, she approached her grandfather's house and knocked on his door. He came to the door now at eighty-seven years of age—

"Yes," he said, his eyes dim with living.

"Grandfather, it's me, Marie Dawn."

"Oh my child," he said and he held her dearly.

Together they embraced and held each other. The Mojave have a saying that your flesh knows its own flesh. Yes; Marie Dawn was home with her grandfather! Grandfather patiently let Marie Dawn ask all the questions and he provided all the answers about the family. Yes, grandmother had passed on. Marie Dawn shared with him her experience with the Mojave people, Hom, the children and how the pony soldiers had imprisoned Hom near here and she was looking for him. Grandfather listened intently and he was pleased that Marie Dawn still followed the universal way. That she found the Great God even in the Land of Hom, Grandfather said,

"Your story does not surprise me, my child, you were always a high spirited person and pretty independent too."

"Can you help me find Hom and free him?"

"Yes my child, he may be here or in South Carolina."

They spent the rest of their time reminiscing, but Marie Dawn's mind was on finding Hom! Her mind was asking, 'Where are you my dear. Are you alright? My dear, I'm coming!' Her mind kept echoing—Hom! Hom! Hom! Hom! Suddenly, Hom sat up in his prison cell thinking someone called his name! He knew it was the voice of another Sumach-ahot person nearby!

There was a celebration for Marie Dawn. Some of her family accepted Dawn's story and others were uncomfortable with it and distanced themselves. Grandfather said this would be so and that she should respect each one's feelings. The mission was to find Hom! Grandfather began searching for Hom and with information he obtained he told Marie Dawn.:

"Hom is in a Kentucky prison nearby here. I'll approach the Commander and see what I can do."

Marie Dawn was elated, she touched her river stone and it was cool!

Grandfather approached the Commander and asked about Hom and how to get his release. The Commander looked up Hom's record and said,

"He is here in my prison but my hands are tied. There's nothing I can do. He was involved in the murder of a soldier on the frontier."

"My granddaughter was there. Hom is a

Prince of the Mojave people and was on a diplomatic mission between the two nations when this event occurred and was wrongly accused of this deed. Would you not take the word of a Kentucky Daughter?"

"As the highest ranking retired Kentucky Colonel, would you take my word for it, Sir?"

The Commander knew of grandfather and respected his authority and his Kentucky gentleman's manner and replied:

"I'll see what I can do, Sir!"

The Commander began an inquiry with Marie Dawn testifying about Hom's innocence. Hom was exonerated and he was given a document that stated this fact. Hom was released. Back at Grandfather's house they all talked about the universal way and grandfather was pleased they had found and followed the way. Together they began planning for the return west, "Back to the Land of Hom!" Grandfather found a receptive family who were planning to go west. He arranged for them to travel with that family with Hom as an assistant. So their journey began.

Note: This story is so lengthy and detailed that I am in the process of writing another book entitled—"Back to the Land of Hom" But that's another story—

They arrived back in the Land of Hom seven moons later. There was much celebration at the return of Hom, Prince and Elder of the Mojave People, both by the People and by Hom's family. There were many *stories from the stones* to tell of their sojourn and the celebration lasted many days and evenings. Dawn and Hom were together again with their family. They could live in—Peace! Peace! Peace! Peace!

Chapter Six

❖

Kinship

Photo by Jeffrey L. Garton

The Clan System of the Fort Mojave Indians

by Lorraine M. Sherer

Reprinted with permission of Southern California Quarterly.

Introduction

The study of the clans or old family system of the Fort Mojave Indians has been a memorable and deeply rewarding experience. Although Fort Mojave Indians have been part of my life since childhood and they have provided generous help since 1952 in preparing a history of their tribe, this is the first time we have embarked on a team research project together. Our aims in making the study were to obtain an authentic description of their ancestral clan system as Mojaves "look at it from the inside" and to prepare a roster of the tribe by clan names to parallel the roster of English names under which they are registered with the Department of the Interior. The clan system has been placed in its historical setting to tell what the Fort Mojaves call "The Story of Our Old Family Names."

The study was conducted through official tribal channels—the Fort Mojave Tribal Council, whose Chairman, Mrs. Frances Malika Stillman, served as the local coordinator and as my chief consultant. Our principal advisor and helper was Oach (Mrs. Lizzie Kimball Hood). These two women assisted with a preliminary study of their clans in 1957-1959, and were instrumental in obtaining the cooperation of other Fort Mojave Indians in this expanded study "to get a record of our old family system". The material contained in this study is based on interviews with Fort Mojave Indians who live in Mojave Village and in Needles, California, and on Fort Mojave Tribal records housed in the office of the Fort Mojave Tribal Council in Mojave Village, as well as extensive information supplied by Mrs. Stillman and Mrs. Hood.

Mrs. Frances Stillman is a full blood Mojave of the *Malika* clan, married to a full blood Mojave of the *Maha* clan. She was born on the Fort Mojave Reservation in 1910. Her father was a *Malika*, the clan of the hereditary great chieftain of the Mojaves. Her mother, Oach, died when she was an infant so she was reared by her old-fashioned grandparents, who grounded her in the tribal ways. Her grandfather was *Thumpah* of the *Oach* clan, her grandmother was *Norge*. She is a graduate of the Fort Mojave School, the Sherman Institute, and the Needles High School. She speaks and writes English fluently in dealing with white people, and speaks Mojave fluently when talking with Mojaves. She served as vice chairman of the Fort Mojave Tribal Council from 1951 to 1956 when the Fort Mojaves set up a new local government after the death of the Great Chieftain. In 1957 the Fort Mojave Tribe adopted a constitution approved by the Secretary of the Interior. Mrs. Stillman was elected chairman of the new Fort Mojave Tribal Council, an office to which she was re-elected in 1963. She was also honored in 1963 by the Business and Professional Women of Needles as "The Woman of the Year."

Oach (Mrs. Hood), her aunt, was born in 1880. She is the oldest *Oach* and the second oldest Fort Mojave woman. She grew up on a farm near the Fort, attended the Fort Mojave School from 1896 to 1904, served as an "outing student" in Los Angeles for nine years, returned to Needles and married a Fort Mojave School graduate. She is bilingual. When she entered the Fort Mojave School in 1896, she was given an English first name and was called "Lizzie Oach". She smiled cryptically when asked about her registered name, "Mrs. Lizzie Kimball Hood". "I was about nineteen" she said, "working for an American family in Los Angeles, as the school used to have us do. I received a letter from the superintendent. It said, 'Your name is Lizzie Kimball'. Later, I married Robin Hood." She calls herself Lizzie Oach Hood. "I always use my Indian name;" she said. There are several *Oach*, but this venerable woman, who died on April 14, 1963, is entitled to be known and remembered simply as Oach.

Malika and Oach consulted other Mojaves to obtain and verify information. When asked to whom credit should be given for contributions to the study, the Chairman of the Fort Mojave Tribal Council replied, "Almost everybody had a hand in it, some more than others. You have the names of the main ones." The main contributors were: *Atalk hear* (Harry Lewis, b. 1880), the oldest of the *Neolge* clan and the Tribal Orator; *Auva halyevatch* (Charles Hamilton, b. 1881) , the oldest of the *Maha* clan and for fifty years a tribal witness and adviser; *Gottah* (Mrs. Kate Wellman Bryan, b. 1867, d. 1965), the oldest *Gottah* and a Tribal Singer; *Oneyuravarya* (Hal O. Davidson, b. 1892, d. 1959), the oldest man of the Whalia clan, the Chief's representative, 1922-1947, head of the interim tribal government, 1947-1951, member of the Fort Mojave Tribal Council, 1951-1957, and Tribal Recorder, 1922-1957; *Achee hemack* (Robert Jenkins, b. 1897, d. 1964), of the *Oach* clan, a Tribal Singer and Chairman of the Fort Mojave Tribal Council, 1951-1957; and *Boudha Whev* (Mrs. Henrietta Graves Peterson, b. 1898), the only woman of the Boudha clan and a Tribal Singer.

Other sources of information used in the study were the Fort Mojave Tribal Records, records and photographs provided by old time residents in the Mojave Valley, documents from the National Archives, and publications by writers who obtained their data first hand from Mojave Indians in Mojave country. The policy has been to incorporate such sources of information in the text where they contribute to the content without burdening the narrative. All other documentation and explanations appear in notes which accompany each chapter.

In organizing the contents, care has been taken to deal with the clan system and old Mojave family names as a possession of the Mojaves as one people, or tribe—the *Aha macave*, regardless of their registration with the Department of the Interior as two tribes on two reservations, the Mojaves on the Colorado River Reservation and the Fort Mojave Indian Tribe. This arbitrary division was made for purposes of allocating lands and has no bearing on the Mojave clan system per se.

A word on terminology. The term "informant" is acceptable in academic research, but unpalatable to Fort Mojaves. Therefore, it is eschewed in this study. Fort Mojaves are consultants, advisors, contributors, acquaintances, friends, whichever word is appropriate. "Friend" is a word not to be used promiscuously. The term "clan" is used rather than "gens" to keep the wording in line with Professor A. L. Kroeber's precedent and with Mojave usage. The term "religion" is used rather than the term "myth". To Fort Mojaves the faith of their fathers and the commandments they live by are their old Mojave religion in the same sense that Christianity, Judaism, Mohammedanism and Buddhism are religions. The name Mojave is used as the tribal name throughout the text because, as my Mojave consultants say, "it comes close to our real name [*Aha macave*] and people are used to it." Except in quoted passages throughout this study, the tribal name is spelled with a *j*, Mojave, and not with an *h*, Mohave. Both forms appear in general usage but the Fort Mojaves have adopted the *j* form as their official spelling.

My greatest pleasure in presenting this report comes from the Fort Mojaves' pronouncement *ahota* (good). My one regret is that the study came too late for Professor A. L. Kroeber's review and appreciation.

The Origin and Characteristics of the Mojave Clan System

Mojaves say that their family or clan names are very old, that they have been handed down to them by their ancestors from time immemorial, or from so long ago that no one knows when, or since First Time when they were given their names by their god *Mutavilya*. Whipple, who made the first published study of the Mojaves, learned nothing about their clans but he did discover that they believed in *Mutavilya (Mat-e-vil)*. In his Mojave vocabulary "*mat-e-vil*" means God. Curtis reported that the totemic names borne by Mojave women were said by Mojaves to have been given them by *Mutavilya*. Bourke quotes Merriman as saying that the Mojaves were named by *Mastamho*, *Mutavilya's* son. "It was *Mutavilya* who gave us our names, Oach said flatly. "*Eachawhat hoomay* (Merriman) was well informed but he was not an authority on religious matters. *Quaskette howa* was." The *Quaskette howa* to whom she referred was the chief medicine man of the Fort Mojaves until his death around 1917. The old medicine man named *Mutavilya* as the Creator who gave the Mojaves their names and their rules for living, and *Mastamho* as his son who provided for the Mojaves and taught them how to live. In 1905, when the Mojaves were renamed, it was commonly accepted among them that *Mutavilya* gave them their Mojave names.

This is the way *Mutavilya* named the Mojave families, told to me by Malika, as she heard it from her grandfather when she was a child.

"The god *Mutavilya*, in First Time, gave the Mojaves their family names, to use and to pass on to their children. When *Mutavilya* named the families he began with the above-things—the sky or heavens, *Neolge*, the sun; *Oach*, the clouds, rain, and winds; *Whalia*, the moon; *Maha*, the small singing birds.

"Then he named for the earth-things—the desert and mountain animals and plants. The families named for the animals of the earth were *Moha*, the mountain sheep and the deer; *Hipa*, the coyote; *Masipa*, the quail; *Necah*, the caterpillar and the worms. The families named for the plants and growing bushes were *Vemacka*, the bean mesquite and certain other desert plants; *Mus*, the screw mesquite; *Chacha*, the corn; *Gottah*, the tobacco; *Kumathee*, the ocotilla cactus; *Quinetha*, the prickly-pear cactus.

"And then he named for the water and the below-earth things: *Shulia*, the beaver; *Boudha*, the frog; *Malika*, the ground squirrel or the wood rat, and other desert rodents. But *Mutavilya* said, 'Do not despise these below-earth things, for they are wise ones'."

The names recited by Malika all appear on the lists of Curtis and of Kroeber. This version of the names and of the manner of naming the Mojave clans, however, puts the names into a frame-work or design which gives depth and significance not apparent otherwise. These clan names, derived from the ancient Mojave religion, belong to an organized schema of three groups, representative of the natural phenomena of sky and air, of the natural products of the earth and of the water, and the below-earth. The totems are all from the natural environment of the Mojave's homeland: the desert, the mountains, and the river. All are useful and beneficent; at least, none are malevolent. The classication is not hierarchical, ascribing higher attributes to one group than to another.

The clans and clan names seem not "to enter into religious activities so far as is known," as Kroeber reported, but the family names are of Mojave religious origin and are venerated as such by the Mojaves.

The clan names are archaic words of totemic import, as Kroeber stated, not the common words that designate the totems in the Mojave language today. For example: the totemic clan name *Oach*, meaning clouds, rain, and wind, is unlike the common words *eque* (cloud), *cuvawa* (rain), *matha* (wind); *Shulia*, meaning beaver, is unlike *aben* (beaver) ; *Mus*, meaning screw mesquite, is unlike the common word *ahieza*.

The Mojave clan system operates according to rules laid down by the Mojaves' ancient deities. Exogamy is a tribal rule. Men and women of the same clan may not marry. Monogamy is also a tribal rule. According to ancient custom, a Mojave may have but one spouse at a time. However, if the couple are incompatible, they may separate, or divorce and remarry. Endogamy is not, and apparently never has been, a tribal rule.

Photo by A.P. Miller, Needles, 1932

Gwegwi nuor of the **Oach** *in 1932 when he was over one-hundred years old. The feather piece on his head is a non-Mojave decoration supplied by the photographer. The gourd rattle however is an authentic Mojave instrument which* **Gwegwi nuor** *always used when he sang the short* **Tomampa**, *the clan song of the Oach. He was a scout in 1859 and was present when the Mojaves surrendered to Lieutenant Colonel William Hoffman. His account, "Mojave History" in the Fort Mojave Tribal Records, provides the names of the clans who were represented in Hoffman's camp.*

The Mojave clan system is patrilineal. Kroeber termed it "a peculiar clan system'. One outstanding peculiarity is that, although the children take the father's clan name, the men and boys are never called by their clan names; they are silent carriers. The girls and women are called by their clan names; they use or bear the names overtly. Malika explained:

"*Mutavilya* gave the names to the men, not to use, but to carry to their daughters to use. Everyone knows the name the man carries if he has daughters, and everyone uses that name in addressing his daughters or in speaking about his daughters. The daughter's name is *Neolge, Oach, Whalia, Mus, Shulia, Masipa*—whatever name her father gives her. When she marries she keeps her family name to use with her other name. It is hers for life and in the next world, but she cannot pass it on to her children. If a man of the *Oach* marries a woman of the *Neolge*, the wife remains *Neolge*; the daughters are called *Oach*; the sons carry the man's family name *Oach* to their daughters and through their sons to their granddaughters. A family name never dies out as long as it has sons to carry the family name to their daughters. If a man has sons only, or if he has no children and no sisters, it is not easy to remember what family he belongs to."

My Mojave friends, when asked a particular man's family name, either replied at once or used one of the following lines of figuring it: "His daughter is *Whalia*, so he is of the Whalia." "His sister is *Mus*, so he is of the *Mus*." Or, "He has no clan name; his mother married a non-Indian."

"The men, then, are never called by their family names?" I asked.

"The men may be spoken of by the family name, as: he is of the *Neolge*, or he is a *Neolge*. It is not proper to say, he is *Neolge*, or to address him *Neolge*."

A Mojave man may introduce himself by his clan name in social gatherings or tribal meetings by saying "I am a *Masipa*," or "I am of the *Masipa*," or whatever his clan name is. Men are referred to by clan names in ceremonials.

"The men are spoken of by family name in the ceremony of departure. My grandfather was named *Thumpah*, but he was of the *Oach*. In my grandfather's obituary, the orator said:

Here lies an *Oach*.
He was one of you.
Let all the *Oach* sing
Or listen.

All the *Oach* sang, and any who could not sing was expected to listen."

A man's clan name not only identifies him during his lifetime, but it also has perpetuity. It links him to his ancestors, is passed on through him to his progeny, and he takes it with him to the next world. Whatever name he may be called as a boy, or as a man, is ephemeral and relatively inconsequential. Only his clan name matters.

A second peculiarity of the Mojave clan system mentioned by Kroeber is that "All the women born in a clan bear an identical name, although they may in addition be known by nicknames or other epithets" In exploring this matter I found that these "epithets or nicknames" were descriptive of the totems, although the women may be called also by pet names or nicknames. Unlike the archaic clan names, the descriptive names are words commonly used today.

The clan name is the equivalent of our surname; the descriptive name is "given" by the parents.

The Mojave place the surname first. For example, take *Kuma-thee Hipak: Kumathee* is the clan name, whose totemic import is ocotilla cactus; *Hipak* is the vernacular, meaning "in blossom."

Because the Mojaves' method of naming the woman seemed difficult to understand without illustrations, I asked Malika to describe it, giving illustrations. She said:

"Each daughter in a family, no matter how many there may be, is called by her family name: Neolge, Oach, Whalia, Shulia, Masipa, whatever family name her father gives her. Because a man may have more than one daughter and the men who are his relatives may have daughters, who are all called by the same family name, each family gives to each of its daughters a descriptive name. In that way, everyone knows which *Neolge, Oach, Whalia, Moha* is which."

I asked Malika to explain further taking as an example her own family beginning with her grandfather and her own mother, *Oach*.

"My grandfather as previously stated, was called *Thumpah*, but he was of the *Oach* family. He had two daughters, named *Oach*. Neither sister would know which one her mother called to, or which should answer, so my mother was called *Oach Choim*, meaning 'left over, dying away, distant thunder, as when you hear the thunderclap and then it dies away'; my aunt was *Oach Hajaav*, meaning 'clouds gathering or clustering into a bank.'

"Each family gives its daughters descriptive names. Oach signifies above-things, such as clouds, rain, and wind. The descriptive names describe the different ways these look or what they do, such as clouds gathering, thunder clouds, light floating clouds, noise of thunder, and flash of lightning. There are many ways to describe the different *Oach*, to tell what they look like, what they do.

"Hugh Hammond's daughter, Elda Hammond Butler, is *Oach Horath*, meaning the crashing sound of thunder, when you see lightning crack the sky. You know Mr. Hammond is of the *Oach* because his daughter is named *Oach*. The late Lina Wagner Mc-Dowell was *Oach Hotheeka*, meaning the wind has blown the clouds in different directions, gusty. You know Mr. Wagner carries the *Oach* name because his daughter used the *Oach* name. Harriet Wilson is *Oach* Shekashek, meaning a rain or windstorm that frightens or terrifies."

Other names of *Oach* women and girls are: *Oach Ami sakohav*, clouds covering a large surface or area of the sky (Mrs. Marceline Morgan Sharp, b. 1931, d. 1963) ; *Oach Quireeckma*, ever moving clouds (Mrs. Glorianna Cameron Davidson, b. 1932); *Oach Hildunuym*, "clouds appearing or coming over and over until it's darkening. If they keep coming, for sure you'll have rain" (Ethelyn Fitzgerald Cachora, b. 1929); *Oach Quethum*, feathery, light floating clouds (Annabel Thomas, b. 1944); *Oach Ahanecut*, rain clouds that cause floods (Mrs. Shirley Harper Eddy, b. 1930); *Oach Jamonamon*, rolling clouds (Kathleen Hammond, b. 1958); *Oach Anyieh*, light from a flash of lightning (Mrs. Dorothy Jenkins Patch, b. 1927); *Oach Eque waepai*, colorful, brilliant clouds (Ophelia Jenkins, b. 1947); *Oach Wilawil*, falling raindrops (Mrs. Thelma Carter Hammond, b. 1897); *Oach Aha heelyu*, reflection of clouds in the water, "the clouds are looking down into the water" (Mrs. Gertrude Van Fleet Short, Colorado River Reservation, b. 1924); *Oach Ahum goyuva*, mirrored clouds, or clouds mirrored in water (Mrs. Rosita Fitzgerald Welsh, b. 1933); *Oach Ami guquiv*, a design or pattern in the sky (Mrs.

Norma Hammond Stanley, b. 1929); *Oach Heelta portma*, "clouds that look like they had been dumped from the sky" (Lorna Cameron, b. 1940); *Oach Hilyodpaka*, many clouds appearing over the horizon (Christine Cameron, b. 1934); *Oach Haep*, gathering clouds (Marlene Hammond, b. 1957). *Oach Ami halaguy*, vanity or admiration of oneself (Wanda La Rose Jenkins, b. 1944); *Oach Qualehseh*, a rainbow among the clouds (Kimberly Sue Cameron, b. 1961).

A few examples from other clans illuminate the Mojaves' mode of naming daughters. The clan name *Neolge* stands for sun or fire. The oldest Fort Mojave *Neolge* is Mrs. Annie McCord Fields (b. 1884). Her descriptive name is *Thonathon*, meaning heat from the sun that wilts things. A two-year-old *Neolge* (Denise Williams, b. 1961) is *Neolge Sahagav*, which means the shooting light rays from the sun. Marsha Williams (b. 1957) is called *Neolge Ami chucare*, descriptive of the sun making bands or streaks of color in the sky. *Neolge Dalack*, meaning the sun radiating warmth and brightness, was the Mojave name of the late Mrs. Minta Armstrong (d. 1962).

The clan name *Whalia* (moon) may be accompanied by a name descriptive of the clear bright moon, the quarter moon shaped like a rocking boat, the moon hidden by clouds and so on. *Whalia Quarai*, clear moon, was Whalia Wilson's name (d. 1930). *Whalia Shukashuk*, a moving, sailing moon, was Mrs. Angie Hamilton's name (d. 1933) . The only known descriptive name of a living *Whalia* is *Whalia Davov*, whose name describes "the moon at certain seasons, balanced with the sun—when you see the moon just coming up, the sun just going down'.' It belongs to Mrs. Lusina Whalia Carter, the oldest Fort Mojave *Whalia* (b. 1888).

Girls and women of the *Maha* clan, or the order of flying-birds, bear such names as *Maha Soovar*, a singing bird (Mrs. Grace Stillman Lewis, b. 1906); *Maha lyava*, a bird in flight, slanting or banking (Mrs. Lucy Morrison Morgan, b. 1890. Mrs. Trilby Wilson McCord who died in the 1920's was called *Maha Alova*, descriptive of the clutching or grasping of a bird's feet. Maha Menvah was the name of Leo Kormes' mother. She had no English name. Her Mojave name described "the sound that birds make when a flock of them takes off at once."

The oldest *Motheha* or nightbird (Lelia

Montgomery McCord, b. 1900) is called simply *Motheha* now. In her younger days she was called *Motheha Hilyameech*, which means the cry or the call of a nightbird. (The two teenage *Motheha's* do not have descriptive names as far as is known.)

Three *Hipa* (coyote) sisters have the following names: *Hipa Chaleel*, descriptive of a coyote hauling something away by mouth (Mrs. Mildred Joann Bryan Fisher, b. 1934); *Hipa Choojkwahj*, descriptive of a coyote uncovering something, that is, like removing the straw from melons (Mrs. Leona Judy Bryan Throssell, b. 1936) ; and *Hipa Ahtrahkoy*, meaning sly fox (Mrs. Winona Bryan Loera, b. 1940). Their aunt (Mrs. Rena Bryan Sands, who died in the 1940's) was called *Hipa Lutabma*. *Lutabma* means something like rejected, left, discarded.

The last Fort Mojave *Shulia* (beaver) was Mrs. Shulia Dickerman Dean (b. 1879, d. 1961). Her Mojave name was *Shulia Chupai*, meaning the leaning works of a beaver piled up on the banks, or logs leaning over. Other known *Shulia* names are *Shulia Ahalyam*, swimming beaver, and *Shulia Chuckgonum*, gnawing beaver.

Only one Fort Mojave *Moha* is living yet (Mrs. Rebecca Dean Knox, b. 1919). Her name is *Moha Dalom*, which signifies mountain sheep or deer refreshing themselves with water; watering deer.

The *Vemacka* (bean mesquite) are extinct now among the Fort Mojaves. The only name that could be recalled belonged to a woman who had no English name. Her Mojave name was *Vemacka Kugoth*, descriptive of the sound of the pounding of mesquite beans into meal.

The *Mus* clan (screw mesquite) use or used such names as *Mus Analya bok*, blossoming mesquite (Mrs. Caroline Gates, b. 1908); *Mus Gwawava*, mesquite branch laden with ripened screw beans (Mrs. Hilda Kormes Twist, d. 1937) and *Mus Hamaote*, meaning a clump of mesquite. *Mus Hamaote* was *Auva halyevatch's* wife (d. 1950). She had no English name.

The *Quinetha*, or prickly pear women, bear such names as *Quinetha Heelyasum*, glowing, alive from the sun (Mrs. Arlene Armstrong Rodriquez, b. 1921); *Quinetha Hipak*, blossoming prickly pear (Mrs. Mary Bricker Miller, b. 1908); *Quinetha Navapalye*, prickly pear blossoms or fruit or leaves growing close together (Mrs. Imogene Bricker Lewis, b. 1924); *Quinetha Dunyum*, prickly pear blossoms, or fruit or leaves, growing so close together as to look stacked or piled on each other (Mrs. Isadora Bricker Bernal, b. 1927); *Quinetha Waipai*, alive, vibrant (Miss Letitia Armstrong, b. November 17, 1942).

The *Kumathee* or ocotilla cactus clan called their daughters such names as *Kumathee Atat*, a thorny ocotilla cactus (Mrs. Ruby Newford Twist, d. 1944); *Kumathee Hilyarbymk*, an ocotilla "leaning over to look at something, or bending over to see" (Mrs. Clara Durand Amador, d. 1963) and *Kumathee Matquisah*, which means "shadow of the self, or my shadow" (Mrs. Ida Kempton Manakoja of the Colorado River Reservation).

The four Fort Mojave *Gottah* (tobacco) have descriptive names. The oldest *Gottah* (Mrs. Kate Wellman Bryan, b. 1867) is called by her tribesmen *Queaque Gottah*, the aged *Gottah*. In her girlhood, she bore the name *Gottah Mashesha*, which meant "the light that shines in your eyes when you are lighting your smoke." The next oldest *Gottah* (Viva Dean Hayes, b. 1895) is *Gottah Neya mathbaum*, which means "smoldering fire—when you are smoking and the light is going out" Mrs. Clara Prosser Harper (b. 1906) bears the Indian name *Gottah Chaump*, which means "putting aside tobacco to smoke later." The youngest *Gottah* is called simply *Gottah*, or *Got* for short, "because she is the only one in Mojave Village; and everyone knows who you mean" *Gottah Hoova*, whose name means "drawing the string of a tobacco pouch;" lives on the Colorado River Reservation (Mrs. Myrtle Little). Oach remembered two *Gottah* who had no English names, *Gottah Suchinya*, "sifting tobacco in the hands to get the coarse tobacco fine;"

Photo by A.P. Miller, 1935.

Oach Quireechma is the Mohave name of one Oach (Mrs. Glorianna Cameron Davidson, b. 1932). Her clan or family name, Oach, signifies clouds, rain, and possibly wind. Her descriptive name Quireechma means ever moving. the two words together are translated "ever moving clouds."

and *Gottah Thavalya*, meaning "when you smoke you kind of swing your arm—that's what it means—swinging light."

Two *Malika* sisters (Mrs. Frances Wilbur Stillman, b. 1910, and Mrs. Mary Wilbur Gutierrez, b. 1905) are called *Malika Chopek* and *Malika Choquesay*. They are the ground squirrel people. *Chopeck* means gathering things, carrying things back and forth. *Choquesay* means bushy, descriptive of the nest of ground squirrels.

The only living *Boudha* (frog people) is *Boudha Whev* whose name means stretching, unwinding, elastic, as a frog stretching in swimming and jumping. Her English name is Mrs. Henrietta Graves Peterson (b. 1898).

Chacha Hoda was the name of a Mojave woman who died in the 1930's. It means beautiful ear of corn. The woman called "Georgia" (d. 1938), who worked for my mother when I was growing up, was *Chacha Wakavar*, which means treasured corn. This name alludes to the precious seed corn put aside for the next year's planting. *Masipa Ahota*, good or beautiful quail, is the name borne by Mrs. Helen Evanston Swick of the Colorado River Reservation. If there is only one woman in a clan, no descriptive name is necessary.

These descriptive names given to the women reveal a people responsive to nature; impressed by the immensity of the sky; observant of the passing aspects of the sun and the moon, the changing forms and portents of the clouds, the direction and force of the winds, the appearance and ways of birds, animals and plants.

As emphasized earlier, one distinctive feature of the Mojave clan system is that Mojave boys and men are never addressed or called by their clan names. Obviously, there must be some appellation which identifies each, and to which he answers. The Mojaves have worked this out ingeniously.

Boys and men are called by vernacular names which are given to them by their parents, relatives, friends, acquaintances and medicine men. Or, they may choose their names. Moreover, they may change their names, and last but not least, they may have more than one name. This leeway seems consistent with the Mojave viewpoint that only the clan name matters.

Masculine names are descriptive names, but never descriptive of the clan name as is the case with the opposite sex. These vernacular names seem to

fall into several categories, such as observations of nature—including human nature—references to geographic landmarks and historical events, allusions to status, roles and occupations, and comical, ludicrous or whimsical nom-deplumes. Many names are metaphors.

The vernacular Mojave names are difficult to translate into English. Not only does the structure of the two languages differ, but the meaning of the words often elude foreign understanding, because they are inlaid in Mojave culture. For example, the name *Mutheel munagh*, translated literally, is *mutheel*, bread, and *munagh*, trail, e.g., Bread-trail. To Mojaves it means a trail of bread used to lure animals into traps. The name Chaquar ear, translated literally, is "Message-tail" To Mojaves it means an afterthought. "You talk and talk and haven't made yourself clear, so you add a P S.—the tail of a message."

The name of the famed scout Charlie Merriman, *Eachawhat thoomay*, signified a red feather or feather headdress worn by men of distinction in the old days. Chief Jack Harrison's name Quichagoy hunak meant an old lady's necklace. It refers to the intricately carved shell necklaces that women prized in the old days. Such necklaces became very rare and were possessed usually by old ladies who had cherished them since girlhood.

One boy born in the thirties was called *Amat kuquiev*, which means weaving a net, or throwing a net over the land. His name refers to a troublesome incident which caused great excitement among the Fort Mojaves. "Some tempers rose. The Government was putting up fences to say where Indian's cattle could range. The Mojaves didn't like all these fences up. They

Photo by A.P. Miller, 1939

*Oach **Hilyadpaka**, meaning "many clouds appearing over the horizon," is the name of **Oach Quireechma's** younger sister. (Miss Christine Cameron, b. 1934).*

had their own understanding among themselves. They called weaving fences in and out over the land *Amat kuquiev*. A boy was named this."

Two old Mojaves who had no English names used their Indian names on a tribal petition in 1923: *Emeechoman*, which means the rising cry of an animal—a warning; and *Mavarr cawumppa*, meaning "ground grain you hate to part with, or treasured ground grain." This latter connotes the frugal use of grain during lean years or years of drought when the river did not overflow its banks to permit planting. Pete *Sulayha*, or Pete of the Sand Dunes, is Clarence Anderson's name (b. 1889). *Sulayha* is a geographic designation of "where he came from." The sand dunes were located just north of Topock, but now lie under the back-waters of Lake Havasu. Warren Mulford of the *Kumathee* (b. 1897) is called *Homar huwhen*, which means shaving or cutting a child's hair close to his (or her) head. This name implies punishment. Mojaves wore their hair long. Employees at the Fort Mojave School sometimes cut hair close, or shaved a child's head.

Names purporting to be comical or ludicrous are particularly hard for outsiders to understand, but to Mojaves who see the incongruities in the metaphor, the names are uproariously funny. For example, one young Mojave, tired of the conventional high-sounding names that his austere father called his sons, announced that his new name was *Hanava muttukuhav*. "It caused a sensation," and inevitably evoked laughter. Its meaning "the overcoat or jacket of a cicada" is too Mojave for a non-Mojave to find hilarious. The name *Atchkayoak nyamanyo*, meaning sandal of a crane, was also mirth provoking. One man who lived near Needles in the first quarter of the century used the English translation of his Indian name—"Chicken-eye." It seemed apropos if one knew that he had one characteristic of a chicken, namely non-blinking eyes. One of his contemporaries was called *Cawpellahmala*, which means a paper bag; another was called *Hookthar itchhamava*, meaning a place where the coyote feasted. These "shockers," however, are few in number and are not typical of masculine names.

Mojave men and boys have been called by the several foregoing types of names for a long time—at least for more than a century. The Great Chieftain of the Mojaves at the time of their surrender, 1859, was of the *Malika* clan. He was called *Homoseh quahote* (spelled various ways), meaning orator of the star. The literal translation is *homoseh*, star; *quahote*, orator.

His son was called *Empote quatacheech*, which means obscured in a cloud of dust, or hidden behind a cloud of dust. The literal translation is *empote*, cloud of dust, and *quatacheech*, hidden behind. A cloud of dust symbolizes war or trouble. The last hereditary and elected Great Chieftain of the Fort Mojaves was *Homoseh quahote's* grandson Pete Lambert (d. 1947). He was called *Sukulai homar* or *Saqueli homar*, which means young plant. His guardian after his father's death was the Mojave War Chieftain *Asukit* (sometimes spelled *Asakeet*) of the *Neolge*. He was called by two names: John, given to him by soldiers at Fort Mojave, and a Mojave name, *Asukit*, which means picked cactus or cactus fruit.

Jo Courtwright, chief of the Middle Section, was of the *Neolge*. He was called *Hachur tupuva*, frostbitten plant. Chief Sherman Ross of the *Oach*, the nominal great chieftain after the tribe punished *Sukulai homar* by curtailing his authority, was "looked up to by the people." He was called *Avi chavar*, meaning next to the highest mountain. Shinny Mike of the *Chacha*, a subchief, and father of the well

Photo by Helen Simone, 1963

Mrs. Frances Malika Stillman, Chairman of the Fort Mljave Tribal Council, and chief consultant in this study of Fort Mojave clans.

❋ ❋ ❋ ❋ ❖ ❍ ❋ ❋ ❋ ❖ ❍ ❋ ❋ ❋ ❍ ❖ ❋ ❋ ❋ ❋ ❋

known Mojave, William McKinley, was called *Ambat chaque*, which means moving, going, or traveling the breeze. George Armstrong of the *Quinetha* was called *Kohee atavaha*, to set free. Frank Stillman of the *Maha* was called *Huyatch humar*, young life. Teddy Roosevelt's father was called *Thou cumahon*, beautiful dawn. One old Mojave scout, who at the age of 102 was featured at the dedication ceremonies opening Parker Dam, was called *Hera anyai*, light of lightning, or flash of lightning. *Gwegwi nuor's* name stood for a gift of livestock, usually beef. *Thumpah's* name meant wasp. Jack Jones Sr. of the *Vemacka*, Kroeber's interpreter, was called *Quichnyailk* racer snake.

Among the men who were deceased during the last twenty years was Steve Smith of the *Oach*, the elected chief of the south Mojaves after the death of *Waporecohaveca*, or smokestack. He was a close friend of Chief Lambert and leader of the Fort Mojave Indian Band. His name, *Chaquar ear*, meant tail of the sage. Dio Lewis of the *Mus* (b. 1884, d. 1962) bore the name *Eachchoyear sipasip*, which means "something piercing the air, as an arrow or a bird. Today it might mean a rocket." Arthur Geonowein of the *Neolge* (d. 1959) was called *Havasu galep*, wilted green leaves. Richard Scott Sr. of the *Neolge* (d. 1959) was called *Avas canum*, running toward something. John Carter of the *Whalia* (d. 1960) had the name *Coona manev*, anxious to bear a message, or anxious to receive a message. The late Jason Peck of the *Oach* was called *Ami nyahott*, which means a pet of the sky or heavens.

Mojave men who are living today are called various descriptive names or metaphors. Harry Lewis of the *Neolge* (b. 1880) is called *Atalk hear*, which means the root of a water plant, said to be edible, but now extinct. Charles Hamilton of the *Maha* (b. 1881) is called *Auva halyevatch*, which literally translated is *auva*, tobacco, and *halyevatch*, sitting in. It means a form seen in tobacco smoke, or a form among tobacco plants. Dewey Hayes of the *Maha* (b. 1881) bears the name *Quechan monuov*, an historical reference meaning Yuman combat. His brother, Webster Hayes (b. 1883), is *A-ah lovalov*, fluttering cottonwood leaves. Clyde Peterson of the *Oach* (b. 1880) is called *Oonya homar*, a newly finished path or road, or literally "young path or young road." Bert Kempton of the *Kumathee* (b. 1880) is called *Sukum munagh*, on the trail of the trader. Maurice Boucher of the *Cha-cha* (b. 1892) is *Herow heilhevow*, someone traveling fast, fast traveler. Robert Jenkins of the *Oach* (b. 1897), who comes from a line

of fishermen, is called *Achee muk*, a fisher, or of fisherman's lineage. Charles Evanston of the *Masipa* (b. 1890) is called *Mutaquesa manyieh*, a pleasant or good spirit. Clifford Johnson of the *Neolge* (b. 1890) is called *Messahi dunyum*. The literal translation is *messa*, daughter, and *dunyum*, repetition or over and over. The name means "having one daughter after another without having a son."

Mojave men may have several names. For example, the chief medicine man my mother knew well when we lived in Needles in 1905-1914 had several names. He was of the *Oach*, but he was called *Kopit kipiton*, meaning Captain or Chief of the Owls; *Quaskette howa*, meaning broken vessel or shattered pottery; Chief Rheumatism Medicine Man, his professional title, and Van Fleet, his United States Army name.

The late Hal Davidson of the *Whalia* had at least three vernacular names: *Oneyuravarya*, unreached destination, his boyhood name; *Aha homee*, high water, his manhood name, which refers to the floodwaters of the Colorado River in the springtime, and *Quachnuor*, writer or recorder, an occupational name.

A Mojave boy or man may change his name for any number of reasons. For example, after motorcars came into use, one little boy was given the name *Cooack anyieh*, by a close friend of the family, who was an enthusiast for the new automobiles. The name means "lights from pressure or push, or lights caused by turning or pushing something" A few years later, the boy objected to his modern name. He wanted an old-fashioned Mojave name. He took the one suggested by his grandmother—*Chuim manyieh*. The meaning of this name is complicated to explain. *Chuim* means "saving for a later time"; *manyieh* means "pleasant." To his parents and grandparents the name had hidden meanings. It embodies the idea of saving pleasure one derives from the pleasant taste of eating something to a later time when it may be appreciated more. His grandmother explained, "In just mixing and straining mesquite meal with water, do not drink it all. Put it away and it will taste better when you are really hungry" As a youth, the boy's name was shortened to *Manyieh*, pleasant.

One middle-aged man asked his friends and acquaintances to help him pick a new name. Of his name he said, "My mother and father called me by that name. It makes me sad. I want to be called by something else." His folks were dead.

The Mojaves' point of view, according to my

Fort Mojave consultants, "is just the opposite of Americans who like old things and want to keep them to remember their parents by, for sentimental reasons" A Mojave may say, "That was my name when I was young (e.g., when his parents were living). I would like to be called something else" One Mojave said, "I called a man by his name once, and my aunt said, 'No. That is his old name. It hurts him. Call him by his new name'."

Mojaves' consideration of feelings is exemplified in the case of Hal Davidson who had served his tribe from young manhood. He had three names before he grew old, lost almost all of his relatives, lost his eyesight, lost his hearing, and could no longer function as the Tribal Recorder. In his old age, the Mojaves called him by none of his earlier names, because these hurt. They called him by the name given to him in appreciation by the Walapais—*Eque tekecuma*, meaning something like "where the clouds bank together."

The names by which men and boys are called epitomize Mojave feelings that a man's true name is his clan name—his heritage from the past, his bequest to his children, and his identification in life and in the Shadow Land. This view is capsuled in the statement, "Only the clan name matters." It is illustrated by the freedom accorded males to be called whatever name or names each takes or accepts.

To make sure that the ideas of the transmission of clan names, and of the names borne by both women and men were clear, I asked Malika for another concrete example, this time from her own immediate family. "This is an important subject, Malika," I told her, "and one that is difficult for outsiders to understand. Your explanation will help to clarify your totemic clan system and the patrilinear descent of your people." She laughed and said, "The big words mean that I will explain how our family names work."

"My husband is of the *Maha*, of the order of birds and flying things: they are the representatives of *soocoomah*, are orators, and advisers in very difficult problems. I am *Malika*, of the things below the earth, the 'understanding people.' Our son will carry his father's name, *Maha*, to our granddaughters. We have five daughters, named *Maha*, the name their father passed to them. We call them Maha. The oldest is *Maha Quechneoch*, meaning the repetition of the singing or calling of birds, over and over. The second *Maha* is called *Maha Heilhochav*, descriptive

of the birds that come picking the seeds when you plant, so you have to plant over again. The third *Maha Munsaaow*, a little red bird that sings sweetly in the valley. The fourth and fifth daughters have no descriptive clan names.

"My husband is not called by the name *Maha*. His name is *Suoppaub*, meaning ripened. My son's name is *Manyieh*, meaning pleasant. I am called by my family name, *Malika*, and a descriptive name *Chopeck*, a gatherer. Each of us has an English name. Mojaves all have English names. We use these for legal purposes, and with outsiders. When we are among ourselves we call each other by our Indian names."

Changes from Mojave to English Names, 1859-1959

The Mojave Indians began the century, 1859-1959, with Mojave names, and ended it with English names. They have preserved their Indian names orally and they use these names when they are talking among themselves. The English names, however, are their legal names, and these are the names they use in their dealings with outsiders.

The shift from Mojave to English names during the past century followed similar courses among the Fort Mojaves and the Colorado River Reservation Mojaves. Because my historical research has been concentrated upon the Fort Mojave Indians, this study in name changes will be confined to the latter.

Alterations in Fort Mojave names began in a small way during the period of military occupation, which began April 21, 1859 and lasted until July 2, 1890. Soldiers at Fort Mojave by-passed the long Indian names of Mojave men by dubbing them Bill, Joe, Sam, Pete, and so on. The official substitution of English first" names, and the modification of men's names, started after Mojave men joined the federal troops as scouts, and when they were employed as policemen, interpreters and laborers by the War Department. The simplification was mainly for record-keeping and payroll purposes. For example, *Asikut* of the *Neolge*, a war chief and leader of the Mojave scouts under General George Crook, was named John Asikut. *Kopeeda* of the *Chacha* clan was called Pete Nelse. The long name of the scout *Thalnaack whoree* of the *Vahath* was shortened to, *Whoree* or *Ouree*, prefaced by Sam—Sam Ouree. These names were accepted easily for they did not

TABLE I
MOJAVE CLANS DURING THE CENTURY 1859-1959

SHERER 1959	KROEBER 1925	CURTIS 1908	BOURKE 1889	CWEGWI NUOR 1859	COMMON NAME–1959
The Above-things: Things of the Sky or Heavens					
Neolge sun, fire	*Nyo'ilcha* sun, fire, deer, eagle beetle	*Nyolch* deer	*Nol-cha* sun	*Neolge*	*ánnah*, sun *ahow*, fire
Oach clouds, rain, wind	*Owich* cloud	*Och* white cloud	*O-cha* rain-cloud	*Oach*	*éque* cloud *cuvawa* rain
(Extinct)	*Mat-hachva* wind	*Matáchwa* wind		*Matavacha*	*mátha* wind
Whalia moon	*Hoalya* moon	*Huálya* moon	*Hual-ga* moon	*Whallia*	*hálya* moon
Maha small flying bird	*Maha* a small bird	*Maha* a kind of bird	*Máha* caterpillar	*Maha*	*soocoomah* small bird
Motheha night bird	*Motheha* screech bird			*Motheha*	*dooláuk* night bird *suthéca* screech owl
(Extinct)	*Kutkilya* owl	*Qutkilye* owl		*que Kellia*	*nyav thee-coopit*, owl
The Earth-things: Desert and Mountain Plants and Animals					
Hipa coyote	*Hipa* coyote	*Hipa* coyote	*Hi-pa* coyote	*Hipah*	*hookthar* coyote
Moha mountain sheep, deer	*Moha* mountain sheep				*ahmo* mountain sheep *akwaka*, deer
Masipa quail	*Masipa* quail possibly coyote		*Ma-si-pa* coyote	*Missiboh*	*ahmah* quail
(Extinct)	*Nyikha* caterpillar or worm		(see *Maha*)	*Ne-ka*	*hamsuquenp* caterpillar or worm

Norge is used by *Neolge* women who have lost a child.

❉ ✦ ❉ ✦ ❉ ◇ ❉ ✦ ❉ ✦ ❉ ✦ ❉ ✦ ❉ ✦ ❉ ◇ ❉ ✦ ❉ ✦ ❉ ◇   The Mojave Indians   133 affect the clan names nor conflict with Mojave customs. The only living woman known to have worked at Fort Mojave, "while the soldiers were there," was *Gottah* (Kate Wellman Bryan). She was called *Gottah*, *Got*, or *Kate*. Again, clan names were not involved.

During most of the period of military occupation the Fort Mojaves were technically under the jurisdiction of the Department of the Interior. "Legally" they belonged on the Colorado River Reservation after it was established in 1865. They refused to leave their ancestral homes in the Mojave Valley, the War Department declined to try to force them onto the reservation, and the Indian Agent there was unable to supervise them. 'Whatever actual supervision or control they had came from the commanders at Fort Mojave. As long as Fort Mojave was garrisoned by the War Department, the Fort Mojaves, if peace abiding, were relatively free to follow their old tribal ways unmolested. This state of affairs came to an end in the midsummer of 1890 when the War Department withdrew its troops and, transferred the post to the Department of the Interior.

Beginning in August, 1890, the Fort Mojaves began to feel the drastic cultural changes demanded by the Department of the Interior. Fort Mojave was converted into a boarding school for Fort Mojave and other "non-reservation" Indians. From 1890 until 1931, a period of forty-one years, all Fort Mojave boys and girls between the ages of six and eighteen were compelled to live at this school or attend an advanced Indian school remote from Fort Mojave. This was the era of de-Indianizing Indians, breaking up tribal ties, rooting out Indian beliefs, customs and native tongue, and civilizing them after the patterns of white men.

Here at the school the children and youth were transformed, outside, into facsimiles of white children of their day—haircuts, clothing, habits of eating, sleeping, toiletry, manners, industry, language, and so on. Five lashes of the whip was the penalty for the first offense of speaking in their native tongue. "The whippings were awful," said Oach with a shudder, "Simply awful."

Between 1890 and 1904 the clan names were not affected. The first two superintendents gave priorities to other changes. The boys and girls who attended the Fort Mojave Indian School, and the Mojave adults employed there, were given English first names, which they used with their Indian names. They were encouraged to take English surnames, if their Indian names were difficult to pronounce and to write. Feminine use of the clan name with an English first name came into practice during this time. In old reports and commencement programs of the Fort Mojave School are found such examples as Nell *Oach*, Alice *Oach*, Bernice *Neolge*, Della *Neolge*, Stella *Moha* (spelled Mopa), Lena *Hipah*. Boys and men had such names as Fred *Unyo hamara*, John Walds *Abob*, Jason *Mynahot*, Robert *Mechaken*.

The Department of the Interior became more and more insistent by 1903 that all Indian families be registered under the same family name in order to provide a basis for land allotments. In 1903, the administration of the Fort Mojave School changed. The new superintendent fell heir to this problem with the Fort Mojaves. He was also given jurisdiction over the Indians within a radius of thirty miles of the Fort Mojave School, which made him the local Indian agent with increased authority.

In 1905, all Fort Mojave Indians, young and old, were required to take English surnames as family names. The school authorities of the Fort Mojave School prepared a list of names and gave the oldest school children first choices of their new family names. Parents were then assigned the family name chosen by their offspring.

This wholesale renaming of the people was a dark hour for the Fort Mojaves. "They could not believe their ears," Oach said. "The old folks shook their heads. What will they [the whites] want next?" Mojave adults were appalled and shaken. Their protests went unheard.

In his annual report to the Commissioner of Indian Affairs, dated August 9, 1905, the superintendent of the Fort Mojave School wrote, "Census—During the fiscal year a great deal of work has been done in the collection and classification of data to be used as follows: In preparing a census, in the establishment of a register of families, in the formulation of annual statistics, in the keeping of a register of births and deaths, etc. Therefore, a census of the Indians within a radius of thirty miles of Fort Mohave is furnished with this report." His report included no clues as to the furor his procedures caused.

Feelings ran high. However, much was at stake. Fort Mojave leaders, deeply concerned over the regaining of their ancestral land, and deeply worried over white settlement upon it, mollified

TABLE I (continued)
MOJAVE CLANS DURING THE CENTURY 1859-1959

SHERER 1959	KROEBER 1925	CURTIS 1908	BOURKE 1889	CWEGWI NUOR 1859	COMMON NAME–1959
The Earth-things: Desert and Mountain Plants and Animals					
*Vemacka** bean mesquite	*Vimaka* bean mesquite		*Vi-ma-ga* a green plant, not identified	*Ve mock*	*ahnalya* bean mesquite
Mus screw mesquite	*Musa* screw mesquite	*Musha* mesquite	*Mus* mesquite	*Moose*	*ahieza* screw mesquite
Chacha corn	*Chacha* corn or food	*Chach* corn		*Chagge*	*tallicha* corn
(Extinct)	*Vahadha* tobacco		*Va-had-ha* tobacco		*auva* tobacco
Gottah or *Gotah* tobacco	*Kata* tobacco, perhaps mescal, that is agave	*Kata* tobacco	*Ko-ta* mescal or tobacco	*Got*	*auva* tobacco
Kumathee ocotilla cactus	*Kumadhiya* ocotilla cactus	*Kumathi* ocotilla cactus	*Ku-mad-ha* ocotilla cactus	*Coomathea*	*attat* ocotilla cactus
Quinetha prickly-pear cactus	*Kwinitha* prickly-pear cactus	*Qinitha* prickly-pear cactus		*Quneathea*	*tapah* prickly-pear cactus
*Teelya*** mescal	*Tilya* mescal	*Tiilya* mescal	*Ti-hil-ya* mescal	*Te ella*	*ahnalya* mescal
Below-earth and Water Beings					
*Shulia**** beaver	*Siulya* beaver	*Shula* beaver	*Shuyl-ya* beaver	*Susuella* Sulloh (?)	*aben* beaver
Boudha frog	*Halypota* frog			*Hall-po-ta*	*hanye* frog
Malika ground squirrel wood rat, desert rodent	*Malyikha* wood rat	*Milika* wood rat	*Ma-li-ka* not identified	*Malike*	*amailk* ground squirrel, desert rodent

Halpote is used by *Boudha* women who have lost a child. *Kusool* or coosool is used by *Shulia* women who have lost a child.

   * Extinct among the Fort Mojaves on November 22. 1959.
  ** Extinct among the Fort Mojaves in 1944.
 *** Extinct among the Fort Mojaves on March 1, 1961.

the chief objectors and influenced the peaceful outward acceptance of "white man's law." A few of the old Indians absolutely refused to take new names. However, the majority of them did take the English names with outer passivity. According to Oach, there was "nothing else they could do." But the Fort Mojaves did not relinquish the old Mojave family names given to them by their Creator. These, like their religion and their native tongue, went underground, to be used only when among themselves.

The method of renaming the Fort Mojaves created numerous confusions in family names. In the first place, the new English surnames did not correspond one-to-one with the old Mojave clan or family names. According to my Fort Mojave consultants, each Mojave clan should have one English surname "to be right." Such was not the case.

In checking the families enrolled by English names in the tribal register in order to identify each by clan name (if it had one), we found that seventeen surviving clans in 1959 had sixty-two different English family names, instead of seventeen as would have been the case had each Mojave clan been given one English family name in 1905. Several names known to have been given in 1905 have disappeared through death.

The number of English surnames per clan in 1959 ranged from one to eighteen. (The names of the clans with their English surnames are shown on *Table II*.) Six clans had one English surname each: *Boudha, Malika, Moha, Motheha, Shulia, Vemacka*. The *Boudha* were registered as *Graves*, the *Malika* as Wilbur, the *Moha* as Dean, the *Motheha* as Kormes, the *Shulia* as Dickerman, and the *Vemacka* as Scott. The *Malika* were given two different names in 1905—Wilbur and Hood. Hood became extinct with the death of Robin Hood in 1945. Twelve clans had from two to eighteen English surnames per clan.

The reason for this proliferation, Oach explained, was that the superintendent and teachers at the Fort Mojave School "could not figure out our family system. It was hard to understand." Malika and Oach both attributed the multi-English names to "mix-ups at the School when they gave us our English names."

Oach and Malika cited a number of examples of the "mix-ups" in names. Two brothers of the *Quinetha* were given two different English surnames at the School—Armstrong (George) and Bricker (John). Both died in the 1930's but both left children. Their children and grandchildren are *Quinetha*, who go by the English family names of Armstrong and Bricker. Two schoolboys of the *Maha*, whose fathers were full brothers, were given different surnames by the school—Stillman (Lute) and Andrews (Charles) Their fathers—who did not go to school—were given the same surnames as their sons. Later, after authorities at the school found the mistake, the elder Andrews was re-named Stillman. His two sons' names, however, remained Andrews. When the boys' sister went to school "the school tried to straighten it out. Her name was Mina Stillman."

A further mix-up among the *Mahas* was that the two brothers who were given the names Andrews and Stillman had a first cousin on the father's side. He was named Hayes (John), not Andrews nor Stillman. All three of these elder relatives (*Mahas*) had children and grandchildren. They go by three names—Andrews, Stillman, Hayes.

Several mix-ups occurred among the *Neolge*. For example: Blake Gates of the *Neolge* had seven children by the same wife. The oldest son was given the name Gates by the school; the other children were named Rockefeller. A second example among the *Neolge*: Harry Lewis, Tom Wilson, Edna Jackson were full brothers and sisters. There was another sister (the mother of Cora Jackson) . The girls were given the name Jackson; their brothers' surnames remained Lewis and Wilson.

The *Masipa* were given two English surnames. Two half-brothers by the same father were named Evanston (Charles) and McDowell (Thomas). Their father had no English name. The *Kumathee* were also given two English surnames. In this case two schoolboys, who were double cousins—their fathers having married sisters—were given the surnames Kempton (Bert) and Mills (Milo).

Children of two completely unrelated clans, the *Neolge* and the Vemacka, were given the same English surname Scott. Time has straightened out this confusion. The *Vemacka* Scotts became extinct with the death of Calvin Coolidge Scott on November 22, 1959. There remain only the Scotts who are *Neolge*.

To complicate matters, the Mojave clans on

TABLE II
CLAN NAMES AND ENGLISH NAMES OF THE FORT MOJAVE INDIANS IN 1959

CLAN NAMES	ENGLISH SURNAMES
Neolge	Anderson, Arrison, Brockman, Burns, Carter, Courtwright, Gates, Geonowein, Hanna, Howard, Jackson, Johnson, Knox, Lewis, McCord, Rockefeller, Scott, Williams
Oach	Cameron, Fitzgerald, Hammond, Harper, Jenkins, Peck, Peterson, Thomas, Van Fleet
Whalia	Davidson, Harrison, Hough, Marble
Maha	Andrews, Hamilton, Harrison, Hayes, Morrison, Shafer, Wilson
Motheha	Kormes
Hipa	Bryan, Charles
Moha	Dean
Shulia	Dickerman
Masipa	Evanston, McDowell
Vemacka	Scott
Mus	Field, Kormes, McCormick aka Shed
Chacha	Boucher, Brown, Hills, Hogan
Gottah	McKenzie, Roosevelt
Kumathee	Kempton, Mills, Mulford
Quinetha	Armstrong, Bricker
Boudha	Graves
Malika	Wilbur

TABLE III
CLANS AMONG THE FORT MOJAVE INDIANS (1963)

ARCHAIC CLAN NAMES	MEANING OF CLAN NAME	VERNACULAR
Neolge	sun or fire	*annah*, sun or *ahow*, fire
Oach	clouds, rain wind	*eque, cuvava, matha*
Whalia	moon	*halya*
Maha	small bird	*soocama*
Motheha	night bird	*doolauk*
Hipa	coyote	*hookthar*
Moha	mountain sheep or deer	*ahmo* or *akwaka*
Masipa	quail	*ahmah*
Mus	screw mesquite	*ahieza*
Chacha	corn	*tallicha*
Gottah	tobacco	*auva*
Kumathee	ocotilla cactus	*attat*
Quinetha	prickly-pear cactus	*apah*
Boudha	frog	*hanye*
Malika	desert rodent	*amailk*

the Colorado River Reservation were given different English names than were their Fort Mojave kin. For example, one name given to the *Malika* was Miller. Their Fort Mojave kin are Wilbur, and in 1905, Hood. Pete Homer, Chairman of the Colorado River Reservation, is of the *Quinetha*. His Fort Mojave kin are Armstrong and Bricker—and until recently, Columbus (Chris Columbus, d. July 9, 1960).

Fort Mojave opinion on this manner of renaming them is divided. Some believed that it was a deliberate plan to break up their clanship system. Others, like Oach, are inclined to take the view she expressed, namely, that the mix-ups were due to the fact that "our family system was hard to understand". The reticence of the Mojaves to divulge their names, their refusal to speak of the dead, and their unusual clan system contributed a share to the confusion.

Regardless of the many mix-ups in acquiring English family names, Fort Mojaves know their clan name—if they have one—and they know their relatives regardless of what English name they bear or on which reservation they are registered.

Photo by Jeffrey L. Garton

Bibliography

Dreamers of the Colorado: The Mojave Indians

Alcock, J. (1990). Raging arroyo. In Lawrence W. Cheek. (Ed.). *Voices in the desert.* San Diego: Harcourt Brace, 1995, pp. 31-33.

Apodaca, P. (1999). Tradition, myth, and performance of Cahuilla bird songs. Unpublished doctoral dissertation, U. of California at Los Angeles.

Brennan, B. (1966). This is river country. *Arizona Highways.* 42(2), 30-38.

Casebier, D. (2007). Precarious foothold on the wild frontier. *Tales of the Mojave Road: the military.* Essex, CA: Mojave Desert & Cultural Assoc., pp. 42-52.

Devereux, G. (1951). Mohave chieftainship in action: a narrative of the first contacts of the Mohave Indians with the United States. *Plateau.* 23(3), 33-43.

Devereux, G. (1956). Mohave dreams of omen and power. *Tomorrow.* 4(3), 17-24.

Devereux, G. (1949). Mohave voice and speech mannerisms. *Word.* 5(3), 268-272.

Fisher, W. (2008). Beading to delight in. (unpublished manuscript).

Furst, J. Leslie. (2001). Mojave pottery, Mojave people. Santa Fe: School of American Research Press. pp. 21-31, 40-44, 85-86, 94-97, 131-141, 144-147, 180-181.

Gorman, F.J.E. (1981). The persistent identity of the Mohave Indians, 1859-1965. In Castlile, G.P., & Kushner, G. (Eds.). *Persistent peoples: cultural enclaves in perspective.* Tucson: U. of Arizona Press. pp. 43-68.

Hammerschlag, C. (1988). Jolene. *The Dancing Healers.* New York: Harper & Row. pp. 88-98.

Hayes, A. & Hayes, C. (2006). The desert southwest: four thousand years of life and art. Berkeley, CA: Ten Speed Press, pp. 140-143.

Herzog, G. (1928). The Yuman musical style. *Journal of American Folklore.* 41(168), 183-231.

Hills, K. (2008). Na u knov em. (I am going to tell you something). Volume 1, Issue 1 • Sept., 28, 2007.

Hills, R. (2008). Dancing to the Mojave Birdsongs (unpublished manuscript).

Hinton, L., & Watahomigie, L.J. (Eds.) (1984). Spirit Mountain: an anthology of Yuman story and song. Tucson: U. of Arizona Press. pp. 3-7, 281, 282, 284-290.

Hunter, L.G. (1979). The Mohave expedition of 1858-9. *Arizona and the West.* 21(2), 137-156.

Japenga, Ann. (2009, June). Lost and Found. *Sierra Magazine.* pp. 42-50.

Johnson, L. (2007). A story from the stones. (unpublished manuscript).

Klasky, P. Song of the land. *The Cultural Conservancy*. Retrieved November 13, 2001, from the web site: http:/www.nativeland.org/mcs.html.

Knight, J. (1999, Summer). The Mojave beading tradition. *Beadwork*, pp. 40-43.

Kroeber, A.L. (1972). More Mohave myths. *University of California Anthropological Records*. 27(xi-xii) 1-161. (Interviews conducted In 1902).

Kroeber, C.B. (1965). The Mohave as nationalist, 1859-1874. *Proceedings of the American Philosophical Society*. 109(3), 173-180.

Palmer, E. (1867). Manufacture of pottery by Mohave Indian women. *Proceedings of the Davenport Academy of Natural Sciences*. 2(1), 32-34.

Sherer, L.M. (1966). Great chieftains of the Mojave Indians. *Southern California Quarterly*. 48(1), 1-35.

Sherer, L.M. (1965, Spring). The clan system of the Fort Mojave Indians. *Southern California Quarterly*. 47(1), 1-72.

Steinbeck, J. (1988). Travels with Charley. New York: Viking Penguin, a division of Penguin Group. pp. 211-218.

Stegner, P. (1995). The teatime moon and the setting sun. In Lawrence W. Cheek. (Ed.). *Voices in the desert*. San Diego: Harcourt Brace. pp. 9-17.

Stewart, K.M. (1947). An account of the Mojave mourning ceremony. *American Anthropologist*. 49(1), 146-148.

Stewart, K.M. (1956, November). Life on the desert: dreamers of the Mojave. *Desert Magazine*. pp. 11-12.

Stewart, K.M. (1956). Mohave. In A. Ortiz. (Ed.). *Handbook of the North American Indians*. Washington, D.C.: Smithsonian Institution Press. Vol. 10, pp. 55-70.

Stewart, K.M. (1970). Mojave Indian shamanism. *The Masterkey*. 48(1), 4-13.

Stewart, K.M. (1947). Mohave warfare. *Southwestern Journal of Anthropology*. 3(3), 257-278.

Thomas, C.F., Jr. (1945). Ah-Ve-Koov-o-Tut, ancient home of the Mojave. *Desert Magazine*. 9(1), 13-17.

Tsosie, M. (1992, Winter). Historic Mojave bead collars. *American Indian Art Magazine*. 18(1), 36-49.

Waitman, L.B. (1970). Fort Mohave. *San Bernadino Museum Association Quarterly*. 18(2-3), 40-48.

Wallace, W.J. (1948). Infancy and childhood among the Mojave Indians. *Primitive Men*. 21(1-2), 19-37.